One Economics • Many Recipes

One Economics • Many Recipes

GLOBALIZATION, INSTITUTIONS, AND ECONOMIC GROWTH

Dani Rodrik

PRINCETON UNIVERSITY PRESS • PRINCETON AND OXFORD

Copyright © 2007 by Princeton University Press

Published by Princeton University Press, 41 William Street, Princeton, New Jersey 08540
In the United Kingdom: Princeton University Press, 3 Market Place, Woodstock,
Oxfordshire OX20 1SY

All Rights Reserved

Library of Congress Cataloging-in-Publication Data

Rodrik, Dani.
One economics, many recipes: globalization, institutions, and economic
growth/Dani Rodrik.
p. cm.
Includes bibliographical references and index.
ISBN-13: 978-0-691-12951-8 (cloth: alk. paper)
1. International economic relations. 2. Globalization—Economic aspects. I. Title.
HF1359.R63 2007
338.9—dc22   2007005575

British Library Cataloging-in-Publication Data is available

This book has been composed in Warnock Typeface
Printed on acid-free paper.
press.princeton.edu
Printed in the United States of America

10   9   8   7   6   5   4   3

Tanıdığim en harika insan
eşim, arkadaşım,
Pınar'ıma

Contents

Acknowledgments

THIS BOOK may carry my name alone, but its contents were shaped also by the contributions and insights of the various collaborators I have been lucky to work with in recent years. It is a pleasant duty to acknowledge them here (in alphabetical order): Ricardo Hausmann, Murat Iyigun, Robert Lawrence, Sharun Mukand, Lant Pritchett, Francisco Rodriguez, Andrés Rodríguez-Clare, Arvind Subramanian, Roberto Unger, and Andres Velasco. They have influenced my thinking in diverse and often subtle ways—sometimes through an offhand remark and at other times through an extended discussion. But brainstorming with them on the issues covered in these pages has been the highlight of my academic career, for which I am deeply grateful.

Among these individuals, two deserve special mention. I doubt that Ricardo Hausmann and Roberto Unger agree about many things—and indeed it is difficult to think of two people with intellectual temperaments that are so different—but each has had a singular impact on my thinking. Ricardo Hausmann, the scholar-practitioner par excellence, has pushed me to think harder and deeper about issues of economic growth than anyone else. His energy, enthusiasm, and devotion to improving the policy environment for growth—and doing it in a way that is intellectually sound and academically rigorous—are unparalleled. Convincing him to join the Kennedy School faculty is unquestionably one of the best things I have done in—and *for*—my professional life. Roberto Unger, whose brilliance never ceases to amaze me, made his entry into my life quite suddenly. Even though we had never met, he phoned me out of the blue one day and asked me to teach a course with him. I don't know what possessed me to say yes. I have joked since that I did not understand a single word of any of his lectures the first time around. But a couple of years into the experience, my views on institutional development had been irrevocably altered. He better than anyone made me understand the multiplicity of market-supporting institutions. With his uncanny ability to articulate my views better than I ever could and extract richer implications than I was able to, he has helped me recognize and overcome—to some extent!—the professional deformations of the economist that I am.

Many others have read some or all of these chapters and have provided feedback at various times. I have benefited in particular from discussions with and comments from Philippe Aghion, Yilmaz Akyüz, Abhijit Banerjee, Nancy Birdsall, Avinash Dixit, Bill Easterly, Eduardo Engel, Ricardo Faini, Ricardo Ffrench-Davis, Arminio Fraga, Jeff Frankel, Richard Freeman, Jeffry Frieden, Murray Gibbs, Steph Haggard, David Held, Gerry Helleiner, K. S. Jomo, Devesh Kapur, Dani Kaufmann, Michael Kremer, Frank Levy, Kamal Malhotra, Maggie McMillan, José Antonio Ocampo, Yung Chul Park, James Robinson, Mark Rosenzweig, Jeffrey Sachs, Gita Sen, Francisco Sercovich, Narcis Serra, Andrei Shleifer, T. N. Srinivasan, Joseph Stiglitz, Dan Trefler, Robert Wade, Michael Weinstein, John Williamson, and Roberto Zagha. Needless to say, not all of these individuals agree with my broad arguments; some disagree with practically every substantive point I make in the following pages. I thank them all, without implicating them in any way.

Without the patient encouragement and prodding over the years of Peter Dougherty of Princeton University Press, I doubt that I would have had the nerve to put this book together. I also gratefully acknowledge financial support from the Carnegie Corporation (chapter 1), Center for International Relations and Development (CIDOB) in Barcelona (chapters 2 and 3), UN Industrial Development Organization (UNIDO, chapter 4), International Monetary Fund (chapter 5), the Munich Society for the Promotion of Economic Research (CESifo, chapter 6), Kennedy School Visions of Government Project (chapter 7), and the UN Development Program (UNDP, chapter 8). Magali Junowicz and Zoe McLaren provided excellent research assistance (on chapter 4 and chapter 8, respectively).

The John F. Kennedy School of Government and Harvard University have provided an unparalleled institutional environment for this work in a number of different ways. At its best, the Kennedy School excels in stimulating research that matters in practice. Many of the ideas in these chapters were first discussed in discussions at weekly meetings of the school's Lunch Group on International Economic Policy (LIEP). The students in the Kennedy School's master's degree program in economic development (MPAID) are an endless source of inspiration: they demand rigorous work that directly speaks to the burning issues of the day. It was only after the MPAID program came into its own that my teaching and research became truly complementary. Harvard's Center for International Development was an excellent source for research assistance and administrative support. I was also lucky to have a succession of extremely talented faculty assistants at the Kennedy School who deserve special thanks for putting up with my demands and disorganization: Joanna Veltri, Mary Gardner, Michele Kane, Zoe McLaren, and Robert Mitchell. The last of these, Robert Mitchell, devoted considerable effort to getting this book in shape for publication in his characteristically efficient and understated manner.

I have dedicated this book to Pinar Doğan, my wife, love of my life, and closest friend. She changed my life from the day that she entered it and taught me more than books and articles ever can.

PUBLICATION INFORMATION

Chapter 1: Original version published as "Growth Strategies" in *Handbook of Economic Growth*, ed. P. Aghion and S. Durlauf, vol. 1A (North-Holland, 2005). Chapter 2: original version published as "Growth Diagnostics" (with Ricardo Hausmann and Andres Velasco), in J. Stiglitz and N. Serra, eds., *The Washington Consensus Reconsidered: Towards a New Global Governance* (Oxford University Press, forthcoming). I thank Hausmann and Velasco for giving me permission to include this paper in this collection. Chapter 3: original version published as "A Practical Approach to Formulating Growth Strategies," in J. Stiglitz and N. Serra, eds., *The Washington Consensus Reconsidered: Towards a New Global Governance* (Oxford University Press, forthcoming). Chapter 4: This is based on an unpublished paper, of the same title, prepared for the UN Industrial Development Organization. Chapter 5: Original version published as "Institutions for High-Quality Growth: What They Are and How to Acquire Them," *Studies in Comparative International Development* 35, no. 3 (2000). Chapter 6: Original version published as "Getting Institutions Right," *CESifo DICE Report*, February 2004. Chapter 7: Original version published as "Governance of Economic Globalization," in J. S. Nye Jr. and J. D. Donahue, eds., *Governance in a Globalizing World* (Brookings Institution Press, 2000). Parts of this paper drew from my "How Far Will International Economic Integration Go?" *Journal of Economic Perspectives* (Winter 2000). Chapter 8: This is an abridged and updated version of a paper originally published as "The Global Governance of Trade as if Development Really Mattered," United Nations Development Program, New York, 2001. Chapter 9: Original version published as "Globalization for Whom?" *Harvard Magazine*, July–August 2002.

One Economics • Many Recipes

Introduction

O N A VISIT to a small Latin American country a few years back, my colleagues and I paid a courtesy visit to the minister of finance. The minister had prepared a detailed PowerPoint presentation on his economy's recent progress, and as his aide projected one slide after another on the screen, he listed all the reforms that they had undertaken. Trade barriers had been removed, price controls had been lifted, and all public enterprises had been privatized. Fiscal policy was tight, public debt levels low, and inflation nonexistent. Labor markets were as flexible as they come. There were no exchange or capital controls, and the economy was open to foreign investments of all kind. "We have done all the first-generation reforms, all the second-generation reforms, and are now embarking on third-generation reforms," he said proudly.

Indeed the country and its finance minister had been excellent students of the teaching on development policy emanating from international financial institutions and North American academics. And if there were justice in the world in matters of this kind, the country in question would have been handsomely rewarded with rapid growth and poverty reduction. Alas, not so. The economy was scarcely growing, private investment remained depressed, and largely as a consequence, poverty and inequality were on the rise. What had gone wrong?

Meanwhile, there were a number of other countries—mostly but not exclusively in Asia—that were undergoing more rapid economic development than could have been predicted by even the most optimistic economists. China has grown at rates that strain credulity, and India's performance, while not as stellar, has confounded those who thought that this country could never progress beyond its "Hindu" rate of economic growth of 3 percent. Clearly, globalization held huge rewards for those who knew how to reap them. What was it that these countries were doing right?

THE PRIMACY OF ECONOMIC GROWTH

These are some of the greatest economic puzzles of our time, and they are the questions around which the chapters in the book revolve.

Fascinating and challenging as they are from a scholarly standpoint, their significance runs much deeper. Our ability to answer these questions will help determine the extent to which the world's poor lift themselves out of destitution, improve their standards of living, achieve better health and education, and attain greater control over their lives. Economic growth *is* the most powerful instrument for reducing poverty. If you look at a map of the world today and ask where there is the greatest incidence of poverty, the simplest answer is: where there has been the least amount of growth since the onset of modern economic growth around the middle of the eighteenth century. Economic growth can be powerful over much shorter periods of time as well. China's rapid growth since 1980 has allowed more than 400 million of its citizens to pull themselves above the poverty line.[1] Of course, growth is not a panacea, and there are certainly cases where health and social indicators have not improved despite sustained growth over periods of a decade or more. But historically nothing has worked better than economic growth in enabling societies to improve the life chances of their members, including those at the very bottom.

As the vignettes with which I started indicate, these have been interesting times for students of economic growth. Some countries have embarked on rapid growth after years of stagnation; others have collapsed following a period of high growth; yet others have never experienced sustained growth. This book represents my attempt to understand the growth successes and failures of the last few decades and to distill general lessons from this experience. My objective is as much to shine a guiding light on future policies as it is to interpret the past. I aim in these essays to elucidate the nature of the institutional arrangements—national and global—that best support economic development over the longer term.

All of this diverse experience with growth has happened in an era of rapid globalization, during which countries have become increasingly open to forces emanating from outside their borders. The fact that they have responded so differently is evidence enough—if any is needed—that *national* policy choices are the ultimate determinant of economic growth. At the same time, successful countries are those that have leveraged the forces of globalization to their benefit. China and India would not have done nearly as well without access to relatively open markets for goods and services in the advanced countries. But their success was also due to their governments' concerted efforts to restructure and diversify their economies. If China and India had nothing other than garments and agricultural products to export, the gains from foreign trade and investment would not have been nearly as large. Understanding how the forces of globalization interact

---

[1] The poverty line here refers to the one-dollar-a-day benchmark. See Chen and Ravallion 2004.

with national economic policies is therefore indispensable as we interpret the past and draw lessons for the future. This helps us rethink global economic governance from a slightly different perspective: instead of asking, "What do countries have to do to live with globalization?" we can ask, "How should the institutions of economic globalization be designed to provide maximal support for national developmental goals?" I devote a good chunk of this book to the latter question.

The chapters that follow cover a wide range of topics—growth, institutions, globalization—but they advance, I think, a unified framework motivated by a number of common predilections and preoccupations. It may be useful to lay out those predilections—some will call them biases—at the outset.

A Credo of Sorts

First, this book is strictly grounded in neoclassical economic analysis. At the core of neoclassical economics lies the following methodological predisposition: social phenomena can best be understood by considering them to be an aggregation of purposeful behavior by individuals—in their roles as consumer, producer, investor, politician, and so on—interacting with each other and acting under the constraints that their environment imposes. This I find to be not just a powerful discipline for organizing our thoughts on economic affairs, but the only sensible way of thinking about them. If I often depart from the consensus that "mainstream" economists have reached in matters of development policy, this has less to do with different modes of analysis than with different readings of the evidence and with different evaluations of the "political economy" of developing nations. The economics that the graduate student picks up in the seminar room—abstract as it is and riddled with a wide variety of market failures—admits an almost unlimited range of policy recommendations, depending on the specific assumptions the analyst is prepared to make. As I will argue in the chapters to come, the tendency of many economists to offer advice based on simple rules of thumb, regardless of context (privatize this, liberalize that), is a derogation rather than a proper application of neoclassical economic principles.

Second, I believe in the importance of a careful reading of the empirical evidence. In particular, our prescriptions need to be based on a solid understanding of recent experience. This may seem like a trivial point to emphasize, but it is remarkable how frequently it is overlooked. It is common for policy advisors to recommend growth strategies to countries without having a solid grasp of the ups and downs of their recent economic performance—that is, without understanding the nature of the growth process in that economy. Econometricians are still hard at work looking for the growth-promoting effects of policies that countries in Latin America and elsewhere embraced enthusiastically a quarter century ago. I am not a purist when it comes to the kind of evidence that matters. In particular, I believe in the need for both cross-country regressions and detailed country studies. Any cross-country regression giving results are that not validated by case studies needs to be regarded with suspicion. But any policy conclusion that derives from a case study and flies in the face of cross-national evidence needs to be similarly scrutinized. Ultimately, we need both kinds of evidence to guide our views of how the world works.

Third, I remain a believer in the ability of governments to do good and change their societies for the better. Government has a positive role to play in stimulating economic development beyond enabling markets to function well. This view is to be contrasted with two alternative perspectives. One of these, the public-choice or rent-seeking perspective, thinks of the government as the malign tool of private interests. When the government interferes, it does so only to enrich supporters, cronies, or the intervening bureaucrats themselves. From this perspective, the more we can restrain government action, the better. The second perspective, that of the political-economy school, does not take an ex ante position on whether government is a positive or negative force, but fully endogenizes the behavior of government, and in doing so leaves it with no room to do anything (whether good or bad) that has not already been foreordained by long-standing structural determinants. To adherents of this perspective, the question "What should the government do?" is meaningless—or at least one that they have difficulty dealing with. While both schools have contributed important insights, I believe they underestimate the roles that serendipity and imperfect knowledge play in policy formulation. In the world of public policy, lots of $100 bills are left lying on the sidewalk. The role of economists is to point those out, while that of political leaders is to engineer the bargains that will allow them to be picked up.

Fourth, I believe that appropriate growth policies are almost always context specific. This is not because economics works differently in different settings, but because the *environments* in which households, firms, and investors operate differ in terms of the opportunities and constraints they present. "You don't understand; this reform will not work here because our entrepreneurs do not respond to price incentives," is not a valid argument. "You don't understand, this reform will not work here because credit constraints prevent our entrepreneurs from taking advantage of profit opportunities" or "because entrepreneurship is highly taxed at the margin" *is a* valid argument—assuming those borrowing constraints or high taxes can be documented. Learning from other countries is always useful—indeed, it is indispensable. But straightforward borrowing (or rejection) of policies without a full understanding of the context that enabled them to be successful (or led them to be failures) is a recipe for disaster. Once one understands that context, there will always be variations on the original policy (or different policies altogether) that will do a better job of producing the intended effects.

A fifth preoccupation is with prioritization, sequencing, selectivity, and targeting of reforms on the most binding constraints. One of the professional deformations of economists is to see an economy's problems almost exclusively from the perspective of their own area of specialty. A trade theorist will turn to developing economies and see lack of openness to trade as the key obstacle to growth. A financial market economist will identify imperfections in credit markets and lack of financial depth as the main culprit. A macroeconomist will worry about budget deficits, levels of debt, and inflation. A political-economy specialist will blame weakness in property rights and other institutions. A labor economist will point to labor-market rigidities. Each of them will then advocate a demanding set of institutional and governance reforms targeted at removing the presumed defect. So trade openness will require not just removal of tariffs and quotas on imports, but also improved governance, less corruption, better education, and smoothly functioning labor and credit markets. Financial depth requires prudential supervision and regulation, an open capital account, appropriate macroeconomic management. Macroeconomic stability requires fiscal rules, central bank independence, adherence to international financial codes, and sundry "structural reforms." Rarely will the advisor ask whether the problem at hand constitutes a truly binding constraint on economic growth, and whether the long list of institutional reforms on offer are well targeted at the economy's present needs. But governments are constrained by limits on their resources—financial, administrative, human, and political. They have to make choices on which constraints to attack first and what kind of reforms to spend political capital on. What they need is not a laundry list, but an explicitly diagnostic approach that identifies priorities based on local realities.

Finally, modesty. Economists have probably had more influence on policy in recent decades than at any other time in world history. But the sad reality is that their influence in the developing world has run considerably ahead of their actual achievements. Winston Churchill famously quipped that Clement Attlee, his rival and successor as prime minister in 1945, was "a modest man, with much to be modest about." To turn the quip on its head, economists are an arrogant bunch, with very little to be arrogant about. I hope the reader will agree that the essays in this book are different, for they were written in a spirit of humility. As social scientists, economists have neither the ability of physicists to fully explain the phenomena around us, nor the expertise of physicians to prescribe effective cures when things go wrong. We can be far more useful when we display greater self-awareness of our shortcomings. The emphasis on pragmatism, experimentation, and local knowledge that permeates the essays in the book is grounded in such considerations.

A Road Map of the Book

The chapters in the book are organized in three parts: growth, institutions, and globalization. Each part includes two substantive chapters plus a shorter piece of synthesis. These essays were written at different times over a period of around six years. All except one (chapter 4) has been published previously. I selected them among my publications not because they are my favorites or are better known, but because they fit well together and are thematically well linked. In preparing them for inclusion in this book, I undertook only some minor updating and edits, mainly to provide for smoother transitions across the chapters and eliminate repetition.

Part A of the book focuses on economic growth: why have some countries grown more rapidly than others, and what we can learn from this experience as we design growth strategies going forward? Chapter 1 offers a broad review of the evidence and presents two key arguments. One is that neoclassical economic analysis is a lot more flexible than its practitioners in the policy domain have generally given it credit for. In particular, first-order economic principles—protection of property rights, market-based competition, appropriate incentives, sound money, and so on—do not map into unique policy packages. Reformers have substantial room for creatively packaging these principles into institutional designs that are sensitive to local opportunities and constraints. Successful countries are those that have used this room wisely. The second argument is that igniting economic growth and sustaining it are somewhat different enterprises. The former generally requires a limited range of (often unconventional) reforms that need not overly tax the institutional capacity of the economy (as discussed in chapter 2). The latter challenge is in many ways harder, as it requires constructing over the longer term a sound institutional underpinning to endow the economy with resilience to shocks and maintain productive dynamism (see chapters 4 and 5). Ignoring the distinction between these two tasks leaves reformers saddled with impossibly ambitious, undifferentiated, and impractical policy agendas.

Chapter 2 (coauthored with Ricardo Hausmann and Andres Velasco) focuses on igniting economic growth. It presents a framework for identifying "binding constraints" on growth, so that reform strategies can focus on areas with the biggest immediate impact. The diagnostics revolve around a decision tree. Starting from the very top, growth can be constrained by inadequate social returns, by a large wedge between social and private returns (lack of appropriability), or by poor access to finance. Economies suffering from each of these different constraints throw out different signals. For example, a finance-constrained economy is one where real interest rates are high, current account deficits are large, and investment is highly responsive to exogenous foreign inflows (e.g., remittances). The diagnostic analysis begins by trying to identify which of these areas presents a more serious constraint, and then moves one level down. For instance, if low social returns are identified as the constraint, the next question turns on whether the reasons for that have to do with poor geography, low human capital, or inadequate infrastructure. The analysis continues in fractal fashion at successively finer levels of resolution until the list of binding constraints is narrowed to a set small enough to be amenable to policy. The chapter discusses the application of this approach to three Latin American countries: El Salvador, Brazil, and Dominican Republic.

Chapter 3 is a shorter, synthetic essay that pulls the key themes in the previous two chapters together and lays out a broad vision for formulating growth strategies. It emphasizes three steps in the process. The first step consists of an analysis of growth diagnostics, along the lines discussed in the previous chapter. The second step involves policy design, where the objective is to remove the identified constraint(s) with targeted, imaginative policies that are cognizant of the local realities. The third step is an ongoing one, requiring the institutionalization of the diagnostic and policy design activities, with the goals of strengthening the institutional infrastructure of the economy and maintaining productive vitality.

This provides a transition to part B of the book, which focuses on institutions specifically. The first chapter in this part (chapter 4) picks up the theme of productive vitality and asks: what kind of institutions best enable developing economies to diversify their productive structures so that they can sustain economic growth in the longer run? The hallmark of development is structural change—the process of pulling the economy's resources from traditional low-productivity activities to modern high-productivity activities. This is far from an automatic process, and requires more than well-functioning markets. It is the responsibility of industrial policy to stimulate investments and entrepreneurship in new activities, especially those in which the economy may end up having comparative advantage. The usual argument against industrial policy is that governments can never pick winners. I show that this is the wrong way of thinking what industrial policy does. Appropriately structured, industrial policy is a *process* of strategic collaboration between the private and public sectors, where the objectives are to identify blockages and obstacles to new investments and to design appropriate policies in response. The chapter describes the institutional features that such an industrial policy regime needs to have.

The focus of chapter 5 is the full gamut of market-supporting institutions that ensure economic prosperity in the long run. The chapter opens with a typology of institutions that allow markets to perform adequately. While we can identify in broad terms institutional prerequisites, I argue that there is no unique mapping between markets and the nonmarket institutions that underpin them. The chapter emphasizes the importance of "local knowledge," and advances the view that a strategy of institution building must not overemphasize best-practice "blueprints" at the expense of experimentation. The question is, how do we design such institutions sensitive to local knowledge and needs? I argue that participatory political systems are the most effective mechanism for processing and aggregating local knowledge. In effect, democracy is a metainstitution for building good institutions. I end the chapter with a range of evidence that shows that participatory democracies enable higher-quality growth.

Chapter 6 concludes part B by providing a guided tour of some of the key issues and controversies spawned by the huge outpouring of literature on institutions in recent years. If we focus on institutions—the rules of the game in a society—as the fundamental determinant of long-run growth, does that mean that economic policies themselves have little role to play? If it is true that colonial history has had a big hand in shaping today's institutional outcomes, does that mean that patterns of development are historically determined? If institutions "trump" geography as a deep determinant of incomes, does that mean that geography is of no consequence? If property rights are critical, does that imply that developing countries should adopt the property rights regimes that prevail in the United States or Europe? I argue in this chapter that the answers to each of these questions is no.

Part C of the book is devoted to globalization. In chapter 7, I identify the central dilemma of the world economy as the tension between the *global* nature of many of today's markets in goods, capital, and services, and the *national* nature of almost all of the institutions that underpin and support them. The needs of efficiency, equity, and legitimacy cannot all be met. If we want to advance economic globalization, we need to give up either on the nation-state or on democracy. If we want to retain the nation-state, we need to give up on either deep economic integration or mass democracy. And if we want to deepen democracy, we must sacrifice either the nation-state or deep integration. But the overall message of the chapter is not a pessimistic one. Our challenge is not markedly different from that confronted by the designers of Bretton Woods system in the aftermath World War II. By designing appropriate institutions of global economic governance—incorporating mechanisms of escape clauses and opt-outs—we can retain much of the benefit of economic globalization while endowing national democracies with the space they need to address domestic objectives.

Chapter 8 works out the implications of this line of reasoning for the international trade regime in particular. I argue that a World Trade Organization whose primary goal was to enable countries to grow out of poverty, rather than maximize the volume of trade, would look different from the WTO we have. In view of how open the global trade regime is currently, the big bucks in terms of growth are no longer in pushing for further increases in market access for developing countries in rich-country markets. The real challenge going forward is to how to make the tightening web of global trade regulations compatible with developmental needs. Connecting with the arguments made earlier in the book, a desirable trade regime would be one that provided much greater policy space to developing countries to pursue domestically crafted growth strategies, possibly including "unorthodox" policies such as export subsidies, trade protection, weak patent rules, and investment performance requirements. It should be possible to design institutional safeguards to ensure that such policy space does not deteriorate into crass protectionism, and the chapter discusses what such safeguards might look like. Under this new vision, the role of the WTO would be to regulate the interface between different national regulatory regimes rather than to narrow the differences among them. Developing countries would no longer short-change themselves by engaging in a game of reciprocal market access instead of ensuring that they have access to the full range of policy tools they need.

Chapter 9 is a short final essay that brings together some of the book's main themes of the relationship between economic growth and globalization. It ends with a proposal that was somewhat tongue-in-cheek when first formulated. If global trade negotiators are serious about making globalization work for developing countries, they should drop everything else on their agenda and focus on a temporary work permit program that allows unskilled workers from poor nations to take up employment (for periods of three to five years at a time) in rich countries. If globalization has an unexplored frontier, it is that of labor mobility. Nothing else promises as big a welfare bang for developing country workers as a relaxation of the restrictions on their international mobility. Remarkably, this pie-in-the-sky proposal has entered policy discussions. Ideas do matter.

A Final Word

Making a book out of a collection of one's previously published essays requires a certain hubris, which sits ill at ease with the spirit of humility that I claimed marks the essays themselves. I can say in my defense that this is not the first time I have attempted an effort of this kind. But previously, each time I put a table of contents together, I found that the book did not hang together. This time seemed different. Important themes—important in the sense that I still believe in them and feel the need to get them across—thread through the essays and connect different parts of the volume together. I will leave it to reviewers to judge whether the proverbial whole is greater than the sum of the parts. But I do hope that even the reader who has encountered some of these essays before will find new nuggets in rereading them in the context of the entire collection.

PART A

Economic Growth

1

Fifty Years of Growth (and Lack Thereof):
An Interpretation

REAL per capita income in the developing world grew at an average rate of 2.1 percent per annum during the four and a half decades between 1960 and 2004.[1] This is a high growth rate by almost any standard. At this pace incomes double every 33 years, allowing each generation to enjoy a level of living standards that is twice as high as the previous generation's. To provide some historical perspective on this performance, it is worth noting that Britain's per capita GDP grew at a mere 1.3 percent per annum during its period of economic supremacy in the middle of the nineteenth century (1820–70) and that the United States grew at only 1.8 percent during the half century before World War I when it overtook Britain as the world's economic leader (Maddison 2001, table B-22, 265). Moreover, with few exceptions, economic growth in the last few decades has been accompanied by significant improvements in social indicators such as literacy, infant mortality, and life expectation.[2] So on balance the recent growth record looks quite impressive.

However, since the rich countries themselves grew at a very rapid clip of 2.5 percent during the period 1960–2004, few developing countries consistently managed to close the economic gap between them and the advanced nations. As figure 1.1 indicates, the countries of East and Southeast Asia constitute the sole exception. Excluding China, this region experienced pretty consistent per capita GDP growth of 3.7 percent over 1960–2004. Despite the Asian financial crisis of 1997–98 (which shows as a slight dip in figure 1.1), countries such as South Korea, Thailand, and Malaysia ended the century with productivity levels that stood significantly closer to those enjoyed in the advanced countries.

[1] This figure refers to the exponential growth rate of GDP per capita (in constant 2000 US$) for the group of low- and middle-income countries. The data come from the World Development Indicators of the World Bank.

[2] According to the World Bank's World Development Indicators, even in sub-Saharan Africa life expectancy rose from 41 in the early 1960s to 50 by the early 1990s, and then fell back to 46 by 2003 under the influence of the AIDS scourge.

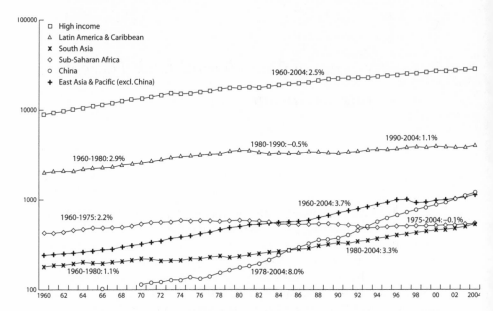

Fig. 1.1. GDP per capita by country groupings (in 2000 US$)
Source: World Bank, World Development Indicators.

Elsewhere, the pattern of economic performance has varied greatly across different time periods. China has been a major success story since the late 1970s, experiencing a stupendous growth rate of 8.0 percent since 1978. Less spectacularly, India has roughly doubled its growth rate since the early 1980s, pulling South Asia's growth rate up to 3.3 percent in 1980–2000 from 1.1 percent in 1960–1980. The experience in other parts of the world was the mirror image of these Asian growth take-offs. Latin America and sub-Saharan Africa both experienced robust economic growth prior to the late 1970s and early 1980s—2.9 percent and 2.2 percent respectively—but then lost ground subsequently in dramatic fashion. Latin America's growth rate collapsed in the "lost decade" of the 1980s, and has remained anemic despite some recovery in the 1990s. Africa's economic decline, which began in the second half of the 1970s, continued throughout much of the 1990s and has been aggravated by the onset of HIV/AIDS and other public-health challenges. Measures of total factor productivity run parallel to these trends in per capita output (see, for example, Bosworth and Collins 2003).

Hence the aggregate picture hides tremendous variety in growth performance, both geographically and temporally. We have high-growth countries and low-growth countries; countries that have grown rapidly throughout, and countries that have experienced growth spurts for a decade or two; countries that took off around 1980 and countries whose growth collapsed around 1980.

This chapter is devoted to the question, what do we learn about growth strategies from this rich and diverse experience? By *growth strategies* I refer to economic policies and institutional arrangements aimed at achieving economic convergence with the living standards prevailing in advanced countries. My emphasis will be less on the relationship between specific policies and economic growth—the stock-in-trade of cross-national growth empirics—and more on developing a broad understanding of the contours of successful strategies. Hence my account harks back to an earlier generation of studies that distilled operational lessons from the observed growth experience, such as Albert Hirschman's *The Strategy of Economic Development* (1958), Alexander Gerschenkron's *Economic Backwardness in Historical Perspective* (1962), and Walt Rostow's *The Stages of Economic Growth* (1965). This chapter follows an unashamedly inductive approach in this tradition.

A key theme in these works, as well as in the present analysis, is that growth-promoting policies tend to be context specific. We are able to make only a limited number of generalizations on the effects on growth, say, of liberalizing the trade regime, opening up the financial system, or building more schools. As I will stress throughout this book, the experience of the last two decades has frustrated the expectations of policy advisors who thought we had a good fix on the policies that promote growth. And despite a voluminous literature, cross-national growth regressions ultimately do not provide us with much reliable and unambiguous evidence on such operational matters.[3] An alternative approach, the one I adopt here, is to shift our focus to a higher level of generality and to examine the broad design principles of successful growth strategies. This entails zooming away from the individual building blocks and concentrating on how they are put together.

The chapter revolves around two key arguments. One is that neoclassical economic analysis is a lot more flexible than its practitioners in the policy domain have generally given it credit for. In particular, first-order economic principles—protection of property rights, contract enforcement, market-based competition, appropriate incentives, sound money, debt sustainability—do not map into unique policy packages. Good institutions are those that deliver these first-order principles effectively. There is no unique correspondence between the *functions* that good institutions perform and the *form* that such institutions take. Reformers have substantial room for creatively packaging these principles into institutional designs that are

---

[3] Easterly (2005) provides a good overview of these studies. See also Temple 1999; Brock and Durlauf 2001; Rodríguez and Rodrik 2001; and Rodríguez 2005.

sensitive to local constraints and take advantage of local opportunities. Successful countries are those that have used this room wisely.

The second argument is that igniting economic growth and sustaining it are somewhat different enterprises. The former generally requires a limited range of (often unconventional) reforms that need not overly tax the institutional capacity of the economy. The latter challenge is in many ways harder, as it requires constructing a sound institutional underpinning to maintain productive dynamism and endow the economy with resilience to shocks over the longer term. The good news is that this institutional infrastructure does not have to be constructed overnight. Ignoring the distinction between these two tasks—starting and sustaining growth—leaves reformers saddled with impossibly ambitious, undifferentiated, and impractical policy agendas.

The plan for the chapter is as follows. The next section sets the stage by evaluating the standard recipes for economic growth in light of recent economic performance. The third section develops the argument that sound economic principles do not map into unique institutional arrangements and reform strategies. The fourth section reinterprets recent growth experience using the conceptual framework of the previous section. The fifth section discusses a two-pronged growth strategy that differentiates between the challenges of igniting growth and the challenges of sustaining it. Concluding remarks are presented in the final section.

WHAT WE KNOW THAT (POSSIBLY) AIN'T SO

Development policy has always been subject to fads and fashions. During the 1950s and 1960s, "big push," planning, and import-substitution were the rallying cries of economic reformers in poor nations. These ideas lost ground during the 1970s to more market-oriented views that emphasized the role of the price system and an outward orientation.[4] By the late 1980s a remarkable convergence of views had developed around a set of policy principles that John Williamson (1990) infelicitously termed the "Washington Consensus." These principles remain at the heart of conventional understanding of a desirable policy framework for economic growth, even though they have been greatly embellished and expanded in the years since.

The left panel in table 1.1 shows Williamson's original list, which focused on fiscal discipline, "competitive" currencies, trade and financial liberalization, privatization and deregulation. These were perceived to be the key elements of what Krugman (1995, 29) has called the "Victorian virtue in economic policy," namely "free markets and sound money."

[4] Easterly (2001) provides an insightful and entertaining account of the evolution of thinking on economic development. See also Lindauer and Pritchett 2002; and Krueger 1997.

TABLE 1.1
Rules of Good Behavior for Promoting Economic Growth

Original Washington Consensus	"Augmented" Washington Consensus (additions to the original 10 items)
1. Fiscal discipline	11. Corporate governance
2. Reorientation of public expenditures	12. Anticorruption
3. Tax reform	13. Flexible labor markets
4. Interest rate liberalization	14. Adherence to WTO disciplines
5. Unified and competitive exchange rates	15. Adherence to international financial codes and standards
6. Trade liberalization	16. "Prudent" capital-account opening
7. Openness to direct foreign investment	17. Nonintermediate exchange rate regimes
8. Privatization	18. Independent central banks/inflation targeting
9. Deregulation	19. Social safety nets
10. Secure property rights	20. Targeted poverty reduction

Toward the end of the 1990s, this list was augmented in the thinking of multilateral agencies and policy economists with a series of so-called second-generation reforms that were more institutional in nature and targeted at problems of "good governance." A complete inventory of these Washington Consensus–plus reforms would take too much space, and in any case the precise listing differs from source to source.[5] I have shown a representative sample of 10 items (to preserve the symmetry with the original Washington Consensus) in the right panel of table 1.1. They range from anticorruption and corporate governance to "flexible" labor markets and social safety nets.

The perceived need for second-generation reforms arose from a combination of sources. First, there was growing recognition that market-oriented policies might be inadequate without more serious institutional transformation, in areas ranging from the bureaucracy to labor markets. For example, trade liberalization will not reallocate an economy's resources appropriately if the labor markets are "rigid" or insufficiently "flexible." Second, there was a concern that financial liberalization might lead to crises and excessive volatility in the absence of a more carefully delineated macroeconomic framework and improved prudential regulation. Hence arose the focus on nonintermediate exchange-rate regimes, central bank

[5] For diverse perspectives on what the list should contain, see Stiglitz 1998; World Bank 1998; Naim 1999; Birdsall and de la Torre 2001; Kaufmann 2002; Ocampo 2002; and Kuczynski and Williamson 2003.

independence, and adherence to international financial codes and standards. Finally, in response to the complaint that the Washington Consensus represented a trickle-down approach to poverty, the policy framework was augmented with social policies and antipoverty programs.

It is probably fair to say that a list along the lines of table 1.1 captures in broad brushstrokes mainstream post–Washington Consensus thinking on the key elements of a growth program. How does such a list fare when held against the light of contemporary growth experience? Imagine that we gave table 1.1 to an intelligent Martian and asked him to match the growth record displayed in figure 1.1 with the expectations that the list generates. How successful would he be in identifying which of the regions adopted the standard policy agenda and which did not?

Consider first the high-performing East Asian countries. Since this region is the only one that has done consistently well since the early 1960s, the Martian would reasonably guess that there is a high degree of correspondence between the region's policies and the list in table 1.1. But he would be at best half right. South Korea's and Taiwan's growth policies, to take two important illustrations, exhibit significant departures from the mainstream consensus. Neither country undertook significant deregulation or liberalization of its trade and financial systems well into the 1980s. Far from privatizing, they both relied heavily on public enterprises. South Korea did not even welcome direct foreign investment. And both countries deployed an extensive set of industrial policies that took the form of directed credit, trade protection, export subsidization, tax incentives, and other nonuniform interventions. Using the minimal scorecard of the original Washington Consensus (left panel of table 1.2), the Martian would award South Korea a grade of 5 (out of 10) and Taiwan perhaps a 6 (Rodrik 1996a).

The gap between the East Asian "model" and the more demanding institutional requirements shown in the right panel of table 1.1 is, if anything, even larger. I provide a schematic comparison between the mainstream "ideal" and the East Asian reality in table 1.2 for a number of different institutional domains, such as corporate governance, financial markets, business-government relationships, and public ownership. Looking at these discrepancies, the Martian might well conclude that South Korea, Taiwan, and (before them) Japan stood little chance to develop. Indeed, so strong were the East Asian anomalies that when the Asian financial crisis of 1997–98 struck, many observers attributed the crisis to the moral hazard, "cronyism," and other problems created by East Asian–style institutions (see MacLean 1999; Frankel 2000a).

The Martian would also be led astray by China's boom since the late 1970s and by India's less phenomenal, but still significant growth pickup since the early 1980s. While both of these countries have transformed their attitudes toward markets and private enterprise during

TABLE 1.2
East Asian Anomalies

Institutional Domain	Mainstream Ideal	"East Asian" Pattern
Property rights	Private, enforced by the rule of law	Private, but government authority occasionally overrides the law (esp. in Korea)
Corporate governance	Shareholder ("outsider") control, protection of shareholder rights	Insider control
Business-government relations	Arm's length, rule based	Close interactions
Industrial organization	Decentralized, competitive markets, with tough antitrust enforcement	Horizontal and vertical integration in production (*chaebol*); government-mandated "cartels"
Financial system	Deregulated, securities based, with free entry. Prudential supervision through regulatory oversight.	Bank based, restricted entry, heavily controlled by government, directed lending, weak formal regulation
Labor markets	Decentralized, deinstitutionalized, "flexible" labor markets	Lifetime employment in core enterprises (Japan)
International capital flows	"Prudently" free	Restricted (until the 1990s)
Public ownership	None in productive sectors	Plenty in upstream industries

this period, their policy frameworks bear very little resemblance to what is described in table 1.1. India deregulated its policy regime slowly and undertook very little privatization. Its trade regime remained heavily restricted late into the 1990s. China did not even adopt a private property rights regime, and it merely appended a market system to the scaffolding of a planned economy (as discussed further below). It is hardly an exaggeration to say that had the Chinese economy stagnated in the last couple of decades, the Martian would be in a better position to rationalize it using the policy guidance provided in table 1.1 than he is to explain China's *actual* performance.[6]

The Martian would be puzzled that the region that made the most determined attempt at remaking itself in the image of table 1.1, namely Latin America, has reaped so little growth benefit out of it. Countries such as Mexico, Argentina, Brazil, Colombia, Bolivia, and Peru did more liberalization, deregulation, and privatization in the course of a few years than East Asian countries have done in four decades. Figure 1.2 shows an index of structural reform for these and other Latin American countries, taken from Lora (2001a). The index measures on a scale from 0 to 1 the extent of trade and financial liberalization, tax reform, privatization, and labor-market reform undertaken. The regional average for the index rises steadily from 0.34 in 1985 to 0.58 in 1999. Yet the striking fact from figure 1.1 is that Latin America's growth rate has remained a fraction of its pre-1980 level. The Martian would be at a loss to explain why growth is now lower given that the quality of Latin America's policies, as judged by the requirements in table 1.1, have improved so much.[7] A similar puzzle, perhaps of a smaller magnitude, arises with respect to Africa, where economic decline persists despite an overall (if less marked) "improvement" in the policy environment.[8]

---

[6] Vietnam, a less well known case than China, has many of the same characteristics: rapid growth since the late 1980s as a result of heterodox reform. Vietnam has benefited from a gradual turn toward markets and greater reliance on private entrepreneurship, but as Van Arkadie and Mallon (2003) argue, it is hard to square the extensive role of the state and the nature of the property rights regime with the tenets of the Washington Consensus.

[7] Lora (2001b) finds that structural reforms captured by this index do correlate with growth rates in the predicted manner, but that the impacts (taking the decade of the 1990s as a whole) are not strong. Another econometric study by Loayza, Fajnzylber, and Calderón (2002) claims that Latin America's reforms added significantly to the region's growth. However, the latter paper uses outcome variables such as trade/GDP and financial depth ratios as its indicators of "policy," and therefore is unable to link economic performance directly to the reforms themselves. This paper also finds a strongly negative dummy for the 1990s—i.e., an unexplained growth reduction.

[8] See also Milanovic 2003 for a closely related Martian thought experiment. Milanovic emphasizes that economic growth has declined in most countries despite greater globalization.

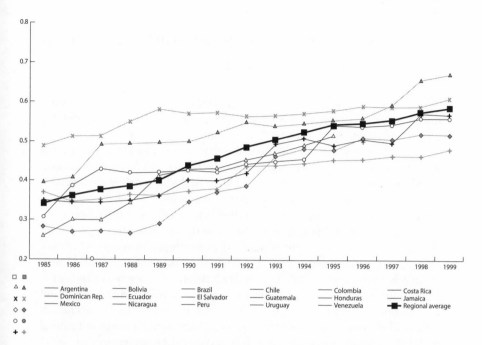

Fig. 1.2. Structural reform index for Latin American Countries
Source: Lora 2001a.

The Martian would recognize that the growth record is consistent with some of the *higher-order* economic principles that inspire the standard policy consensus. A semblance of property rights, sound money, fiscal solvency, market-oriented incentives—these are elements common to all successful growth strategies.[9] Where they have been lacking, economic performance has been lackluster at best. But the Martian would also have to conclude that the mapping from our more detailed policy preferences (such as those in table 1.1) to economic success is quite imperfect. He would wonder if we could not do better.

[9] Here is how Larry Summers (2003) summarizes the recent growth evidence: "[The] rate at which countries grow is substantially determined by three things: their ability to integrate with the global economy through trade and investment; their capacity to maintain sustainable government finances and sound money; and their ability to put in place an institutional environment in which contracts can be enforced and property rights can be established. I would challenge anyone to identify a country that has done all three of these things and has not grown at a substantial rate." Note how these recommendations are couched not in terms of specific policies (maintain tariffs below x percent, raise the government primary surplus above y percent, privatize state enterprises, and so on), but in terms of "abilities" and "capacities" to get certain outcomes accomplished. I will suggest below that these "abilities" and "capacities" do not map neatly into the standard policy preferences, and can be generated in a variety of ways.

INDETERMINATE MAPPING FROM ECONOMIC PRINCIPLES TO INSTITUTIONAL ARRANGEMENTS

Here is another thought experiment. Imagine a Western economist was invited to Beijing in 1978 in order to advise the Chinese leadership on a reform strategy. What would she recommend, and why?

The economist would recognize that reform must start in the rural areas since the vast majority of the poor live there. An immediate recommendation would be the *liberalization of agricultural markets* and the *abolition of the state order system* under which peasants had to make obligatory deliveries of crops at low, state-controlled prices. But since price liberalization alone would be inadequate to generate the appropriate supply incentives under a system of communal land ownership, the economist would also recommend the *privatization of land*. Next, the economist would have to turn her attention to the broader implications of price liberalization in agriculture. Without access to cheap grains, the state would be left without a source of implicit tax revenue, so *tax reform* must be on the agenda as well. And in view of the rise of food prices, there must be a way to respond to urban workers' demand for higher wages. State enterprises in urban areas must be *corporatized*, so that their managers are in a position to adjust their wages and prices appropriately.

But now there are other problems that need attention. In an essentially closed and noncompetitive economy, price-setting autonomy for large state enterprises entails the exercise of monopoly power. So the economist would likely recommend *trade liberalization* in order to "import" price discipline from abroad. Openness to trade in turn calls for other complementary reforms. There must be *financial sector reform* so that financial intermediaries are able to assist domestic enterprises in the inevitable adjustments that are called forth. And, of course, there must be *social safety nets* in place so that those workers who are temporarily displaced have some income support during the transition.

The story can be embellished by adding other required reforms, but the message ought to be clear. By the time the Western economist is done, the reform agenda she has formulated looks very similar to the Washington Consensus (see table 1.3). The economist's reasoning is utterly plausible, which underscores the point that the consensus is far from silly: it is the result of systematic thinking about the multiple, often complementary reforms needed to establish property rights, put market incentives to work, and maintain macroeconomic stability. But while this particular reform program represents a logically consistent way of achieving these

TABLE 1.3
The Logic of the Washington Consensus and a Chinese Counterfactual

Problem		Solution
Low agricultural productivity	→	Price liberalization
Production incentives	→	Land privatization
Loss of fiscal revenues	→	Tax reform
Urban wages	→	Corporatization
Monopoly	→	Trade liberalization
Enterprise restructuring	→	Financial sector reform
Unemployment	→	Social safety nets

end goals, it is not the only one that has the potential of doing so. In fact, in view of the administrative and political constraints that such an ambitious agenda is likely to encounter, there may be better ways of getting there.

How can we be sure of this? We know this because China took a very different approach to reform—one that was experimental in nature and relied on a series of policy innovations that departed significantly from Western norms. What is important to realize about these innovations is that in the end they delivered—for a period of a couple of decades at least— the very same goals that the Western economist would have been hoping for: market-oriented incentives, property rights, macroeconomic stability. But they did so in a peculiar fashion that, given the Chinese historical and political context, had numerous advantages.

For example, the Chinese authorities liberalized agriculture only *at the margin* while keeping the plan system intact. Farmers were allowed to sell surplus crops freely at a market-determined price only after they had fulfilled their obligations to the state under the state order system. As Lau, Qian, and Roland (2000) explain, this ingenious system generated efficiency without creating any losers. In particular, it was a shortcut that neatly solved a conundrum inherent in wholesale liberalization: how to provide microeconomic incentives to producers while insulating the central government from the fiscal consequences of liberalization. As long as state quotas were set below the fully liberalized market outcome (so that transactions were conducted at market prices at the margin) and were not ratcheted up (so that producers did not have to worry about the quotas creeping up as a result of marketed surplus), China's dual-track reform in effect achieved full allocative efficiency. But it entailed a different inframarginal distribution—one that preserved the income streams of initial claimants. The dual-track approach was eventually employed in other areas as well, such as industrial goods (e.g., coal and steel) and labor markets (employment contracts). Lau et al. (2000) argue that the system was critical to achieve political support for the reform process, maintain its momentum, and minimize adverse social implications.

Another important illustration comes from the area of property rights. Rather than privatize land and industrial assets, the Chinese government implemented novel institutional arrangements such as the household responsibility system (under which land was "assigned" to individual households according to their size) and township and village enterprises (TVEs). The TVEs were the growth engine of China until the mid-1990s (Qian 2003), with their share in industrial value added rising to more than 50 percent by the early 1990s (Lin, Cai, and Li 1996, 180), so they deserve special comment. Formal ownership rights in TVEs were vested not in private hands or in the central government, but in local communities (townships or villages). Local governments were keen to ensure the prosperity of these enterprises, as their equity stake generated revenues directly for them. Qian (2003) argues that in the environment characteristic of China, property rights were effectively more secure under direct local government ownership than they would have been under a private-property-rights legal regime. The efficiency loss caused by the absence of private control rights was probably outweighed by the implicit security guaranteed by local government control. It is difficult to explain otherwise the remarkable boom in investment and entrepreneurship generated by such enterprises.

Qian (2003) discusses other examples of "transitional institutions" China employed to fuel economic growth—fiscal contracts between central and local governments, anonymous banking—and one may expand his list by including arrangements such as special economic zones. The main points to take from this experience are the following. First, China relied on highly unusual, nonstandard institutions. Second, these unorthodox institutions worked precisely because they produced orthodox results, namely market-oriented incentives, property rights, macroeconomic stability, and so on. Third, it is hard to argue, in view of China's stupendous growth, that a more standard, "best-practice" set of institutional arrangements would have necessarily done better. Of course, it is entirely possible that these Chinese-style institutions will turn out to be dysfunctional in the longer run and therefore in need of reform themselves. My point is simply that they sparked an unprecedented rate of economic growth in a manner that is hard to envisage the mainstream alternatives accomplishing.

China's experience helps lay out the issues clearly because its institutional innovations and growth performance are both so stark. But the Chinese experience with nonstandard growth policies is hardly unusual; in fact, it is more the rule than the exception. The (other) East Asian anomalies noted previously (table 1.2) can be viewed as part of the same pattern: nonstandard practices in the service of sound economic principles. I summarize a few non-Chinese illustrations in table 1.4.

TABLE 1.4
How to Understand and Rationalize Institutional Anomalies: Four Illustrations

Objective	What is the Problem?	Institutional Response	Prerequisites	Institutional Complements
Financial deepening (saving mobilization and efficient intermediation)	Asymmetric information (investors know more about their projects than lenders do) and limited liability	"Financial restraint" (Hellmann et al. 1997): controlled deposit rates and restricted entry; creation of rents to induce better portfolio risk management, better monitoring of firms, and increased deposit mobilization by banks	Ability to maintain restraint at *moderate* levels; positive real interest rates; macroeconomic stability; avoid state capture by financial interests	*Finance:* highly regulated financial markets (absence of security markets and closed capital accounts to prevent cherry picking and rent dissipation); *politics:* state "autonomy" to prevent capture and decay into "crony capitalism"
Spurring investment and entrepreneurship in nontraditional activities	Economies of scale together with interindustry linkages depress private return to entrepreneurship/ investment below social return.	"Industrial policy as a coordination device" (Rodrik 1995a): credit subsidies (Korea) and tax incentives (Taiwan) for selected sectors; protection of home market coupled with export subsidies; public enterprise creation for upstream products; arm-twisting and cajoling by political leadership; socialization of investment risk through implicit investment guarantees	High level of human capital relative to physical capital; relatively competent bureaucracy to select investment projects	*Trade:* need to combine import protection (in selected sectors) with exposure to competition in export markets to distinguish high-from low-productivity firms; *business-government relations:* "embedded autonomy" (Evans 1995) to enable close interactions and information exchange while preventing state capture and decay into "crony capitalism"

TABLE 1.4 (cont.)

Objective	What is the Problem?	Institutional Response	Prerequisites	Institutional Complements
Productive organization of the workplace	Trade-off between information sharing (working together) and economies of specialization (specialized tasks)	"Horizontal hierarchy" (Aoki 1997)	(Unintended) fit with prewar arrangements of military resource mobilization in Japan	*Corporate governance:* insider control to provide incentive for accumulating long-term managerial skills; *labor markets:* lifetime employment and enterprise unionism to generate long-term collaborative teamwork; *financial markets:* main bank system to discipline firms and reduce the moral hazard consequences of insider control; *politics:* "bureau-pluralism" (regulation protection) to redistribute benefits to less productive, traditional sectors
Reduce antiexport bias	Import-competing interests are politically powerful and opposed to trade liberalization	Export-processing zone (Rodrik 1999a)	Saving boom; elastic supply of foreign investment; preferential market access in EU	*Dual labor markets:* segmentation between male and female labor force, so that increased female employment in the EPZ does not drive wages up in the rest of the economy

Consider, for example, the case of financial controls. I noted earlier that few of the successful East Asian countries undertook much financial liberalization early in their development process. Interest rates remained controlled below market-clearing levels, and competitive entry (by domestic or foreign financial intermediaries) was typically blocked. It is easy to construct arguments as to why this was beneficial from an economic standpoint. Table 1.4 summarizes the story laid out by Hellmann, Murdock, and Stiglitz (1997), who coin the term *financial restraint* for the Asian model. Where asymmetric information prevails and the level of savings is suboptimal, Hellman et al. argue that creating a moderate amount of rents for incumbent banks can generate useful incentives. These rents induce banks to do a better job of monitoring their borrowers (since there is more at stake) and to expand efforts to mobilize deposits (since there are rents to be earned on them). Both the quality and the level of financial intermediation can be higher than under financial liberalization. These beneficial effects are more likely to materialize when the preexisting institutional landscape has certain properties—for example, when the state is not "captured" by private interests and the external capital account is restricted (see last two columns of table 1.4). When these preconditions are in place, the economic logic behind financial restraint is compelling.

The second illustration in table 1.4 comes from South Korea's and Taiwan's experiences with industrial policy. The governments in these countries rejected the standard advice that they take an arm's length approach to their enterprises and actively sought to coordinate private investments in targeted sectors. Once again, it is easy to come up with economic models that provide justification for this approach. I have argued (Rodrik 1995a) that the joint presence of scale economies and interindustry linkages can depress the private return to investment in nontraditional activities below the social return. Industrial policy can be viewed as a "coordination device" to stimulate socially profitable investments. In particular, the socialization of investment risk through implicit bailout guarantees may be economically beneficial despite the obvious moral hazard risk it poses. However, once again, there are certain prerequisites and institutional complements that have to be in place for this approach to make sense (see table 1.4).

The third illustration in table 1.4 refers to Japan and concerns the internal organization of the workplace, drawing on Aoki's (1997) work. Aoki describes the peculiar institutional foundations of Japan's postwar success as having evolved from a set of arrangements originally designed for wartime mobilization and centralized control of resources. He presents Japan's team-centered approach to work organization and its redistribution of economic resources from advanced to backward sectors—arrangements that he terms "horizontal hierarchy" and "bureau-pluralism," respectively—as solutions to particular informational and distributive dilemmas the Japanese economy faced in the aftermath of World War II. Unlike the previous authors, however, he views this fit between institutions and economic challenges as having been unintended and serendipitous.

Lest the reader think this is solely an East Asian phenomenon, an interesting example of institutional innovation comes from Mauritius (Rodrik 1999a). Mauritius owes a large part of its success to the creation in 1970 of an export-processing zone (EPZ), which enabled an export boom in garments to European markets. Yet instead of liberalizing its trade regime across the board, Mauritius combined this EPZ with a domestic sector that was highly protected until the mid-1980s, a legacy of the policies of import-substituting industrialization (ISI) followed during the 1960s. The industrialist class that had been created with these policies was naturally opposed to the opening up of the trade regime. The EPZ scheme provided a neat way around this difficulty (Wellisz and Saw 1993). The creation of the EPZ generated new profit opportunities, without taking protection away from the import-substituting groups. The segmentation of labor markets was particularly crucial in this regard, as it prevented the expansion of the EPZ (which employed mainly female labor) from driving wages up in the rest of the economy, and thereby disadvantaging import-substituting industries. New profit opportunities were created at the margin, while leaving old opportunities undisturbed. At a conceptual level, the story here is essentially very similar to the two-track reforms in China described earlier. To produce the results it did, however, the EPZ also needed a source of investible funds, export-oriented expertise, and market access abroad, which were in turn provided by a terms-of-trade boom, entrepreneurs from Hong Kong, and preferential market access in Europe, respectively (Rodrik 1999a; Subramanian and Roy 2003).

In reviewing cases such as these, we may read too much into them after the fact. In particular, we need to avoid several fallacies. First, we cannot simply assume that institutions take the form that they do *because* of the functions that they perform (the functionalist fallacy). Aoki's account of Japan is a particularly useful reminder that a good fit between form and function might be the unintended consequence of historical forces. Second, it is not correct to ascribe the positive outcomes in the cases just reviewed only to their anomalies (the ex post rationalization fallacy). Many accounts of East Asian success emphasize the standard elements—fiscal conservatism, investment in human resources, and export orientation (see, for example, World Bank 1993). As I will discuss below, East Asian institutional anomalies have often produced perverse results when employed in other settings. And it is surely not the case that all anomalies are economically functional.

The main point I take from these illustrations is robust to these fallacies, and has to do with the "plasticity" of the institutional structure that neoclassical economics is capable of supporting. All of the above institutional anomalies are compatible with, and can be understood in terms of, neoclassical economic reasoning ("good economics"). Neoclassical economic analysis does not determine the form that institutional arrangements should or do take. What China's case and other examples discussed above demonstrate is that the higher-order principles of sound economic management do not map into unique institutional arrangements.

In fact, principles such as appropriate incentives, property rights, sound money, and fiscal solvency all come institution-free. We need to operationalize them through a set of policy actions. The experiences above show us that there may be multiple ways of packing these principles into institutional arrangements. Different packages have different costs and benefits depending on prevailing political constraints, levels of administrative competence, and market failures. The preexisting institutional landscape will typically offer both constraints and opportunities, requiring creative shortcuts or bold experiments. From this perspective, the "art" of reform consists of selecting appropriately from a potentially infinite menu of institutional designs.

A direct corollary of this line of argument is that there is only a weak correspondence between the higher-order principles of neoclassical economics and the specific policy recommendations in the standard list (as enumerated in table 1.1). Once again, an example may clarify the point. Consider one of the least contentious recommendations in the list, having to do with trade liberalization. Can the statement "Trade liberalization is good for economic performance" be derived from first principles of neoclassical economics? Yes, but only if a *large* number of side conditions are met:

- The liberalization must be complete or else the reduction in import restrictions must take into account the potentially quite complicated structure of substitutability and complementarity across restricted commodities.[10]
- There must be no microeconomic market imperfections other than the trade restrictions in question, or if there are some, the second-best interactions that are entailed must not be adverse.[11]

[10] There is a large theoretical literature on partial trade reform, which shows the difficulty of obtaining unambiguous characterizations of the welfare effects of incomplete liberalization. See Hatta 1977a and 1977b; Anderson and Neary 1992; and Lopez and Panagariya 1992. For an applied general equilibrium analysis of how these issues can complicate trade reform in practice, see Harrison, Rutherford, and Tarr 1993.

[11] For an interesting empirical illustration on how trade liberalization can interact adversely with environmental externalities, see Lopez 1997.

• The home economy must be "small" in world markets, or else the liberalization must not put the economy on the wrong side of the "optimum tariff."[12]

• The economy must be in reasonably full employment, or if not, the monetary and fiscal authorities must have effective tools of demand management at their disposal.

• The income redistributive effects of the liberalization should not be judged undesirable by society at large, or if they are, there must be compensatory tax-transfer schemes with low enough excess burden.[13]

• There must be no adverse effects on the fiscal balance, or if there are, there must be alternative and expedient ways of making up for the lost fiscal revenues.

• The liberalization must be politically sustainable and hence credible so that economic agents do not fear or anticipate a reversal.[14]

All these theoretical complications could be sidestepped if there were convincing evidence that in practice trade liberalization systematically produces improved economic performance. But even for this relatively uncontroversial policy, it has proved difficult to generate unambiguous evidence (see Rodríguez and Rodrik 2001; Vamvakidis 2002; and Yanikkaya 2003).[15]

The point is that even the simplest of policy recommendations—"liberalize foreign trade"—is contingent on a large number of judgment calls about the economic and political context in which it is to be implemented.[16] Such judgment calls are often made implicitly. Rendering them explicit has a double advantage: it warns us about the potential minefields that await the standard recommendations, and it stimulates creative thinking on alternatives (as in China) that can sidestep those minefields. By

---

[12] This is not a theoretical curiosum. Gilbert and Varangis (2003) argue that the liberalization of cocoa exports in West African countries has depressed world cocoa prices, with most of the benefits being captured by consumers in developed countries.

[13] The standard workhorse model of international trade, the factor-endowments model and its associated Stolper-Samuelson theorem, comes with sharp predictions on the distributional effects of import liberalization (the "magnification effect").

[14] Calvo (1989) was the first to point out that lack of credibility acts as an intertemporal distortion. See also Rodrik 1991.

[15] Recent empirical studies have begun to look for nonlinear effects of trade liberalization. In a study of India's liberalization, Aghion et al. (2003) find that trade liberalization appears to have generated differentiated effects across Indian firms depending on prevailing industrial capabilities and labor market regulations. Firms that were close to the technological frontier and in states with more "flexible" regulations responded positively, while others responded negatively. See also Helleiner 1994 for a useful collection of country studies that underscores the contingent nature of economies' response to trade liberalization.

[16] This is one reason why policy discussions on standard recommendations such as trade liberalization and privatization now often take the formulaic form, "Policy x is not a panacea; in order to work, it must be supported by reforms in the areas of a, b, c, d, and so on."

contrast, when the policy recommendation is made unconditionally, as in the mainstream consensus (Washington or post-Washington), the gamble is that the policy's prerequisites will coincide with our actual draw from a potentially large universe of possible states of the world.

I summarize this discussion with the help of tables 1.5, 1.6, and 1.7, dealing with microeconomic policy, macroeconomic policy, and social policy, respectively. Each table contains three columns. The first column displays the ultimate goal that is targeted by the policies and institutional arrangements in the three domains. Hence microeconomic policies aim to achieve static and dynamic efficiency in the allocation of resources. Macroeconomic policies aim for macroeconomic and financial stability. Social policies target poverty reduction and social protection.

The next column displays some of the key higher-order principles that economic analysis brings to the table. Allocative efficiency requires property rights, the rule of law, and appropriate incentives. Macroeconomic and financial stability requires sound money, fiscal solvency, and prudential regulation. Social inclusion requires incentive compatibility and appropriate targeting. These are the "universal principles" of sound economic management. They are universal in the sense that it is hard to see what any country would gain by systematically defying them. Countries that have adhered to these principles—no matter how unorthodox their manner of doing so—have done well, while countries that have flouted them have typically done poorly.

From the standpoint of policymakers, the trouble is that these universal principles are not operational as stated. In effect, the answers to the real questions that preoccupy policymakers—how far should I go in opening up my economy to foreign competition, should I free up interest rates, should I rely on payroll taxes or the VAT, and the others listed in the third column of each table—cannot be directly deduced from these principles. This opens up space for a multiplicity of institutional arrangements that are compatible with the universal, higher-order principles.

These tables clarify why the standard recommendations (table 1.1) correlate poorly with economic performance around the world. The Washington Consensus, in its various forms, has tended to blur the line that separates column 2 from column 3. Policy advisors have been too quick in jumping from the higher-order principles in column 2 to taking unconditional stands on the specific operational questions posed in column 3. And as their policy advice has yielded disappointing results, they have moved on to recommendations with even greater institutional specificity (as with "second-generation reforms"). As a result, sound economics has often been delivered in unsound form.

I emphasize that this argument is not one about the advantages of gradualism over shock therapy. In fact, the set of ideas I have presented is

TABLE 1.5
Sound Economics and Institutional Counterparts: Microeconomics

Objective	Universal Principles	Plausible Diversity in Institutional Arrangements
Productive efficiency (static and dynamic)	*Property rights*: Ensure potential and current investors can retain the returns to their investments.	What type of property rights? Private, public, cooperative?
	Incentives: Align producer incentives with social costs and benefits.	What type of legal regime? Common law? Civil law? Adopt or innovate?
	Rule of law: Provide a transparent, stable, and predictable set of rules.	What is the right balance between decentralized market competition and public intervention?
		Which types of financial institutions/corporate governance are most appropriate for mobilizing domestic savings?
		Is there a public role to stimulate technology absorption and generation (e.g., "protection" of intellectual property rights)?

TABLE 1.6
Sound Economics and Institutional Counterparts: Macroeconomics

Objective	Universal Principles	Plausible Diversity in Institutional Arrangements
Macroeconomic and Financial Stability	*Sound money*: Do not generate liquidity beyond the increase in nominal money demand at reasonable inflation.	How independent should the central bank be?
		What is the appropriate exchange-rate regime (dollarization, currency board, adjustable peg, controlled float, pure float)?
	Fiscal sustainability: Ensure public debt remains "reasonable" and stable in relation to national aggregates.	Should fiscal policy be rule-bound, and if so, what are the appropriate rules?
	Prudential regulation: Prevent financial system from taking excessive risk.	Size of the public economy.
		What is the appropriate regulatory apparatus for the financial system?
		What is the appropriate regulatory treatment of capital account transactions?

TABLE 1.7
Sound Economics and Institutional Counterparts: Social Policy

Objective	Universal Principles	Plausible Diversity in Institutional Arrangements
Distributive justice and poverty alleviation	*Targeting:* Redistributive programs should be targeted as closely as possible to the intended beneficiaries.	How progressive should the tax system be?
		Should pension systems be public or private?
	Incentive compatibility: Redistributive programs should minimize incentive distortions.	What are the appropriate points of intervention: educational system? access to health? access to credit? labor markets? tax system?
		What is the role of "social funds"?
		Redistribution of endowments (land reform, endowments-at-birth)?
		Organization of labor markets: decentralized or institutionalized?
		Modes of service delivery: NGOs, participatory arrangements., etc.

largely orthogonal to the long-standing debate between the adherents of the two camps (see for example Lipton and Sachs 1990; Aslund, Boone, and Johnson 1996; Williamson and Zagha 2002). The strategy of gradualism presumes that policymakers have a fairly good idea of the institutional arrangements that they want to achieve ultimately, but that for political and other reasons they can proceed only step by step in that direction. The argument here is that there is typically a large amount of uncertainty about what those institutional arrangements are, and therefore that the process required is more one of "search and discovery" than one of gradualism. The two strategies may coincide when policy changes reveal information *and* small-scale policy reforms have a more favorable ratio of information reve-lation to risk of failure.[17] But it is best not to confuse the two strategies. What stands out in the cases of real success, as I will further illustrate below, is not gradualism per se but an unconventional mix of standard and nonstandard policies well attuned to the reality on the ground.

BACK TO THE REAL WORLD

Previously we had asked our Martian to interpret economic per-formance in the real world from the lens of the standard reform agenda. Suppose we now remove the constraint and ask him to summarize the styl-ized facts as he sees them. Here is a list of four stylized facts that he would come up with.

1. In practice, growth spurts are associated with a narrow range of policy reforms.

One of the most encouraging aspects of the comparative evidence on economic growth is that it often takes very little to get growth started. To appreciate the point, it is enough to turn to table 1.8, which lists 83 instances of growth accelerations. The table shows all cases of significant growth accelerations since the mid-1950s that can be identified statistically. The definition of a growth acceleration is the following: an increase in an economy's per capita GDP growth of 2 percentage points or more (relative to the previous five years) that is sustained over at least eight years. The timing of the growth acceleration is determined by fitting a spline centered on the candidate break years, and selecting the break that maximizes the fit of the equation (see Hausmann, Pritchett, and Rodrik 2005 for details on the procedure).[18]

[17] For example, Dewatripont and Roland (1995) and Wei (1997) present models in which gradual reforms reveal information and affect subsequent political constraints.

[18] The selection strategy allows multiple accelerations, but they must be at least five years apart. We require postacceleration growth to be at least 3.5 percent, and also rule out recoveries from crises.

TABLE 1.8

Episodes of Rapid Growth, by Region, Decade, and Magnitude of Acceleration

Region	Decade	Country	Year	Growth Before	Growth After	Difference in Growth
Sub-Saharan	1950s and	NGA	1967	−1.7	7.3	9.0
Africa	1960s	BWA	1969	2.9	11.7	8.8
		GHA	1965	−0.1	8.3	8.4
		GNB	1969	−0.3	8.1	8.4
		ZWE	1964	0.6	7.2	6.5
		COG	1969	0.9	5.4	4.5
		NGA	1957	1.2	4.3	3.0
	1970s	MUS	1971	−1.8	6.7	8.5
		TCD	1973	−0.7	7.3	8.0
		CMR	1972	−0.6	5.3	5.9
		COG	1978	3.1	8.2	5.1
		UGA	1977	−0.6	4.0	4.6
		LSO	1971	0.7	5.3	4.6
		RWA	1975	0.7	4.0	3.3
		MLI	1972	0.8	3.8	3.0
		MWI	1970	1.5	3.9	2.5
	1980s and	GNB	1988	−0.7	5.2	5.9
	1990s	MUS	1983	1.0	5.5	4.4
		UGA	1989	−0.8	3.6	4.4
		MWI	1992	−0.8	4.8	5.6
South Asia	1950s/60s	PAK	1962	−2.4	4.8	7.1
	1970s	PAK	1979	1.4	4.6	3.2
		LKA	1979	1.9	4.1	2.2
	1980s	IND	1982	1.5	3.9	2.4
East Asia	1950s and	THA	1957	−2.5	5.3	7.8
	1960s	KOR	1962	0.6	6.9	6.3
		IDN	1967	−0.8	5.5	6.2
		SGP	1969	4.2	8.2	4.0
		TWN	1961	3.3	7.1	3.8
	1970s	CHN	1978	1.7	6.7	5.1
		MYS	1970	3.0	5.1	2.1
	1980s and	MYS	1988	1.1	5.7	4.6
	1990s	THA	1986	3.5	8.1	4.6
		PNG	1987	0.3	4.0	3.7
		KOR	1984	4.4	8.0	3.7
		IDN	1987	3.4	5.5	2.1
		CHN	1990	4.2	8.0	3.8

TABLE 1.8 (*cont.*)

Region	Decade	Country	Year	Growth Before	Growth After	Difference in Growth
Latin America	1950s and	DOM	1969	−1.1	5.5	6.6
and Caribbean	1960s	BRA	1967	2.7	7.8	5.1
		PER	1959	0.8	5.2	4.4
		PAN	1959	1.5	5.4	3.9
		NIC	1960	0.9	4.8	3.8
		ARG	1963	0.9	3.6	2.7
		COL	1967	1.6	4.0	2.4
	1970s	ECU	1970	1.5	8.4	6.8
		PRY	1974	2.6	6.2	3.7
		TTO	1975	1.9	5.4	3.5
		PAN	1975	2.6	5.3	2.7
		URY	1974	1.5	4.0	2.6
	1980s and	CHL	1986	−1.2	5.5	6.7
	1990s	URY	1989	1.6	3.8	2.1
		HTI	1990	−2.3	12.7	15.0
		ARG	1990	−3.1	6.1	9.2
		DOM	1992	0.4	6.3	5.8
Middle East and	1950s and	MAR	1958	−1.1	7.7	8.8
North Africa	1960s	SYR	1969	0.3	5.8	5.5
		TUN	1968	2.1	6.6	4.5
		ISR	1967	2.8	7.2	4.4
		ISR	1957	2.2	5.3	3.1
	1970s	JOR	1973	−3.6	9.1	12.7
		EGY	1976	−1.6	4.7	6.3
		SYR	1974	2.6	4.8	2.2
		DZA	1975	2.1	4.2	2.1
	1980s and 1990s	SYR	1989	−2.9	4.4	7.3
OECD	1950s and	ESP	1959	4.4	8.0	3.5
	1960s	DNK	1957	1.8	5.3	3.5
		JPN	1958	5.8	9.0	3.2
		USA	1961	0.9	3.9	3.0
		CAN	1962	0.6	3.6	2.9
		IRL	1958	1.0	3.7	2.7
		BEL	1959	2.1	4.5	2.4
		NZL	1957	1.5	3.8	2.4
		AUS	1961	1.5	3.8	2.3
		FIN	1958	2.7	5.0	2.2
		FIN	1967	3.4	5.6	2.2

TABLE 1.8 (*cont.*)

Region	Decade	Country	Year	Growth Before	Growth After	Difference in Growth
	1980s and	PRT	1985	1.1	5.4	4.3
	1990s	ESP	1984	0.1	3.8	3.7
		IRL	1985	1.6	5.0	3.4
		GBR	1982	1.1	3.5	2.5
		FIN	1992	1.0	3.7	2.8
		NOR	1991	1.4	3.7	2.2

Source: Hausmann, Pritchett, and Rodrik 2005.

Most of the usual suspects are included in the table: for example, Taiwan 1961, Korea 1962, Indonesia 1967, Brazil 1967, Mauritius 1971, China 1978, Chile 1986, Uganda 1989, Argentina 1990, and so on. But the exercise also yields a large number of much less well known cases, such as Egypt 1976 or Pakistan 1979. In fact, the large number of countries that have managed to engineer at least one instance of transition to high growth may appear as surprising. As I will discuss later, most of these growth spurts have eventually collapsed. Nonetheless, an increase in growth of 2 percentage points (and typically more) over the better part of a decade is nothing to sneer at, and it is worth asking what produces it.

In the vast majority of the cases listed in table 1.8, the "shocks" (policy or otherwise) that produced the growth spurts were apparently quite mild. Asking most development economists about the policy reforms of Pakistan in 1979 or Syria in 1969 would draw a blank stare. This reflects the fact that not much reform was actually taking place in these cases. Apparently, small changes in the background environment can yield a significant increase in economic activity.

Even in the well-known cases, policy changes at the outset have been typically modest. The gradual, experimental steps toward liberalization that China undertook in the late 1970s were discussed above. South Korea's experience in the early 1960s was similar. The military government led by Park Chung Hee that took power in 1961 did not have strong views on economic reform, except that it regarded economic development as its key priority. It moved in a trial-and-error fashion, experimenting at first with various public investment projects. The hallmark reforms associated with the Korean miracle, the devaluation of the currency and the rise in interest rates, came in 1964 and fell far short of full liberalization of currency and financial markets. As these instances illustrate, an attitudinal change on the part of the top political leadership toward a more market-oriented, private-sector-friendly policy framework often plays as large a role as the scope of policy reform itself. Perhaps the most important example of this can be found in India: such an attitudinal change appears to have had a particularly important effect in the Indian takeoff of the early 1980s, which took place a full decade before the economic liberalization of 1991 (DeLong 2003; Rodrik and Subramanian 2005).

This is good news because it suggests countries do not need an extensive set of institutional reforms in order to start growing. Instigating growth is a lot easier in practice than the standard recipe, with its long list of action items, would lead us to believe. This should not be surprising from the standpoint of growth theory. When a country is so far below its potential steady-state level of income, even moderate movements in the right direction can produce a big growth payoff. Nothing could be more encouraging to policymakers, who are often overwhelmed and paralyzed by the apparent need to undertake policy reforms on a wide and ever-expanding front.

2. The policy reforms that are associated with these growth transitions typically combine elements of orthodoxy with unorthodox institutional practices.

No country has experienced rapid growth without minimal adherence to what I have termed higher-order principles of sound economic governance—property rights, market-oriented incentives, sound money, fiscal solvency. But as I have already argued, these principles have often been implemented via policy arrangements that are quite unconventional. I illustrated this using examples such as China's two-track reform strategy, Mauritius's export-processing zone, and South Korea's system of "financial restraint."

It is easy to multiply the examples. When Taiwan and South Korea decided to reform their trade regimes to reduce antiexport bias, they did so not via import liberalization (which would have been a Western economist's advice) but through selective subsidization of exports. When Singapore decided to make itself more attractive to foreign investment, it did so not by reducing state intervention but by greatly expanding public investment in the economy and through generous tax incentives (Young 1992). Botswana, which has an admirable record with respect to macroeconomic stability and the management of its diamond wealth, also has one of the largest levels of government spending (in relation to GDP) in the world. Chile, a country that is often cited as a paragon of virtue by the standard checklist, has also departed from it in some important ways: it has kept its largest export industry (copper) under state ownership; it has maintained capital controls on financial inflows through the 1990s; and it has provided significant financial, technological, organizational, and marketing assistance to its fledgling agro-industries.

In all these instances, standard desiderata such as market liberalization and outward orientation were combined with public intervention and government selectivity of some sort. The former element in the mix ensures that any economist so inclined can walk away from the success cases with a renewed sense that the standard policy recommendations really "work." Most egregiously, China's success is often attributed to its turn toward markets—which is largely correct—and then, with an unjustified leap of logic, is taken as a vindication of the standard recipe—which is largely incorrect. It is not clear how helpful such evaluations are when so much of what these countries did is unconventional and fits poorly with the standard agenda.[19]

It is difficult to identify cases of high growth where unorthodox elements have not played a role. Hong Kong is probably the only clear-cut case. Hong Kong's government has had a hands-off attitude toward the economy in almost all areas, the housing market being a major exception. Unlike Singapore, which followed a free trade policy but otherwise undertook extensive industrial policies, Hong Kong's policies have been as close to laissez-faire as we have ever observed. However, there were important prerequisites to Hong Kong's success, which illuminate once again the context-specificity of growth strategies. Most important, Hong Kong's important entrepôt role in trade, the strong institutions imparted by the British, and the capital flight from Communist China had already transformed the city-state into a high-investment, high-entrepreneurship economy by the late 1950s. As figure 1.3 shows, during the early 1960s Hong Kong's investment rate was already more than *three times* higher than that in South Korea or Taiwan. The latter two economies would not reach Hong Kong's 1960 per capita GDP until the early 1970s. Hence Hong Kong did not face the same challenge that Taiwan, South Korea, and Singapore did to crowd in private investment and stimulate entrepreneurship (see chapter 4). It would be a mistake to deduce from Hong Kong's experience that the other East and Southeast Asian economies—confronted with very different initial conditions—would have done equally well under laissez-faire policies.

It goes without saying that not all unorthodox remedies work. And those that work sometimes do so only for a short while. Consider, for

---

[19] Another source of confusion is the mixing up of policies with outcomes. Successful countries end up with much greater participation in the world economy, thriving private sectors, and a lot of financial intermediation. What we need to figure out, however, are the policies that produce these results. It would be a great distortion of the strategy followed by countries such as China, South Korea, Taiwan, and others to argue that these outcomes were the result of trade and financial liberalization, and privatization.

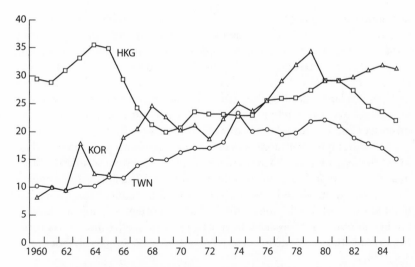

Fig. 1.3. Investment as a share of GDP in East Asia
Source: Penn World Tables 6.1.

example, Argentina's experiment in the 1990s with a currency board. Most economists would consider a currency board regime as too risky for an economy of Argentina's size insofar as it puts monetary policy on automatic pilot and removes the exchange rate as a policy tool. (Hong Kong has long operated a successful marketing board.) But the currency board sought to purchase credibility for Argentine policymakers and to counteract the effects of more than a century of financial mismanagement. It was a short-cut aimed at convincing foreign and domestic investors that the rules of the game had changed irrevocably. Indeed, as the Argentinean economy began to grow rapidly in the first half of the 1990s, it looked like the gamble was working. Had the Asian crisis of 1997–98 and the Brazilian devaluation of 1999 not forced Argentina off its currency board, it would have been easy to construct a story ex post about the virtues of the currency board as a growth strategy. Under better external circumstances, the credibility gained might have more than offset the disadvantages. The problem in this case was the unwillingness to pull back from the experiment even when it became clear that the regime had left the Argentine economy with a hope-lessly uncompetitive real exchange rate. The lesson is that institutional innovation requires a pragmatic approach that avoids ideological lock-in.

3. Institutional innovations do not travel well.

The more discouraging aspect of the stylized facts is that the pol-icy packages associated with growth accelerations—and particularly the nonstandard elements therein—tend to vary considerably from country to country. China's two-track strategy of reform differs significantly from India's gradualism. South Korea's and Taiwan's more protectionist trade strategy differs markedly from the open trade policies of Singapore (and Hong Kong). Even within strategies that seem superficially similar, a closer look reveals large variation. Taiwan and South Korea both subsidized non-traditional industrial activities, but the former did it largely through tax incentives and the latter largely through directed credit.[20]

Attempts to emulate successful policies elsewhere often fail. When in the Soviet Union Gorbachev tried to institute a system similar to China's household responsibility system and two-track pricing during the middle to late 1980s, it produced few of the beneficial results that China had obtained.[21] Most developing countries have export-processing zones of one kind or another, but few have been as successful as the one in Mauritius. Import-substituting industrialization (ISI) worked in Brazil, but not in Argentina.[22]

In light of the arguments made earlier, this experience should not be altogether surprising. Successful reforms are those that package sound economic principles around local capabilities, constraints, and opportunities. Since these local circumstances vary, so do the reforms that work. An immediate implication is that growth strategies require considerable local knowledge. It does not take a whole lot of reform to stimulate economic growth—that is the good news. The bad news is that it may be quite difficult to identify where the binding constraints or promising opportunities lie (see chapter 2). A certain amount of policy experimentation may be required in order to discover what will work. China represents the apotheosis of this experimental approach to reform. But it is worth noting that many other instances of successful reform were preceded by failed experiments. In South Korea, President Park's developmental efforts initially focused on the creation of white elephant industrial projects that ultimately went nowhere (Soon 1994, 27–28). In Chile, Pinochet's entire first decade can be viewed as a failed experiment in "global monetarism."

Economists can have a useful role to play in this process: they can identify the sources of inefficiency, describe the relevant trade-offs, figure out general-equilibrium implications, predict behavioral responses, and so on. But they can do these well only if their analysis is adequately embedded

---

[20] On the institutional differences among East Asian economies, see Haggard 2004.

[21] Murphy, Shleifer, and Vishny (1992) analyze this failure and attribute it to the inability of the Soviet state to enforce the plan quotas once market pricing was allowed (albeit at the margin). This had been critical to the success of the Chinese approach.

[22] TFP growth averaged 2.9 and 0.2 percent per annum in Brazil and Argentina, respectively, during 1960–73. See Rodrik 1999a; and Collins and Bosworth 1996.

within the prevailing institutional and political reality. The hard work needs to be done at home. In the next two chapters, I will develop these ideas further.

4. Sustaining growth is more difficult than igniting it, and requires more extensive institutional reform.

The main reason that few of the growth accelerations listed in table 1.8 are etched in the consciousness of development economists is that most of them did not prove durable. In fact, as discussed earlier, over the last four decades few countries except for a few East Asian ones have steadily converged to the income levels of the rich countries. The vast majority of growth spurts tend to run out of gas after a while. The experience of Latin America since the early 1980s and the even more dramatic collapse of sub-Saharan Africa are emblematic of this phenomenon. In a well-known paper, Easterly, Kremer, Pritchett, and Summers (1993) were the first to draw attention to a related finding, namely the variability in growth performance across time periods. The same point is made on a broader historical canvas by Goldstone (forthcoming).

Hence growth in the short to medium term does not guarantee success in the long term. A plausible interpretation is that the initial reforms need to be deepened over time with efforts aimed at strengthening the institutional underpinning of market economies. It would be nice if a small number of policy changes—which, as argued above, is what produces growth accelerations—could produce growth over the longer term as well, but this is obviously unrealistic. I will discuss some of the institutional prerequisites of sustained growth later in the chapter (and in greater detail in chapters 4 and 5). But the key to longer-term prosperity, once growth is launched, is to develop institutions that maintain productive dynamism and generate resilience to external shocks.

For example, the collapse of growth experienced by many developing countries in the period from the mid-1970s to the early 1980s seem to be related mainly to their inability to adjust to the volatility exhibited by the external environment at that time. In these countries, the effects of terms-of-trade and interest-rate shocks were magnified by weak institutions of conflict management (Rodrik 1999b). This, rather than the nature of microeconomic incentive regimes in place (e.g., import-substituting industrialization), is what caused growth in Africa and Latin America to grind to a halt after the mid-1970s and early 1980s. The required macroeconomic policy adjustments set off distributive struggles and proved difficult to undertake. Similarly, the weakness of Indonesia's institutions explains why that country could not extricate itself from the 1997–98 East Asian financial crisis (see Temple 2003), while South Korea, for example, engineered a rapid turnaround. These examples are also a warning that continued growth in China cannot be taken for granted: without stronger institutions in areas ranging from financial markets to political governance, the Chinese economy may well find itself having outgrown its institutional underpinnings.[23]

A TWO-PRONGED GROWTH STRATEGY

As the evidence discussed above reveals, growth accelerations are feasible with minimal institutional change. The deeper and more extensive institutional reforms needed for long-term convergence take time to implement and mature. And they may not be the most effective way to raise growth at the outset because they do not directly target the most immediate constraints and opportunities facing an economy. At the same time, such institutional reforms can be much easier to undertake in an environment of growth rather than stagnation. These considerations suggest that successful growth strategies are based on a two-pronged effort: a short-run strategy aimed at stimulating growth, and a medium- to long-run strategy aimed at sustaining growth.[24] The rest of this section takes up these two stages in turn. A more extended discussion is offered in the chapters that follow.

An Investment Strategy to Kick-Start Growth

The most important question in the short run for an economy stuck in a low-activity equilibrium is how to get entrepreneurs excited about investing in the home economy. "Invest" here has to be interpreted broadly, as referring to all the activities that entrepreneurs undertake, such as expanding capacity, employing new technology, producing new products, searching for new markets, and so on. As entrepreneurs become energized, capital accumulation and technological change are likely to go hand in hand—too entangled with each other to separate out cleanly.

What sets this process into motion? There are two kinds of answers in the literature. One approach emphasizes the role of government-imposed barriers to entrepreneurship. In this view, excessive government

---

[23] Young (2000) argues that China's reform strategy may have made things worse in the long run, by increasing the number of distorted margins.

[24] A similar distinction is also made by Ocampo (2003), who emphasizes that many of the long-run correlates of growth (such as improved institutions) are the result, and not the instigator, of growth. There is also an analogue in the political science literature in the distinction between the political prerequisites of initiating and sustaining reform (see Haggard and Kaufman 1983).

intervention, policy biases toward large and politically connected firms, institutional failures (in the form of licensing and other regulatory barriers, inadequate property rights and contract enforcement), and high levels of policy uncertainty and risk create dualistic economic structures and repress entrepreneurship. The removal of the most egregious forms of these impediments is then expected to unleash a flurry of new investments and entrepreneurship. According to the second view, the government has to do more than get out of the private sector's way: it needs to find means of crowding in investment and entrepreneurship with some positive induce-ments. In this view, economic growth is not the natural order of things, and establishing a fair and level playing field may not be enough to spur productive dynamism. The two views differ in the importance they attach to prevailing, irremovable market imperfections and their optimism with regard to governments' ability to design and implement appropriate policy interventions.

GOVERNMENT FAILURES

A good example of the first view is provided by the strategy of development articulated in Stern (2001). In a deliberate evocation of Hirschman's *The Strategy of Economic Development* (1958), Stern outlines an approach with two pillars: building an appropriate "investment climate" and "empowering poor people." For our present discussion, the former is the relevant part of his approach. Stern defines "investment climate" quite broadly, as "the policy, institutional, and behavioral environment, both present and expected, that influences the returns and risks associated with investment" (2001, 144–45). At the same time, he recognizes the need for priorities and the likelihood that they will be context specific. He empha-sizes the favorable dynamics that are unleashed once a few, small things are done right.

In terms of actual policy content, Stern's illustrations make clear that he views the most salient features of the investment climate to be government-imposed imperfections: macroeconomic instability and high inflation, high government wages that distort the functioning of labor markets, a large tax burden, arbitrary regulations, burdensome licensing requirements, corruption, and so on. He recommends using enterprise surveys and other techniques to uncover which of these problems bite the most, and then focusing reforms on the corresponding margin. Similar per-spectives can be found in Johnson, McMillan, and Woodruff 2000), Fried-man et al. (2000), and Aslund and Johnson (2003). The title of Shleifer and Vishny's (1998) book aptly summarizes the nature of the relevant con-straint in this view: *The Grabbing Hand: Government Pathologies and Their Cures.*

MARKET FAILURES

The second approach focuses not on government-imposed constraints, but on market imperfections inherent in low-income environments that block investment and entrepreneurship in nontraditional activities. In this view, economies can get stuck in a low-level equilibrium because of the nature of technology and markets, even when government policy does not penalize entrepreneurship. There are many versions of this latter approach, and some of the main arguments are summarized in the taxonomy presented in table 1.9. I distinguish here between stories that are based on learning spillovers (a nonpecuniary externality) and those that are based on market-size externalities induced by scale economies. See also the useful discussion of these issues in Ocampo 2003, which takes a more overtly structuralist perspective.

As Acemoglu, Aghion, and Zilibotti (2002) point out, two types of learning are relevant to economic growth: (*a*) adaptation of existing technologies, and (*b*) innovation to create new technologies. Early in the development process, the kind of learning that matters the most is of the first type. There are a number of reasons why such learning can be subject to spillovers. There may be a threshold level of human capital beyond which the private return to acquiring skills becomes strongly positive (as in Azariadis and Drazen 1990). There may be learning-by-doing that is either external to individual firms or cannot be properly internalized because of imperfections in the market for credit (as in Matsuyama 1992). Or there may be learning about a country's own cost structure, which spills over from the incumbents to later entrants (as in Hausmann and Rodrik 2003). In all these cases, the relevant learning is underproduced in a decentralized equilibrium, with the consequence that the economy fails to diversify into nontraditional, more advanced lines of activity. There then exist policy interventions that can improve matters. With standard externalities, the first-best takes the form of a corrective subsidy targeted at the relevant distorted margin. In practice, constraints on revenue, administration, or information may make resort to second-best interventions inevitable.

The second main group of stories shown in table 1.9 relates to the existence of coordination failures induced by scale economies. The big-push theory of development, articulated first by Rosenstein-Rodan (1943) and formalized by Murphy, Shleifer, and Vishny (1989), is based on the idea that moving out of a low-level steady state requires coordinated and simultaneous investments in a number of different areas. A general formulation of such models can be provided as follows. Let the level of profits in a given modern-sector activity depend on n, the proportion of the economy that is already engaged in modern activities: $\pi^m(n)$, with $d\pi^m(n)/dn > 0$. Let

TABLE 1.9

A Taxonomy of "Natural" Barriers to Industrialization

A. Learning externalities
    1. Learning-by-doing (e.g., Matsuyama 1992)
    2. Human capital externalities (e.g., Azariadis and Drazen 1990)
    3. Learning about costs (e.g., Hausmann and Rodrik 2003)

B. Coordination failures (market-size externalities induced by IRS)
    1. Wage premium in manufacturing (e.g., Murphy, Shleifer, and Vishny 1989)
    2. Infrastructure (e.g., Murphy, Shleifer, and Vishny 1989)
    3. Specialized intermediate inputs (e.g., Rodrik 1995a, 1996b)
    4. Spillovers associated with wealth distribution (e.g., Hoff and Stiglitz 2001)

---

profits in traditional activities be denoted π^t. Suppose modern activities are unprofitable for an individual entrant if no other entrepreneur already operates in the modern sector, but highly profitable if enough entrepreneurs do so: $\pi^m(0) < \pi^t$ and $\pi^m(1) > \pi^t$. Then $n = 0$ and $n = 1$ are both possible equilibria, and industrialization may never take hold in an economy that starts with $n = 0$. The precise mechanism that generates profit functions of this form depends on the model in question. Murphy, Shleifer, and Vishny (1989) develop models in which the complementarity arises from demand spillovers across final goods produced under scale economies or from bulky infrastructure investments. Rodríguez-Clare (1996), Rodrik (1996b), and Trindade (2005) present models in which the effect operates through vertical industry relationships and specialized intermediate inputs. Hoff and Stiglitz (2001) discuss a large class of models with coordination failure characteristics.

The policy implications of such models can be quite unconventional, requiring the crowding in of private investment through subsidization, jawboning, public enterprises, and the like. Despite the "big push" appellation, the requisite policies need not be wide-ranging. For example, socializing investment risk through implicit investment guarantees, a policy followed in South Korea, is welfare enhancing in Rodrik's (1996b) framework because it induces simultaneous entry into the modern sector. It is also costless to the government, because the guarantees are never called on insofar as the resulting investment boom pays for itself. Hence, when successful, such policies will leave little trail on government finances or elsewhere.[25]

---

[25] On South Korea's implicit investment guarantees, see Amsden 1989. During the Asian financial crisis, these guarantees became an issue, and they were portrayed as evidence of crony capitalism (MacLean 1999).

Both types of models listed in table 1.9 suggest that the propagation of modern, nontraditional activities is not a natural process and that it may require positive inducements. One such inducement that has often worked in the past is a sizable and sustained depreciation of the real exchange rate. For a small open economy, the real exchange rate is defined as the relative price of tradables to nontradables. In practice, this price ratio tends to move in tandem with the nominal exchange rate, the price of foreign currency in terms of home currency. Hence currency devaluations (supported by appropriate monetary and fiscal policies) increase the profitability of tradable activities across the board. From the current perspective, this has a number of distinct advantages. Most of the gains from diversification into nontraditional activities are likely to lie within manufactures and natural-resource-based products (i.e., tradables) rather than services and other nontradables. Second, the magnitude of the inducement can be quite large, since sustained real depreciations of 50 percent or more are quite common. Third, since tradable activities face external competition, the activities that are encouraged tend to be precisely the ones that face the greatest market discipline. Fourth, the manner in which currency depreciation subsidizes tradable activities is completely market-friendly, requiring no micromanagement on the part of bureaucrats. For all these reasons, a credible, sustained real exchange rate depreciation may constitute the most effective industrial policy there is.[26] It may substitute for, and render unnecessary, more activist industrial policies (of the type that will be discussed in chapter 4).

WHERE TO START?

The two sets of views outlined above—the government failure and market failure approaches—can help frame policy discussions and identify important ways of thinking about priorities in the short run. The most effective point of leverage for stimulating growth obviously depends on

[26] Large real exchange rate changes have played a big role in some of the more recent growth accelerations—Chile and Uganda since the mid-1980s, for example. In both cases, a substantial swing in relative prices in favor of tradables accompanied the growth take-off. In Chile, the more than doubling of the real exchange rate following the crisis of 1982–83 (the deepest in Latin America at the time) is commonly presumed to have played an instrumental role in promoting diversification into nontraditional exports and stimulating economic growth. It is worth noting that import tariffs were raised significantly as well (during 1982–85), giving import-substituting activities an additional boost. The depreciation in Uganda was even larger. By contrast, large real depreciations did not play a major role in early growth accelerations in East Asia during the 1960s (Rodrik 1997a). Polterovich and Popov (2002) provide theory and evidence on the role of real exchange rate undervaluations in generating economic growth.

local circumstances. It is tempting to think that the right first step is to remove government-imposed obstacles to entrepreneurial activity before worrying about "crowding in" investments through positive inducements. But this may not always be a better strategy. Certainly when inflation is in triple digits or the regulatory framework is so cumbersome that it stifles any private initiative, removing these distortions will be the most sensible initial step. But beyond that, it is difficult to say in general where the most effective margin for change lies. Asking businesspeople their views on the priorities can be helpful, but not decisive. When learning spillovers and coordination failures block economic takeoff, enterprise surveys are unlikely to be revealing unless the questions are very carefully crafted to elicit relevant responses.

One of the lessons of recent economic history is that creative interventions can be remarkably effective even when the "investment climate," judged by standard criteria, is pretty lousy. South Korea's early reforms took place against the background of a political leadership that was initially quite hostile to the entrepreneurial class.[27] China's TVEs have been stunningly successful despite the absence of private property rights and an effective judiciary. Conversely, the Latin American experience of the 1990s indicates that the standard criteria do not guarantee an appropriate investment climate. Governments can certainly deter entrepreneurship when they try to do too much; but they can also deter entrepreneurship when they do too little.

It is sometimes argued that heterodoxy requires greater institutional strength and therefore lies out of reach of most developing countries. But the evidence does not provide much support for this view. It is true that the selective interventions I have discussed in the case of South Korea and Taiwan were successful in part due to unusual and favorable circumstances. But elsewhere, heterodoxy served to make virtue out of institutional weakness. This is the case with China's TVEs, Mauritius's export-processing zone, and India's gradualism. In these countries, it was precisely institutional weakness that rendered the standard remedies impractical. It is in part because the standard reform agenda is institutionally so highly demanding—a fact now recognized through the addition of so-called second-generation reforms—that successful growth strategies are so often based on unconventional elements (in their early stages at least).

It is nonetheless true that the implementation of the market failure approach requires a reasonably competent and noncorrupt government.

---

[27] One month after taking power in a military coup in 1961, President Park arrested some of the leading businessmen in Korea under the newly passed Law for Dealing with Illicit Wealth Accumulation. These businessmen were subsequently set free under the condition that they establish new industrial firms and give up the shares to the government (Amsden 1989, 72).

For every South Korea, there are many Zaires where policy activism is an excuse for politicians to steal and plunder. Finely tuned policy interventions can hardly be expected to produce desirable outcomes in settings such as the latter. And to the extent that Washington Consensus policies are more conducive to honest behavior on the part of politicians, they may well be preferable on this account. On this, however, the evidence is ambiguous. Most policies, including those of the Washington Consensus type, are corruptible if the underlying political economy permits or encourages it. Consider, for example, Russia's experiment with mass privatization. It is widely accepted that this process was distorted and delegitimized by asset grabs on the part of politically well-connected insiders. Washington Consensus policies themselves cannot legislate powerful rent-seekers out of existence. Rank ordering different policy regimes requires a more fully specified model of political economy than the reduced-form view that automatically associates governmental restraint with less rent-seeking.[28]

I close this section with the usual refrain: the range of strategies that have worked in the past is quite diverse. A traditional import-substituting industrialization (ISI) model was quite effective in stimulating growth in a large number of developing countries (e.g., Brazil, Mexico, Turkey). So was East Asian–style outward orientation, which combined heavy-handed interventionism at home with single-minded focus on exports (South Korea, Taiwan). Chile's post-1983 strategy was based on quite a different style of outward orientation, relying on large real depreciation, absence of explicit industrial policies (but quite a bit of support for nontraditional exports in agro-industry), saving mobilization through pension privatization, and discouragement of short-term capital inflows. The experience of countries such as China and Mauritius is best described as two-track reform. India comes as close to genuine gradualism as one can imagine. Hong Kong represents probably the only case where growth has taken place without an active policy of crowding in private investment and entrepreneurship, but here too special and favorable preconditions (mentioned earlier) limit its relevance to other settings.

In view of this diversity, any statement on what ignites growth has to be cast at a sufficiently high level of generality. A diagnostic framework, of the type laid out in the next chapter, has the advantage that it can point us to the ailments that are most crippling in a given context and help us focus our energies on the most effective remedies.

[28] In Rodrik 1995b, I compared export subsidy regimes in six countries, and found that the regimes that were least likely to be open to rent-seeking ex ante—those with clear-cut rules, uniform schedules, and no arm's-length relationships between firms and bureaucrats—were in fact less effective ex post. Where bureaucrats were professional and well monitored, discretion was not harmful. Where they were not, the rules did not help.

An Institution-Building Strategy to Sustain Growth

In the long run, the main thing that ensures convergence with the living standards of advanced countries is the acquisition of high-quality institutions. The growth-spurring strategies described above have to be complemented over time with a cumulative process of institution building to ensure that growth does not run out of steam and that the economy remains resilient to shocks. This point has now been amply demonstrated both by historical accounts (North and Thomas 1973; Engerman and Sokoloff 1994) and by econometric studies (Hall and Jones 1999; Acemoglu, Johnson, and Robinson 2001; Rodrik, Subramanian, and Trebbi 2004; Easterly and Levine 2003). However, these studies tend to remain at a very aggregate level of generality and do not provide much policy guidance (a point that is also made in Besley and Burgess 2002).

The empirical research on national institutions has generally focused on the protection of property rights and the rule of law. But one should think of institutions along a much wider spectrum. In its broadest definition, institutions are the prevailing rules of the game in society (North 1990). High-quality institutions are those that induce socially desirable behavior on the part of economic agents. Such institutions can be both informal (e.g., moral codes, self-enforcing agreements) and formal (legal rules enforced through third parties). It is widely recognized that the relative importance of formal institutions increases as the scope of market exchange broadens and deepens. One reason is that setting up formal institutions requires high fixed costs but low marginal costs, whereas informal institutions have high marginal costs (Li 1999; Dixit 2004, chap. 3).

The last two centuries of economic history in today's rich countries can be interpreted as an ongoing process of learning how to render capitalism more productive by supplying the institutional ingredients of a self-sustaining market economy: meritocratic public bureaucracies, independent judiciaries, central banking, stabilizing fiscal policy, antitrust and regulation, financial supervision, social insurance, political democracy. Just as it is silly to think of these as the *prerequisites* of economic growth in poor countries, it is equally silly not to recognize that such institutions eventually become necessary to achieve full economic convergence. In this connection, one may want to place special emphasis on democratic institutions and civil liberties, not only because they are important in and of themselves, but also because they can be viewed as metainstitutions that help society make appropriate selections from the available menu of economic institutions. In chapter 5, I will provide a taxonomy of market-supporting institutions and discuss these issues further.

However, the earlier warning not to confuse institutional *function* and institutional *form* becomes once again relevant here. Appropriate regulation, social insurance, macroeconomic stability, and the like can be provided through diverse institutional arrangements. While one can be sure that some types of arrangements are far worse than others, it is also the case that many well-performing arrangements are functional equivalents. Function does not map uniquely into form. It would be hard to explain otherwise how social systems that are so different in their institutional details as those of the United States, Japan, and Europe have managed to generate roughly similar levels of wealth for their citizens. All these societies protect property rights, regulate product, labor, and financial markets, have sound money, and provide for social insurance. But the rules of the game that prevail in American capitalism are very different from those in Japanese capitalism. Both differ from the European style. And even within Europe, there are large differences between the institutional arrangements in, say, Sweden and Germany. There has been only modest convergence among these arrangements in recent years, with the greatest amount of convergence taking place probably in financial market practices and the least in labor market institutions (Freeman 2000).

There are a number of reasons for institutional nonconvergence. First, differences in social preferences, say over the trade-off between equity and opportunity, may result in different institutional choices. If Europeans have a much greater preference for stability and equity than Americans, their labor market and welfare-state arrangements will reflect that preference. Second, complementarities among different parts of the institutional landscape can generate hysteresis and path dependence. An example of this would be the complementarity between corporate governance and financial market practices of the Japanese "model," as discussed previously. Third, the institutional arrangements that are required to promote economic development can differ significantly, both between rich and poor countries and among poor countries. This too has been discussed previously.

There is increasing recognition in the economics literature that high-quality institutions can take a multitude of forms and that economic convergence need not necessarily entail convergence in institutional forms (North 1994; Freeman 2000; Pistor 2002; Mukand and Rodrik 2005; Berkowitz, Pistor, and Richard 2003; Djankov et al. 2003; Dixit 2004).[29] North (1994, 8) writes, "Economies that adopt the formal rules of another economy will have very different performance characteristics than the first economy because of different informal norms and enforcement [with the

---

[29] Furthermore, as Roberto Unger (1998) has argued, there is no reason to suppose that today's advanced economies have already exhausted all the useful institutional variations that could underpin healthy and vibrant economies.

implication that] transferring the formal political and economic rules of successful Western economies to third-world and Eastern European economies is not a sufficient condition for good economic performance." Freeman (2000) discusses the variety of labor market institutions that prevail among the advanced countries and argues that differences in these practices have first-order distributional effects, but only second-order efficiency effects. Pistor (2002) provides a general treatment of the issue of legal transplantation, and shows how importation of laws can backfire. In related work, Berkowitz, Pistor, and Richard (2003) find that countries that developed their formal legal orders internally, adapted imported codes to local conditions, or had familiarity with foreign codes ended up with much better legal institutions than those that simply transplanted formal legal orders from abroad. Djankov et al. (2003) base their discussion on an "institutional possibility frontier" that describes the trade-off between private disorder and dictatorship, and argue that different circumstances may call for different choices along this frontier. And Dixit (2004, 4) summarizes the lessons for developing countries thus: "It is not always necessary to create replicas of western style state legal institutions from scratch; it may be possible to work with such alternative institutions as are available, and build on them."

Mukand and Rodrik (2005) develop a formal model to examine the costs and benefits of institutional "experimentation" versus "copycatting" when formulas that have proved successful elsewhere may be unsuitable at home. A key idea is that institutional arrangements that prove successful in one country create both positive and negative spillovers for other countries. On the positive side, countries whose underlying conditions are sufficiently similar to those of the successful "leaders" can imitate the arrangements prevailing there and forgo the costs of experimentation. This is one interpretation of the relative success that transition economies in the immediate vicinity of the European Union have experienced. Countries such as Poland, the Czech Republic, or the Baltic republics share a similar historical trajectory with the rest of Europe, have previous experience with capitalist market institutions, and envisaged full EU membership within a reasonable period (de Menil 2003). The wholesale adoption of EU's *acquis communautaire* may have been the appropriate institution-building strategy for these countries. On the other hand, countries may be tempted or forced to imitate institutional arrangements for political or other reasons, even when their underlying conditions are too dissimilar for the strategy to make sense.[30]

---

[30] In Mukand and Rodrik 2005 it is domestic politics that generate inefficient imitation. Political leaders may want to signal their type (and increase the probability of remaining in power) by imitating standard policies even when they know they will not work as well as alternative arrangements. But one can also appeal to the role of IMF and World Bank conditionality in producing this kind of outcome.

Institutional copycatting may have been useful for Poland, but it is much less clear that it was relevant or practical for Ukraine or Kyrgyzstan. The negative gradient in the economic performance of transition economies as one moves away from western Europe provides some support for this idea (see Mukand and Rodrik 2005).

Even though it is recent, this literature opens up a new and exciting way of looking at institutional reform. In particular, it promises an approach that is less focused on so-called best practices or the superiority of any particular model of capitalism, and more cognizant of the context-specificity of desirable institutional arrangements. Dixit's (2004) monograph outlines a range of theoretical models that help structure our thinking along these lines.

CONCLUDING REMARKS

Richard Feynman, the irreverent physicist who won the Nobel Prize in 1965 for his work on quantum electrodynamics, relates the following story. Following the award ceremony and the dinner in Stockholm, he wandered into a room where a Scandinavian princess was holding court. The princess recognized him as one of the awardees and asked him what he got the prize for. When Feynman replied that his field was physics, the princess said it was too bad. Since no one at the table knew anything about physics, she said, they could not talk about it. Feynman disagreed:

> "On the contrary," I answered. "It's because somebody knows *something* about it that we can't talk about physics. It's the things that nobody knows anything about that we *can* discuss. We can talk about the weather; we can talk about social problems; we can talk about psychology; we can talk about international finance . . . so it's the subject that nobody knows anything about that we can all talk about!" (Feynman 1985, 310)

This is not the place to defend international finance (circa 1965) against the charge Feynman levels. But suppose Feynman had picked on economic growth instead of international finance. Would growth economists have a plausible riposte? Is the reason we all talk so much about growth that we understand so little about it?

It is certainly the case that growth theory is now a much more powerful tool than it was before Solow put pencil to paper. And cross-country regressions have surely thrown out some useful correlations and stylized facts. But at the more practical end of things—how do we make growth happen?—things have turned out to be somewhat disappointing. By the mid-1980s, policy-oriented economists had converged on a new consensus regarding the policy framework for growth. We thought we knew a lot about what governments needed to do. But as my Martian thought experiment at the beginning of the chapter underscores, reality has been unkind to our expectations. If Latin America were booming today and China and India were stagnating, we would have an easier time fitting the world to our policy framework. Instead, we are straining to explain why unorthodox, two-track, gradualist reform paths have done so much better than sure-fire adoption of the standard package.

Very few policy analysts think that the answer is to go back to old-style protectionism or economic populism, even though their record was certainly respectable for a very large number of countries. Certainly no one believes that central planning is a credible alternative. But by the same token, few are now convinced that liberalization, deregulation, and privatization on their own hold the key to unleashing economic growth. Maybe the right approach is to give up looking for "big ideas" altogether (as argued explicitly by Lindauer and Pritchett 2002; and implicitly by Easterly 2001). But that would be overshooting too. Economics is full of big ideas on the importance of incentives, markets, budget constraints, and property rights. It offers powerful ways of analyzing the allocative and distributional consequences of proposed policy changes. The key is to realize that these principles do not translate directly into specific policy recommendations. That translation requires the analyst to supply many additional ingredients that are contingent on the economic and political context, and cannot be done a priori. Local conditions matter not because economic principles change from place to place, but because those principles come institution-free and filling them out requires local knowledge.

Therefore, the real lesson for the architects of growth strategies is to take economics more seriously, not less seriously. But the relevant economics is that of the seminar room, with its refusal to make unconditional generalizations and its careful examination of the contingent relation between the economic environment and policy implications. Rule-of-thumb economics, which has long dominated thinking on growth policies, can be safely discarded.

2

Growth Diagnostics

(COAUTHORED WITH RICARDO HAUSMANN
AND ANDRÉS VELASCO)

MOST well-trained economists would agree that the standard policy reforms included in the Washington Consensus have the potential to promote growth. What the experience of the last few decades has shown, however, is that the impact of these reforms is heavily dependent on circumstances (see chapter 1). Policies that work wonders in some places may have weak, unintended, or negative effects in others.[1] This calls for an approach to reform that is much more contingent on the economic environment, but one that also avoids an "anything goes" attitude of nihilism. This chapter shows that it is possible to develop a unified framework for analyzing and formulating growth strategies that is both operational and based on solid economic reasoning. The key step is to develop a better understanding of how the *binding constraints* on economic activity differ from setting to setting. This understanding can then be used to derive policy priorities accordingly, in a way that uses efficiently the scarce political capital of reformers.

This approach is motivated by three considerations. First, while development is a broad concept entailing the raising of human capabilities in general, increasing economic growth rates is the central challenge that developing nations face. Higher standards of living are the most direct route to improvements in social and human indicators. Reform strategies should be principally targeted at raising rates of growth—that is, they should be growth strategies.

Second, trying to come up with an identical growth strategy for all countries, regardless of their circumstances, is unlikely to prove productive.

---

[1] As Al Harberger (2003, 15) had to concede recently: "When you get right down to business, there aren't too many policies that we can say with certainty deeply and positively affect growth."

Growth strategies are likely to differ according to domestic opportunities and constraints. There are of course general, abstract principles—such as property rights, the rule of law, market-oriented incentives, sound money, and sustainable public finances—that are desirable everywhere. But turning these general principles into operational policies requires considerable knowledge of local specificities.

Third, it is seldom helpful to provide governments with a long list of reforms, many of which may not be targeted at the most binding constraints on economic growth. Governments face administrative and political limitations, and their policymaking capital is better deployed in alleviating binding constraints than in going after too many targets all at once. So growth strategies require a sense of priorities.

This chapter develops a framework for growth diagnostics—that is, a strategy for figuring out the policy priorities. The strategy is aimed at identifying the most binding constraints on economic activity, and hence the set of policies that, once targeted on these constraints at any point in time, is likely to provide the biggest bang for the reform buck.

The proposed methodology can be conceptualized as a decision tree (see figure 2.1, discussed below). We start by asking what keeps growth low. Is it inadequate returns to investment, inadequate private appropriability of the returns, or inadequate access to finance? If it is a case of low returns, is that due to insufficient investment in complementary factors of production (such as human capital or infrastructure)? Or is it due to poor access to imported technologies? If it is a case of poor appropriability, is it due to high taxation, poor property rights and contract enforcement, labor-capital conflicts, or learning and coordination externalities? If it is a case of poor finance, are the problems with domestic financial markets or with external ones? And so on.

The chapter offers a discussion of the kind of evidence that would help answer these questions one way or another. It also illustrates the practical implications of this approach by drawing on examples from specific countries.

Aside from providing a useful manual for policymakers, this approach has the advantage that it is broad enough to embed existing development strategies as special cases. It can therefore unify the literature and help settle prevailing controversies. For example, the diagnostic framework clarifies that doctrinal differences on development policy—between proponents of the Washington Consensus and of state-led strategies, or between enthusiastic globalizers and cautious globalizers—are grounded in divergent evaluations of the nature of the binding constraints on growth. Making these differences explicit, and clarifying the nature of the evidence that can resolve them, can move us forward to a more productive policy agenda.

The outline of the chapter is as follows. We first lay out the conceptual framework, linking the terminology of "binding constraints" to standard economic models. In particular, we relate the framework to theories of second-best and partial reform and of endogenous growth. We next cast the framework in the form of a decision tree, and discuss the nature of the evidence required to move along the nodes of the tree. In the final section we carry out an empirical analysis for several "archetypal" cases, each representing a different syndrome, or combination of binding constraints.

THINKING ABOUT REFORM AND GROWTH: A FRAMEWORK

We begin with a formal treatment of our approach. This should help clarify how our discussion of "binding constraints" and "growth diagnostics" relates to conventional economic theory. We show that our approach is grounded on the standard theories of second-best and partial reform. These conceptual foundations provide structure to our framework, even though we naturally have to take a number of shortcuts when we make it operational. We begin with a general treatment, and then provide a more stylized model that allows us to discuss a number of illustrations.

An economy that is underperforming and in need of reform is by definition one where market imperfections and distortions are rampant. These distortions can be government-imposed (e.g., taxes on production) or inherent to the functioning of certain markets (e.g., human capital externalities, information asymmetries, and so on). They prevent the best use of the economy's resources and, in particular, keep the economy far below its attainable productivity frontier. At this level of generality, we need not take a position on the nature of these distortions, although we will later do so. At this point it suffices to note that, regardless of how they arise, such distortions drive a wedge between private and social valuations of specific economic activities.

Let us denote these wedges by $\tau = \{\tau_1, \tau_2, \ldots, \tau_k\}$ with τ_i representing the distortion in activity i. Let us focus also on the problem of a policymaker bent on maximizing social welfare subject to the standard resource constraints, but also constrained by these preexisting distortions or wedges in the economy. The distortions can be modeled as constraints on the policymaking problem that take the general form

$$\mu_i^s(\tau, \ldots) - \mu_i^p(\tau, \ldots) - \tau_i = 0, \tag{1}$$

where $\mu_i^s(\tau, \ldots)$ and $\mu_i^p(\tau, \ldots)$ represent net marginal valuations of activity i by society and by private agents, respectively. Of course, they depend not just on the set τ of distortions, but on levels of consumption, labor supply, asset-holdings, and so forth. Equations of this type are nothing other than restatements of the first-order conditions for the private sector. For example, a tax on investment (or a learning externality) keeps the private return on capital accumulation below the social return, with the result that the economy underinvests. Note that the private and social valuation functions for each activity will depend in general equilibrium on all the wedges in the system. What this means is that the distortion in any one activity also affects the first-order condition for other activities. That is the essence of the second-best problems that we will explore below.

How does welfare depend on these distortions? If u is welfare of the average member of society, then the gain in welfare from reducing one of the distortions marginally is

$$\frac{du}{d\tau_j} = -\lambda_j + \sum_i \lambda_i \frac{\partial[\mu_i^s(\tau,\ldots)-\mu_i^p(\tau,\ldots)]}{\partial \tau_j} \tag{2}$$

and $\lambda_i \geq 0$, $i = \{1, 2, \ldots, k\}$ are the Lagrange multipliers corresponding to the constraints associated with each of the distortions.

The interpretation of this expression is as follows. Assume, without loss of generality, that the initial value of τ_j is strictly positive. The wedge created by the distortion in market j can be thought of as a tax that reduces the equilibrium level of activity in that market by keeping the net private return below the social return. The first term on the right-hand side of equation (2) captures the direct effect of a small change in τ_j: a small reduction in τ_j increases aggregate welfare by an amount given by the multiplier associated with the jth constraint, λ_j. In other words, λ_j is the marginal welfare benefit from reducing the distortion in market j, disregarding the effect on other distorted activities. The more costly is the distortion, the higher the magnitude of λ_j. At the other end of the spectrum, when activity j is undistorted ($\tau_j = 0$), the constraint ceases to bind, since the planner's first-order conditions coincide with those of private agents, and $\lambda_j = 0$.

Turn now to the second term on the right-hand side of equation (2). When activity j is the sole distorted activity, this term vanishes since $\lambda_i = 0$ for all $i \neq j$. In this case, only the direct effect matters. But when there are other distorted activities in the economy, which is the typical case in a reforming economy, we need to track the interaction effects across distorted margins, which is what the term with the summation does. This second term captures the effect of changing τ_j on the weighted sum of the gaps between social and private valuations, with the weights corresponding to each distorted activity's own Lagrange multiplier. If on balance the effect is to reduce these gaps, everything else constant, then the reduction in τ_j produces an additional welfare benefit. If, on the other hand, these interactions tend to increase the gap between private and social valuations at the margin, the welfare gain is reduced.[2] Conceivably, the reduction in τ_j could even produce a welfare loss. This is a typical second-best complication.

Consider an illustration with two activities: j = intermediate input production; and ℓ = final good production. Suppose both activities are protected by import tariffs, given by τ_j and τ_ℓ respectively. Let us consider the partial effect of reducing τ_j while keeping τ_ℓ constant. A reduction in τ_j produces a direct welfare gain that would be captured by its own multiplier. But it also produces an indirect effect downstream in the production of the final good. Since the final good is protected, private valuations of producing the good exceed social valuations. A reduction in the intermediate-good tariff, τ_j, aggravates this distortion by increasing private profitability further. The increased gap between private and social valuations reduces the welfare gain from the reduction in τ_j. Indeed, if λ_ℓ is sufficiently high relative to λ_j, implying that the distortion in the final-good activity is particularly severe, the tariff reform could even result in a welfare loss.

As a second, macroeconomic illustration consider the case of a single-good economy with two periods (today and tomorrow). Let j = goods today and l = goods tomorrow. Suppose the government maintains a restriction on international borrowing, which means that the social marginal valuation of expenditure today exceeds its private marginal valuation: $\lambda_j > 0$. Relaxation of the borrowing restriction would normally enhance domestic welfare. But suppose that for moral-hazard reasons households and firms discount tomorrow's expenditure at a heavier rate than is socially optimal ($\mu_\ell{}^s(\cdot) - \mu_\ell{}^p(\cdot) > 0$, with corresponding $\lambda_\ell > 0$). In this case, relaxing today's borrowing restriction would aggravate the latter distortion. As before, if λ_ℓ is sufficiently high relative to λ_j, removing the borrowing restriction could make the economy worse off.

With this broad framework as a background, consider now several archetypal reform strategies.

Wholesale Reform

One way to eliminate all ambiguities and uncertainties with regard to the consequences of reform strategies is to simultaneously eliminate all distortions. If all the wedges are tackled and eliminated simultaneously, the

---

[2] Note that in equilibrium, the gaps between social and private valuations for the non-i activities have to revert to their original values, since the wedges for these activities have not changed. What restores the equilibrium is the (privately optimal) adjustments in the consumption, production, or accumulation levels that enter the valuation functions. So, for example, an increase in the private valuation of producing a good would normally result in an increase in the quantity supplied, with a corresponding decline in the marginal valuation.

multipliers associated with each of them go to zero, and none of the second-best issues we have highlighted remains relevant. Wholesale reform is guaranteed to improve welfare. The best possible economic growth rate is achieved by eliminating all obstacles that stand in its way.

But notice what this strategy requires. It requires us not only to have complete knowledge of all prevailing distortions, it also necessitates that we have the capacity to remove them all in their entirety. This strategy is technically correct, but practically impossible.

Do as Much Reform as You Can, as Best You Can

The second strategy, which seems to characterize the prevailing approach today, is to ignore the basic economics of the framework outlined above and to simply go for whatever reforms seem to be feasible, practical, politically doable, or enforceable through conditionality. This is a laundry-list approach to reform that implicitly relies on the notions that (a) any reform is good; (b) the more areas reformed, the better; and (c) the deeper the reform in any area, the better.

The framework above shows why this approach, even if practical, is faulty in its economic logic. First, the principle of the second-best indicates that we cannot be assured that any given reform taken on its own can be guaranteed to be welfare promoting, in the presence of multitudes of economic distortions. Second, welfare need not be increasing in the number of areas that are reformed—except in the limiting case of wholesale reform, as discussed above. Third, in the presence of second-best interactions, more extensive reform in any given area is as likely to fall prey to adverse interactions as an incremental approach.

Second-Best Reform

A more sophisticated version of the previous strategy is one that explicitly takes into account the second-best interactions discussed above. Thus, one could envisage a reform strategy that is less ambitious than the wholesale approach, but that recognizes the presence of the second term in equation (2), namely the possibility that interactions across distorted markets have the potential to both augment and counter the direct welfare effects. Under this strategy, one would give priority to reforms that engender positive second-best effects, and downplay or avoid altogether those that cause adverse effects. As the examples given above show, partial trade reform or capital-account liberalization may reduce welfare unless more extensive reforms in trade and in financial markets are done at the same time.

The difficulty with a second-best reform strategy is that many, if not most, of these second-best interactions are very difficult to figure out and quantify ex ante. The strategy requires having a very good sense of the behavioral consequences of policy changes across different markets and activities. The state of the art (based largely on static computable general equilibrium models) is not very encouraging in this respect. In practice, most of the second-best interactions remain obscure, and tend to be revealed after the fact rather than ex ante.

Target the Largest Distortions

If second-best interactions cannot be fully figured out and it is impractical to remove all distortions at once, reformers may instead focus on eliminating or reducing the biggest distortions in the economy—that is, the largest wedges (τ_j) between private and social valuations. This would be an application of what is known as the concertina method in the literature on trade theory: order distortions from largest to smallest in proportional terms, start by reducing the largest of these to the level of the next largest, and proceed similarly in the next round. Under certain (fairly restrictive) conditions,[3] this strategy can be shown to be welfare improving.

However, even leaving aside its limited theoretical applicability, this approach has two severe shortcomings. First, it does require us to have a complete list of distortions, even those that do not take the form of explicit taxes or government interventions. Distortions that arise from market failures or imperfect credibility, for example, are unlikely to show up on our radar screen unless we have reason to look for them. Second, the concertina method does not guarantee that the reforms with the biggest impacts on economic welfare and growth will be the ones undertaken first. It may well turn out that the highest "tax" is on some activity with very limited impact on growth. For example, there may be very high taxes on international borrowing, yet their removal could have miniscule effect on growth if the economy is constrained not by savings but by investment demand. For these reasons, this strategy is of uncertain benefits, especially in the short run.

Focus on the Most Binding Constraints

The approach advocated here is to design reform priorities according to the magnitude of the direct effects—that is, the size of the λ_j. This is

---

[3] The (sufficient) condition is that the activity whose tax is being reduced be a net substitute (in general equilibrium) to all the other goods. See Hatta 1977a and 1977b.

the most practical strategy, as well as the most promising with regard to the likely bang from reform. The idea behind the strategy is simple: if (a) for whatever reason the full list of requisite reforms is unknowable or impractical, and (b) figuring out the second-best interactions across markets is a near-impossible task, the best approach is to focus on the reforms where the direct effects can be reasonably guessed to be large. As equation (2) indicates, as long as reform focuses on the relaxation of the distortions with the largest λ's associated with them, we have less to worry that second-best interactions will greatly diminish or possibly reverse the welfare effects. The principle to follow is simple: go for the reforms that alleviate the most binding constraints, and hence produce the biggest bang for the reform buck. Rather than utilize a spray-gun approach, in the hope that we will somehow hit the target, focus on the bottlenecks directly.

Whether these binding constraints can be effectively identified is a practical and empirical matter, and the rest of the chapter is devoted to arguing that this can be done in a reasonable manner. In practice, the approach we take starts by focusing not on specific distortions (the full list of which is unknowable, as we argued above), but on the proximate determinants of economic growth (saving, investment, education, productivity, infrastructure, and so on). Once we know where to focus, we then look for associated economic distortions whose removal would make the largest contribution to alleviating the constraints on growth.

MOVING FROM THEORY TO PRACTICE

How can one apply the results of this rather abstract analysis of policy reform and its pitfalls? How do we locate the distortion(s) with the largest potential impact on economic growth?

Our strategy is to start with some of the proximate determinants of economic growth. As we discuss below, economic growth depends on the returns to accumulation (broadly construed), on their private appropriability, and on the cost of financing accumulation. The first stage of the diagnostic analysis aims to uncover which of these three factors poses the greatest impediment to higher growth. In some economies, the "constraint" may lie in low returns, in others it may be poor appropriability, and in yet others too high a cost of finance.

The next stage of the diagnostic analysis is to uncover the specific distortions that lie behind the most severe of these constraints. If the problem seems to be poor appropriability, is that due to high taxes, corruption, or macro instability? If the problem is with the high cost of finance, is that due to fiscal deficits or poor intermediation? This approach enables the design of remedies that are as closely targeted as possible.

To begin putting together a list of possible candidates, consider the determinants of growth and the role of distortions in a standard model. The standard endogenous growth model yields the result that, along a balanced growth path, consumption and capital grow according to

$$\frac{\dot{c}_t}{c_t} = \frac{\dot{k}_t}{k_t} = \sigma[r(1-\tau)-\rho], \tag{3}$$

where a dot over a variable denotes the rate of change over time, and where other definitions are as follows:

- c = consumption
- k = capital
- r = the rate of return on capital
- τ = the tax rate on capital, actual or expected, formal or informal
- ρ = the world rate of interest
- σ = elasticity of intertemporal elasticity in consumption.

In addition, the private return on capital r is given by

$$r = r(a, \theta, x), \tag{4}$$

where

- a = indicator of total factor productivity
- x = availability of complementary factors of production, such as infrastructure or human capital.
- θ = index of externality (a higher θ means a larger distortion).

These two equations summarize the possible factors that can affect growth performance. An exercise of *growth diagnostics* simply consists of reviewing and analyzing these factors to ascertain which of these factors is the most binding constraint on growth. As the analysis above reveals, all factors (including market distortions and policy wedges) are likely to matter for growth and welfare. The challenge is to identify the one that provides the largest positive direct effect, so that even after taking into account second-best interactions and indirect effects, the net impact of a policy change is beneficial (and hopefully sizable).

It helps to divide the factors affecting growth into two categories.

High Cost of Financing Domestic Investment

This is a case in which growth is low because, for any return on investment, accumulation is kept down by a high ρ. Stretching definitions slightly, we can interpret ρ as the rate of interest relevant for investment decisions in the economy in question. In turn, this could be connected to two kinds of policy problems:

• Bad international finance: country risk is too high, foreign direct investment conditions are unattractive, debt maturity and denomination increase macro risk, there remain excessive regulations on the capital account, etc.
• Bad local finance: when domestic capital markets work badly, collateral cannot be aggregated properly among domestic borrowers (Caballero and Krishnamurthy 2003) and the risk of banking crises and nonpayment rises. Both of these increase the cost of capital, especially foreign capital.

Low Private Return to Domestic Investment

The other component of the growth equation is given by the private expected return on domestic investment, given by $r(1 - \tau)$. A low such return can be due to

• high τ: high tax rates and/or inefficient tax structure and/or high expected expropriation risk
• high θ: large externalities, spillovers, coordination failures
• low a: low productivity, too little technology adoption or "self-discovery," weak public incentives
• low x: insufficient human capital, inadequate infrastructure, high transport, telecommunications or shipping costs

Moving Down the Multilemma

The logical structure of the analysis can be portrayed in the form of a decision tree, shown in figure 2.1. The tree naturally organizes the policy questions, which can be asked in logical order.

Is the problem one of inadequate returns to investment, inadequate private appropriability of the returns, or inadequate access to finance? If it is a case of low returns to investment, is that due to insufficient supply of complementary factors of production (such as human capital or infrastructure)? Or is it due to poor access to appropriate technologies? If it is a case of poor appropriability, is it due to high taxation, poor property rights and contract enforcement, labor-capital conflicts, or learning externalities?

Or alternatively: if it is a case of poor finance, are the problems with domestic financial markets or external ones?

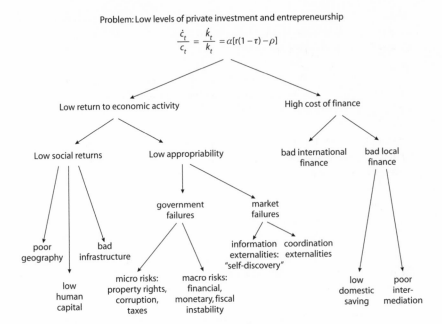

Problem: Low levels of private investment and entrepreneurship

$$\frac{\dot{c}_t}{c_t} = \frac{\dot{k}_t}{k_t} = \alpha[r(1-\tau)-\rho]$$

Fig. 2.1. Growth diagnostics

Moving down the branches of the decision tree is tantamount to discarding candidates for the most binding constraint on growth. The overarching lesson from our theoretical analysis is that it is this constraint, once identified, that deserves the most attention from policymakers.

COUNTRY EXPERIENCES: IDENTIFYING

THE BINDING CONSTRAINTS

We now have a framework to think of growth diagnostics. In this section we apply our approach to three countries with three very different growth experiences: Brazil, El Salvador, and the Dominican Republic.

The first two countries have had lackluster growth in spite of quite impressive reforms. The last had a sustained period of very rapid growth triggered by rather modest reforms, but more recently has stumbled into a financial crisis from which it has had difficulty extricating itself fully.

Both Brazil and El Salvador made major efforts at dealing with their perceived problems during the 1990s. Brazil returned to democracy in the 1980s, started opening up its economy in the early 1990s, stopped

TABLE 2.1

GDP Growth Rates (% real change per annum)

	1998–2003	1993–2003	1990–2000	1980–2000
Brazil	1.4	2.7	2.7	2.7
Dominican Republic	4.8	5.1	4.8	4.3
El Salvador	2.6	3.7	4.6	1.5
OECD	2.3	2.4	2.7	2.9
United States	3.0	3.2	3.2	3.3

Source: Economist Intelligence Unit.

megainflation in the mid-1990s through exchange-rate-based stabilization, implemented privatization and financial reform, and after 1999 was able to maintain price stability while floating the currency and improving its fiscal surplus. El Salvador stopped its civil war, negotiated successful peace agreements, reformed its judiciary and police, stabilized prices, opened up the economy, privatized utilities and social security, and improved social services. Both countries underwent a brief period of decent growth—or should we say recovery—but more recently growth has been quite lackluster. As table 2.1 indicates, in spite of the improvements in the political and policy framework over the 1993–2003 decade, Brazil grew more slowly than the United States and barely 0.3 percentage points faster than the OECD average, in spite of the fact that its rate of demographic growth—and the rate at which its working-age population expands—is over one percentage point per year higher. In other words, there was no catch-up or convergence. Moreover, both economies slowed down quite significantly in the 1998–2003 period. And future prospects look modest. In the context of a very favorable external environment and coming back from three years of stagnant GDP per capita, which should have left underutilized resources, Brazil was barely able to grow at 5.1 percent in 2004, a rate that was clearly above its sustainable level, as it involved a reduction in the rate of unemployment by over by 1.2 percentage points. El Salvador grew at a 2 percent rate in 2003–4, and prospects for the future do not look much different. The obvious question is why. What is keeping these economies from converging toward higher levels of income in spite of the policy improvements? What is the growth diagnostic? What should the authorities focus on in each country?

It will be useful to contrast El Salvador and Brazil to the Dominican Republic, a country with a much less impressive reform effort and with significantly weaker institutions. Its reform history starts with a currency crisis in the late 1980s addressed with an effective stabilization policy and some trade liberalization, but the reforms were nowhere as significant as in the other two countries. Nonetheless, the Dominican Republic achieved more than a decade of very fast growth interrupted only in 2002 by a banking crisis.

In terms of the present analysis, Brazil and El Salvador look like cases of wholesale reform that eliminated some distortions but not necessarily the most binding constraints. The Dominican Republic, by contrast, appears to have found a way around its binding constraint with minor reform efforts. Its eventual crash indicates that as growth proceeds, the shadow prices of other constraints—such as those of weak institutions—increase and that they may eventually become the binding constraint on growth.

Brazil versus El Salvador

Brazil and El Salvador are obviously very different countries in terms of size, history and structure. But they share one feature: lackluster growth in spite of significant reform. The case of El Salvador is particularly puzzling: broad ranging reforms were associated with a short-lived growth spurt and then relative stagnation since 1996.[4] Let us apply our framework to see if Brazil and El Salvador share a similar diagnostic.

For a long time, promoting saving and capital accumulation was the dominant idea in development policy. Under this view, low growth could be explained by an insufficient increase in the supply of factors of production, physical capital in particular. While "capital fundamentalism" has long been discarded (along with Soviet-style planning), it has been replaced more recently with a focus on human capital. Increasing the supply of human capital—through a greater health and education effort—is expected to lead to a faster accumulation of these assets and hence to a higher level of income. Can the poor growth performance in Brazil and El

---

[4] A recent World Bank study (Loayza, Fajnzylber, and Calderón 2002) implicitly finds that the decline in the rate of growth in El Salvador after 1996 is difficult to explain. In their model, improvements in secondary school enrollment, availability of private domestic credit, the increase in openness and in phone lines, the low inflation rate, and the absence of banking crises should have compensated for the increase in the initial level of income, the declining output gap, the increased real appreciation of the currency, and the adverse terms-of-trade shifts. This should have left growth unchanged in the second half of the 1990s relative to the first half. Instead, growth declined by 2.8 percent. Hence, they are unable to account for the growth decline. In line with this, López (2003) attributes the growth decline to "temporary," business-cycle-related factors—an unsustainable boom in the early 1990s followed by a pricking of the bubble in the second half of the decade. This leaves open the question of why the economy has not performed better in the first decade of the new century and why prospects are not more encouraging.

TABLE 2.2

Savings, Investment, and the Current Account (as percentage of GDP, average 1990–2000)

Country	Gross National Savings	Gross Fixed Capital Formation	Current Account Balance
Brazil	18.7	20.8	−2.2
Dominican Republic	18.9	22.2	−3.2
El Salvador	15.6	17.4	−1.8

Source: Penn World Tables 6.1.

Salvador be explained by a weak effort at saving and education? Can these variables explain the difference from the Dominican Republic?

On the face of it, there are two elements that make this argument compelling for El Salvador and Brazil. Both countries have low savings and investment rates (table 2.2). The investment rate averaged around 20.8 percent and 17.4 percent for Brazil and El Salvador, respectively, during the decade of the 1990s. The saving rate in the 1990s (including the remittances as part of national income) was even lower, as both countries ran current account deficits that averaged 2.2 percent in Brazil and 1.8 percent in El Salvador.

Second, both countries have relatively low educational attainment. The supply of education in both countries—measured as the average years of schooling of the labor force—is at the bottom of Latin American countries, although it grew in both countries at over one year per decade in the 1990s.

When would lack of an adequate saving and educational effort be a basic reason for a country's stagnant growth performance? For this story to be plausible, one should be able to observe high returns to both capital and schooling. The economy must be willing to gobble up additional resources, but prevented from doing so because they are not adequately provided. Hence, we should observe the tightness of the constraint in the price society is willing to pay for the scarce resource.

Let us deal first with savings. If savings were scarce, one would observe a high foreign debt or a high current account deficit—a signal that the country is using or has already used up its access to foreign savings, given the paucity of domestic savings. Alternatively, one would observe a high willingness to remunerate savings through high interest rates to depositors or government bondholders.

Here Brazil and El Salvador provide completely different stories. Time and again, Brazil has had serious difficulties with its balance of payments. In 1998, with a debt level already very high (in relation to exports), the scarcity of savings was reflected in a spread on external bonds of 1,226 basis points and in a real ex post overnight (SELIC) interest rate of over 30 percent. In January 1999 the country was forced to devalue: the real multilateral exchange rate depreciated by 37.4 percent in 1999. The current account deficit was reduced in dollars to an average of 24 billion per annum for the following three years (1999–2001). The spread on external bonds averaged a still hefty but lower 758 basis points, and the domestic real ex post overnight interest rate declined to a still high 10 percent. This amount of foreign borrowing also proved unsustainable, and a new balance-of-payments crisis ensued in 2002. The spread on external bonds averaged 2,160 basis points during a three-week period in August 2002 and averaged 1,446 for the year, in spite of massive international official support led by the International Monetary Fund. The real exchange rate depreciated by an additional 38.3 percent in 2002. Lack of external financing, a domestic recession, and real depreciation forced the current account to finally turn around, moving to surplus in 2003.

In short, the country has been trying to cope with the paucity of domestic savings by both attempting to attract foreign savings and by remunerating domestic savings at very high real rates. Time and again, the country has borrowed so much from abroad that it has been perceived as being on the brink of bankruptcy (as indicated by the spread on its foreign debt). In addition, Brazil's growth performance has moved pari passu with the tightness of the external constraint. When the external constraint is relaxed—say, because of an increase in the general appetite for emerging market risk or because of higher commodity prices, as more recently—the economy is able to grow. But when the external constraint tightens, real interest rates increase, the currency depreciates, and growth declines. This suggests that growth is limited by the availability of savings.

The situation in El Salvador is very different. In the past the country has not used up its access to foreign savings: its total gross external debt stands at less than 30 percent of GDP, and it enjoys an investment grade credit rating. Nor is the country currently using foreign savings rapidly: the current account deficit has averaged 2 percent of GDP in the past five years. Savings are not remunerated at high rates: the country needs to pay among the lowest interest rates in the region to attract demand for deposits or government bonds. Its banks have more liquidity than domestic credit demand can soak up, and are actively lending to enterprises in neighboring countries. In terms of average real lending rates, Brazil and El Salvador are at opposite extremes, with El Salvador exhibiting the lowest lending rates and Brazil exhibiting the highest. And perhaps the most telling indicator that El Salvador is not saving-constrained is that the external savings that the dramatic boost in remittances has enabled have not been converted into

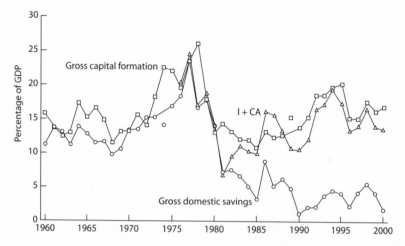

Fig. 2.2. Domestic savings, national savings (including remittances) and investment

Source: Penn World Tables 6.1.

Note: National savings equals gross fixed capital formation plus the current account surplus.

investment. As figure 2.2 shows, the decline in domestic savings has substituted almost one-for-one for the increase in remittances, with no discernible effect on the total investment effort. So there are no symptoms that El Salvador's growth is constrained by lack of savings.

In fact, Brazil and El Salvador are also at opposite extremes in terms of the cost of domestic financial intermediation. In a comparative study by Barth and Levine (2001), the net interest margin was reported to be 11.5 percent in Brazil and 3.7 percent in El Salvador, while the overhead costs were 9.8 percent in Brazil and 3.2 percent in El Salvador. In spite of this, credit to the private sector was almost the same in both countries (25.8 in Brazil and 27.5 in El Salvador).

All this suggests that El Salvador is a country where investment is constrained by low returns to capital (low investment demand), not by low availability of savings. The country invests little not because it cannot mobilize the resources to invest—although savings are low—but because the country does not find productive investments in which to deploy the resources. There is ample access to foreign borrowing, deposit rates are low, and intermediation costs are among the lowest in Latin America. In terms of our decision tree in figure 2.1, it seems clear that El Salvador is a low-return country.

Brazil, by contrast, is a high-return country. In spite of very high overnight real interests and very high intermediation costs, investment has

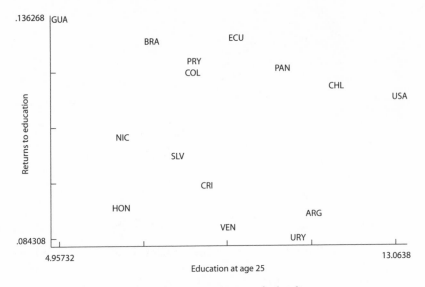

Fig. 2.3. Returns to education and years of schooling
Source: Calculations based on surveys collected by the Inter-American Development Bank

outstripped domestic savings, and the country has used its capacity to borrow abroad from the rest of the world to the hilt. Clearly, the investment rate in Brazil and credit to the private sector would be dramatically higher if the prevailing cost of capital were that of El Salvador.

A similar contrast between the two countries emerges when we turn to education. If education were the constraint on growth, one would expect to see high returns to the few who get educated. Figure 2.3 shows a scatterplot of returns to education and years of schooling for a sample of 14 Latin American countries and the United States. The picture that emerges is clear: while the years of schooling of the labor force are low both in El Salvador and in Brazil, the returns are quite different. Brazil has just about the highest returns in Latin America, while El Salvador is below the regional average. Hence, the evidence suggests that lack of educational effort is not at present a principal source of low growth in El Salvador, while it may well be part of the story in Brazil.

What is at stake here is whether a sudden increase in the supply of more educated citizens is likely to unleash significantly faster growth. If growth is being constrained by other factors, other things equal, more education is likely to lead mainly to lower returns to human capital, not to higher incomes. In this respect, Brazil and El Salvador look quite different.

Hence, the challenge in El Salvador is to identify what constraints may be behind the low returns to investment, while the challenge in Brazil is to explain why the country is constrained in external markets and why domestic savings do not rise to exploit the large returns to investment.

Misdiagnoses in El Salvador

As figure 2.1 indicates, low investment in El Salvador may be the consequence of many potential distortions that keep private returns low, even if social returns are high. One possibility is that the social returns are not privately appropriable. Appropriability problems can emerge from many fronts. We can group these into four major areas:

- High taxes: Actual or expected explicit taxes make private returns low and hence investment unattractive, although social returns may be high.
- Macroeconomic imbalances: Unsustainable fiscal or external accounts usually presage the need for implicit taxation or expropriation through surprise inflation, depreciation, default, or banking crises. In anticipation, country risk and interest rates rise, further depressing investment.
- Poor definition and protection of property rights: Productive investments may be limited by the expectation that investors will not be able to appropriate the returns because their claims are ill-defined or poorly protected, through corruption, judicial manipulation, or outright crime. Measures to avoid these problems create additional high transaction costs that may render investment unattractive.
- Uncertainty: Doubts—deriving from political or other factors—regarding the commitment to the current rules of the game create excessive risks about the environment in which projects will evolve.

The issues involved here are multiple and complex. We will review them quickly and assess their relative importance in El Salvador.

CONCERNS ABOUT EXCESSIVELY HIGH TAXATION

This is not a problem that can explain low growth in El Salvador. The country has a very moderate income tax with a marginal rate at 25 percent, well below the rate that global corporations pay in their home country. Moreover, the country has eliminated the double taxation of capital. The value added tax, at 13 percent, is moderate by regional standards and a fraction of that applied in western Europe. Tariffs are low, and the economy is one of the most open in the region.

In fact, it is easier to argue that El Salvador may be suffering from the opposite problem. Tax revenue may be so low that the government lacks the resources to provide an adequate supply of public goods needed to make economic activity productive. The Global Competitiveness Report of 2002–3, which views smaller government spending as a virtue, ranks El Salvador in fourteenth place in a sample of 80 countries in terms of low government spending. Unfortunately, the world leader in this indicator is Haiti. Even within Latin American countries, El Salvador's public spending appears low. This may be a reason why the country ranks poorly in measures of the quality of infrastructure (especially in roads, rail, and ports) and public education.

We conclude that excessive current or expected explicit taxation is not a sensible explanation of El Salvador's development challenge.

CONCERNS ABOUT MACRO STABILITY

When the economy is on an unsustainable path—for example, when the country as a whole or the government is accumulating obligations at a rate that will compromise its ability to abide by them—participants in the economy know that the current rules of the game will need to be abandoned and act to protect themselves from the expected changes rather than engage in productive investments. Problems of macro stability can be generated by imbalances arising from different areas. The fiscal accounts may be in deficit, and public debt may be increasing faster than the capacity to service it. Longer-term fiscal commitments, in particular the actuarial liabilities of the government vis-à-vis the pension system, may bankrupt an otherwise solvent government. Monetary policy may be too loose, causing a loss of international reserves and an eventual large depreciation. Banks may be taking excessive risk, which can result in a disruptive crisis that often weakens both fiscal and monetary stability. The country may be running large external imbalances that translate into reserve loss or a rapidly rising external debt and signal the need for eventual currency depreciation. The real exchange rate may be misaligned, limiting the profitability and growth of export- and import-competing sectors.

The question is to what extent the relatively disappointing growth of the last few years can be interpreted mainly as the outcome of limitations on these fronts. It is worth noting that the Global Competitiveness Report 2002–3 ranked El Salvador as number 33 out of 80 countries in the world in terms of its macro environment, well ahead of all Central American countries and most Latin American countries, except for Chile. Underpinning this ranking was the country's low inflation rate, low bank spreads, good access to credit, moderate fiscal deficit, small government, and good credit rating. While macro problems may appear in the future, especially if insufficient attention is paid to them, it seems reasonable to argue that El Salvador's low growth in the past five to six years cannot be easily explained in terms of macroeconomic imbalances. The puzzle is precisely why a relatively good macro environment has not generated faster growth.

CONCERNS ABOUT CONTRACT ENFORCEMENT AND PROPERTY RIGHTS

The role of institutions in development has received increasing attention in recent years. Could it be that El Salvador is being held back by an inadequate institutional environment?

Our answer is negative. The Heritage Foundation ranked El Salvador seventeenth in the world in 2002 in terms of "economic freedom" and third in Latin America (behind only Chile and the Bahamas). According to López (2003, 2), El Salvador ranks "always near the top in terms of the World Bank's Country Policy and Institutional Assessment ratings." On the financial front, El Salvador ranks very favorably in indicators associated with credit availability and cost. This is telling because financial markets are particularly sensitive to problems of contract enforcement. Moreover, in 2003 the World Economic Forum ranked El Salvador third among Latin American countries in terms of low corruption and low tax evasion (after much wealthier Chile and Uruguay) and second in the efficiency with which it uses its public funds (after Chile).

If anything, El Salvador looks like a country with very good institutions for its low level of income. In fact, it ranks better than Brazil in most indicators in spite of the fact that it has a level of per capita income that, at US$3,530 for 2003, is less than half that of Brazil (US$7,720). It is hard to argue that a bad institutional framework is keeping returns to capital low.

INFRASTRUCTURE, LABOR, AND REAL EXCHANGE RATE MISALIGNMENT

Other stories in the decision tree involve rigid labor markets and bad infrastructure. Here again, it is hard to make the case that these factors are critical to the growth story. Electricity and telecommunications have been privatized and have undergone a major expansion. While the country ranks low in the Global Competitiveness Report in terms of roads, ports, and rail infrastructure, there have also been important recent improvements in these areas with scant impact on the investment rate of other sectors.

The same can be said of labor institutions. The country has relatively few restrictions on hiring and firing and low payroll taxes. These limited sources of rigidity cannot account for low investment returns.

However, the country does have a high minimum wage in relation to the average wage. In addition, the country is dollarized, which means that the exchange rate cannot move to clear the labor market. The real exchange rate appreciated quite dramatically between 1974 and 1994 but has remained stable in the decade since then. Such a long-term stable level in the context of low current account deficits cannot be anything other than an equilibrium phenomenon (as the labor market should clear in less than a decade!). In part, the appreciation reflects the rise in remittances, which represented 17.6 percent of GDP in 2002. These external flows increase the supply of foreign exchange and in addition are caused by a contraction in the domestic supply of labor. Both effects tend to appreciate the real exchange rate. Hence, even if the exchange rate is misaligned by some measures, it does not seem to be unsustainable or to be generating fears of a currency crisis down the road. In this sense, it does not seem to be a central explanation for the mediocre growth of recent yeas.

INNOVATION AND THE DEMAND FOR INVESTMENT

The third element in our growth framework is productivity and innovation. What we have in mind here is not innovation and R&D in the sense that these terms are used in the advanced economies, but the ability to identify and generate higher-productivity activities within the Salvadoran context. These are new, nontraditional products that could be profitably produced in El Salvador, but which do not currently attract investment because of various market shortcomings (see chapter 4 and Hausmann and Rodrik 2003 for a general discussion).

El Salvador is facing bad news in its traditional sectors, and the speed at which it comes up with new ideas in other areas has been insufficient to compensate. The country has lost its cotton industry. Coffee is in crisis. Nobody has been able to make a decent living in the international sugar market. These "ideas," after creating hundreds of thousands of jobs in El Salvador, are in some sense dying. To achieve growth, new productive ideas must take their place. The speed at which these ideas appear and their economic significance are critical. The only important new sector has been the maquila industry, and this barely represents 480 million dollars (slightly more than 3 percent of GDP) in net exports. The absence of new ideas explains why the expected return to current investment ideas is low, and why investment and growth are low. It is not because of lack of savings. It is not mainly because of fear of taxation, expropriation, or fraud. It is because the actual real returns to investment are low given the absence of profitable investment opportunities.

El Salvador has opened up to the world, stimulated foreign investment, and endeavored to protect property rights. Is that not the way to encourage innovation and secure sufficiently rapid technological advances? The Salvadoran experience suggests that the answer may well be negative. The reason is that the innovation that matters to countries such as El Salvador—identifying and operating profitable new activities—is substantially more problematic than this simple picture assumes.

The problem with innovation is that it is hard to create but easy to copy or imitate. This means that part (or most) of the returns to innovation spill over to other people. This reduces the expected private return to innovation and hence may cause it to be inadequately supplied. In response to this, the world has opted to consider the output of innovators as an item of property that needs protection: hence the development of patents, copyrights, and other forms of intellectual property rights protection. These grant monopoly power over an idea to its creator.

The development process in less advanced countries is largely about structural change: it can be characterized as one in which an economy finds out—self-discovers—what it can be good at, out of the many products and processes that already exist. The problem is that the ideas that are valuable at low levels of development are typically not patentable. For example, the idea that an Ethiopian seed—coffee—could be planted in the hills of Central America was of historic importance, leading to a dramatic transformation of the fabric of society, but yet not patentable.

New ideas that lead to new sectors may require specific public capital or changes in rules and regulations that were designed in ignorance of their negative consequences to the sector. Coffee requires not education, research, and training in general, but in the specifics of coffee. Road and infrastructure networks need to take account of the areas where the new activities can expand. New forms of contracting, transacting, and financing may be required. The whole maquila industry requires a specific form of custom treatment.

The problems of self-discovery in tradable activities are likely to be potentially more important and the payoffs to addressing them much larger. They are more important because, contrary to nontradable activities, in which the first domestic supplier is by definition a monopolist, in the tradable sector, any new firm in a given country will start operating in a market where foreign suppliers already exist, limiting the rents of discovery. The payoffs can be larger in the tradable sector because the productive ideas can be scaled up to supply the world market, not just the more limited local market to which nontradable activities are restricted by definition.

In conclusion, it is problems with self-discovery that seem to be the binding constraint on growth in El Salvador. A growth strategy for this country needs to focus on these specific problems.[5]

Explaining Slow Growth in Brazil

Unlike El Salvador, Brazil is not in such dire need of ideas on where to invest. It has more ideas than investible funds. That is why the balance

---

[5] Chapter 4 provides a general discussion of the type of policies needed to encourage self-discovery. The specific policies needed in the Salvadoran context are discussed in Hausmann and Rodrik 2005.

between supply and demand for these funds occurs at such a high interest rate.

This first analysis clearly eliminates a set of potential diagnoses and policies from the list of priorities. It is true that Brazil suffers from an inadequate business environment, high taxes, high prices for public services, low supply of infrastructure, insecure property rights and judicial enforcement, and inadequate education relative to some best-practice benchmark. But our framework would discard them as priority areas for policy reform. This is because all these factors should depress private investment by keeping private returns low. But in spite of the subpar atmosphere, private returns are very high, and investment is constrained by the inability of the country to mobilize enough domestic and foreign savings to finance the existing investment demand at reasonable interest rates. If the country were to embark on a campaign to improve the business environment, it would make investment even more attractive and consequently would increase investment demand. In addition, it may improve the productivity of the projects that get undertaken (although this is not necessarily so). However, in the first instance, this would not relax the constraint on savings, which is where the binding constraint resides. In fact, some reforms that improve the business environment, such as lower taxes, lower public sector prices, and improved infrastructure and education may in fact lower public savings and thus reduce total savings. In addition, the increased demand for investment will translate mostly into a higher real interest rate, which will complicate public debt dynamics and generate more adverse selection in private financial markets (and hence, potentially worse investments). The overall health of the economy may show little improvement or even deteriorate. This is a case in which reforms that are apparently good may cause overall negative effects given the way reforms interact with other existing distortions, through the second-best logic described previously.[6]

THE PROBLEM WITH EXTERNAL SAVINGS

As argued above, Brazil has often been rationed in international capital markets, to which it has been paying a hefty premium to access funds. These markets have been concerned by the fact that the country already owes an uncomfortably large amount of money, and hence asset prices tend to go up when markets hear about positive innovations to the current account, implying that the country will stop its borrowing binge.

---

[6] Interestingly, the World Bank in its 2002 New Growth Agenda for Brazil came to the opposite view, stressing the importance of improving the investment climate in Brazil in order to trigger higher growth.

Hence, the recent large reduction in country risk that took place between 2002 and 2005 (table 2.2) did not coincide with an increase in external savings (i.e., an increase in the current account deficit) as would be the case if the dominant change were an increase in the supply of external savings. Instead, the decline in country risk coincided with a rapid decline in foreign savings, indicating that it was the demand curve for external savings that did most of the work. Hence, country risk seems to move in tandem with the demand for external savings, as would be the case when there is a highly inelastic supply of external savings.

Models of sovereign risk assume that what makes international lending enforceable is a means to punish opportunistic behavior by the borrower. Since Eaton and Gersovitz (1981) a typical assumption is that lenders can impose trade sanctions, and hence the volume of international trade is related to the credit ceiling lenders would like to avoid breaching.

In this context, Brazil has been a very closed economy, with almost twice the population of Mexico but less than half of its exports. This means that its credit ceiling should be limited by this fact. While the export-to-GDP ratio has risen in recent years, this has been due more to the decline in the dollar value of GDP at market prices than to the increase in exports, especially until 2002. If we take GDP at its purchasing power parity, exports are below 10 percent of output. Hence, while the external debt looks high as a share of GDP, it looks astronomical as a share of exports.

One can imagine a policy to make foreign investors even more eager to lend by raising the credit ceiling. However, ceteris paribus, this is bound to lead to a short-lived acceleration of growth until the economy reaches its new credit ceiling. Hence, we conclude that while the external constraint clearly binds, it is a reflection of the fact that the country has already used its borrowing capacity to the hilt. Some relaxation of that borrowing capacity would lead to faster growth in the transition to the new credit ceiling. But clearly, the underlying problem must be the conflict between the relatively healthy demand for investment and the inadequate level of domestic savings.

EXPLAINING INADEQUATE DOMESTIC SAVINGS

A more sustained relaxation of the constraint on growth would involve an increase in the domestic savings rate. This raises the question of what is keeping it low at present, in spite of high real interest rates.

In searching for an answer, it is useful to note some fiscal characteristics of Brazil.

- At 34 percent of GDP, the country has by far the highest public revenue share in Latin America and one of the highest in the developing world.

• In spite of this, public savings have been negative by more than 2 percent of GDP: public investment has averaged less than 2 percent of GDP between 1999 and 2002, while the fiscal deficit averaged 4.4 percent.

• To achieve its high level of taxation, the country is forced to use distortionary levies at very high rates, such as a cascading sales tax, a tax on financial transactions, and very hefty payroll taxes, which Heckman and Pages (2000) estimate at 37.6 percent of wages.

• In spite of the extraordinary level of taxation, fiscal balance is precarious. According to the IMF, general government debt as a share of GDP stood at 95.1 percent in 2002, while the overall deficit averaged 4.3 percent of GDP between 1999 and 2004.

• The high taxes and low savings reflect a very high level of current spending and transfers. For example, social security expenditures stand at 8.5 percent of GDP, which is unusually high given the country's relatively young demography. They reflect the country's low retirement age and generous terms for its mostly middle-class public and formal sector employees.

High taxation and negative public savings must have adverse effects on aggregate saving: they reduce the disposable income of the formal private sector, and the resources thus mobilized are not used to increase public savings. This may be an important part of the explanation behind the low saving equilibrium. In addition, since equilibrium is reached at a high real interest rate, the positive effect that high interest rates may have on stimulating private savings is offset by the negative effect it has on public savings as the cost of servicing the inherited stock of public debt is raised.

High taxation and negative savings reflect the existence of a very high level of entitlements or waste, and a high level of inherited debt. This forces the country to choose among a very high tax rate, high public sector prices, low investment in infrastructure, and low subsidies for human capital. All these choices are bad for growth because they depress the private return to capital. But returns are already very high, and investment is constrained by lack of loanable funds. If high taxation and the paucity of public goods were in themselves the binding constraint, the private return to investment would be low and equilibrium between savings and investment would be established at a lower return to capital. This is an important distinction because it goes to the heart of the question about what to emphasize in reform: should it be the impact on aggregate savings (such as fiscal consolidation) or on the implications for private returns to capital (such as lower taxation)? This analysis points us in the direction of the former. The first goal has to be to improve national savings.

What are the policy implications? One alternative is to lower government entitlements and waste, with the resources used to increase public savings. The direct effect would be a higher level of aggregate savings, a lower interest rate, better public debt dynamics, and lower intermediation margins, all of which could have a positive effect on foreign savings if the latter is affected by fears of fiscal insolvency. Lowering the burden of pensions through a social security reform may be an effective way to achieve this result.

In the absence of this first-best policy, the question is whether a progrowth strategy can be based on an apparently antigrowth set of policy measures such as increases in taxation and public prices and cuts in infrastructure and human capital subsidies. The analysis above would suggest an affirmative response. The microeconomic inefficiencies of taxation and suboptimal spending structures are not binding because reducing them would increase the returns to capital but would not generate the means to exploit those returns.

The Dominican Republic: Growth and Then Crash

The Caribbean is an unlikely place to find a success story. The region once seemed naturally destined to produce sugar cane, the source of its wealth since the seventeenth century. With the heavy protection of sugar in Europe and the United States, the Caribbean lost its obvious export crop. States in the region are too small to embark on import substitution industrialization, although some tried with disastrous consequences. The Dominican Republic had been lucky because in addition to sugar it had a gold mine. However, this resource was exhausted in the 1980s. The country had to reinvent itself, and with no obvious way to do so.

The country had quite precarious political and bureaucratic institutions. The difficulties of the 1980s had wreaked havoc with its macro balances. A balance-of-payments crisis erupted in 1991, and the country dealt with it swiftly and made modest structural reforms: a unification of its exchange rate regime and some trade liberalization. This triggered a sustained period of high growth that essentially lasted a decade until it ended quickly in the 2002 banking crisis. Yet even in a period of extreme financial turmoil in 2002–4, the economy did not contract, as happened in most other places in the region, namely, Argentina, Colombia, Ecuador, Uruguay, and Venezuela.

What explains its success and its current problems? Why did the achievement of macro balance and some reform lead to such fast growth in the Dominican Republic and not in other places? In retrospect, the answer seems to be lie with three main drivers of growth: tourism, maquila and remittances.

Remittances tripled in the last decade to a level of US$2.1 billion in 2002, or 9.9 percent of GDP. Tourism did even better. It increased from

US$0.7 billion in 1991 to US$2.5 billion in 2000 (11.8 percent of GDP). Net maquila exports per capita doubled to a level of about US$200 per capita in 2000–2001, the highest in the Americas including NAFTA-member Mexico.

Now, these three engines of growth are dependent on some institutional setup. Tourism requires some level of investor, personal, and environmental security. While it would be ideal to assure these three elements for all sectors of the economy, relatively closed all-inclusive resorts can do with a more targeted provision of these public goods, using private security and infrastructure. So the country created an adequate environment for that industry to take off.

By the same token, maquila is an exception to the general laws that apply to other activities. With a sufficiently effective institutional framework for this sector, it can take off even if the rest of the economy is stranded with ineffective institutions and regulations.

In this sense, the Dominican Republic is a good example of an alternative path to institutional development. Such a path would involve attending to the institutional and public good requirements of sectors that see high potential returns and that can be scaled up significantly to become important. In other words, the reforms are geared at solving the specific institutional problems that potentially important new sectors face, so as to increase their expected rate of return and allow an investment boom to start there.

As these "enclave" sectors grow and generate employment and income, they contribute directly or indirectly to the tax base and to domestic intermediate demand. This is the time to fix the bottlenecks in the rest of the economy. This resembles a game of curling in which, as the stone slides, the players work feverishly to polish the ice so that the stone keeps sliding forward. Trade liberalization will make the rest of the economy more like the maquila sector. Personal security and environmental standards can be upgraded in the rest of the country. This will bring benefits to all, including those tourists who might actually venture beyond the grounds of the resort.

Clearly, the problem with this strategy is that the economy might outgrow its relatively weak institutional setting. It is hard to know which institution will crack. It could be that economic success makes foreign lending available to the government without the budget institutions to keep fiscal discipline, as happened in many Latin American countries in the 1970s when they were showered for the first time with syndicated foreign loans. It could be that the stakes of the political game become so high that the political process is disrupted.

None of this happened in the Dominican Republic. Fiscal balance was maintained, and the political process became, if anything, more institutionalized. However, the financial system did grow very fast with the economic expansion and became more integrated with the rest of the world. Imposing prudential regulatory standards on rapidly expanding banks proved institutionally and politically difficult. Some banks were politically influential, and as a group they were capable of blocking legislation and administrative actions by a technically and politically weak regulator. When September 11, 2001, brought a sudden stop to the flow of international tourism, a Ponzi scheme in the banking system was uncovered. Through some mix of limited institutional competence and inadequate political independence, managing this crisis involved converting over 20 percent of GDP in bank losses into the public debt.

As usual, these bank rescues involve drastic expansions of domestic credit by the central bank. The Dominican central bank had no international reserves with which to sterilize money creation. The exchange rate quickly depreciated from 17.8 R$/US$ in January 2003 to 34.9 R$/US$ in July 2003 and 48.6 by June 2004. This massive depreciation caused an acceleration of inflation to over 65 percent in the year to June 2004.

These changes wreaked havoc with the fiscal accounts. The new debt issued by the central bank raised the quasi-fiscal deficit by over 2 percent of GDP. The depreciation increased the domestic resource cost of the foreign currency public debt. The domestic value of the public debt almost tripled, from less than 20 percent of GDP to over 50 percent of GDP. In addition, a system of indirect subsidies for liquefied petroleum gas (LPG) and for electricity, which had prices fixed in pesos, became much more expensive to sustain. Unable to impose harsher adjustment measures in an already difficult situation, the government decided to limit price increases for these goods, but this meant a level of fiscal subsidy that it was unable to pay. Massive shortages of electricity and gas ensued.

The moral of the story is clear. Igniting economic growth may not require the infinite laundry list of reforms that have become the current consensus on best practices. But once the economy is on the path of growth, the onus is on policymakers to solve the institutional and other constraints that will inevitably become more binding.

CONCLUSIONS

An important advantage of the growth-diagnostics framework is that it encompasses all major strategies of development and clarifies the circumstances under which each is likely to be effective. Strategies that focus on resource mobilization through foreign assistance and increased domestic national saving pay off when domestic returns are both high and privately appropriable. Strategies that focus on market liberalization and opening up to the world economy work best when social returns are high and the most serious obstacle to their private appropriation is government-imposed taxes and restrictions. Strategies that emphasize industrial policy are appropriate when private returns are depressed not by the government's errors of commission (what it does), but its errors of omission (what it fails to do).

As the discussion of El Salvador, Brazil, and the Dominican Republic illustrates, each of these circumstances throws out different diagnostic signals. An approach to development that determines the action agenda on the basis of these signals is likely to be considerably more effective than a laundry list of institutional and governance reforms that may or may not be well targeted on the most binding constraints to growth.

3

Synthesis: A Practical Approach to Growth Strategies

THE CENTRAL economic paradox of our time is that "development" is working while "development policy" is not. On the one hand, the last quarter century has witnessed a tremendous and historically unprecedented improvement in the material conditions of hundreds of millions of people living in some of the poorest parts of the world. On the other hand, development policy as it is commonly understood and advocated by influential multilateral organizations, aid agencies, Northern academics, and Northern-trained technocrats has largely failed to live up to its promise. We are faced with the confluence of two seemingly contradictory trends.

Let us start with the successes. According to the latest World Bank estimates, there were roughly 400 million fewer "poor" people in the world in 2001 than two decades earlier, when poverty is measured by the one-dollar-a-day standard. That represents a striking decline in the *absolute* number of the poor, not just in the relative incidence of poverty. What has made these gains possible is the sharp increase in economic growth in some of the poorest and most populous countries of the world, China and India in particular. China's growth rate since 1978 has been nothing short of spectacular, bringing considerable poverty reduction in its wake. In fact, the reduction in poverty in China alone accounts for the full 400 million global reduction, with the gains and losses in the rest of the world canceling each other out. The number of people below the one-dollar-a-day line has fallen somewhat in South Asia, but increased sharply in sub-Saharan Africa. In Latin America, the incidence of poverty has remained roughly constant, while the number of poor people has increased.

As we saw in chapter 1, these regional disparities in performance match up very poorly against reform efforts, when the latter are judged by the standard yardsticks of stabilization, liberalization, and privatization. The high-performing economies have bucked conventional wisdom on what makes for good economic reform. China and Vietnam liberalized their economies in a partial, two-track manner, did not undertake ownership reform, and protected themselves from GATT (General Agreement on Tariffs and Trade) and WTO rules (in the case of China until very recently). India reformed very gradually, and only after a decade of strong economic growth. By any conventional measure of structural reform, these economies would be considered laggards. Given the policies in place in China, Vietnam, and India, it is hardly an exaggeration to say that it would have been easier to explain their performance if these countries had failed abysmally instead of succeeding the way that they did.

Meanwhile, Latin America, which adopted the standard agenda with great enthusiasm and undertook a considerable amount of "structural reform," ended up growing slower not only relative to Asian countries but also relative to its own historical benchmarks. Reform in sub-Saharan Africa may have been more halting than in Latin America, but still, few can deny that this region now has much greater price stability than in the 1970s, is considerably more open to international trade, and gives much smaller role to parastatals and much greater role to markets. Yet the African successes have remained few, fleeting, and far in between. It is apparent that reform efforts have not directly targeted the public health, governance, and resource mobilization problems to which the continent has fallen prey.

To downplay the importance of these disappointments requires that we go through a number of contortions, none of which is particularly convincing. One counterargument is that countries in Latin America and Africa have simply not undertaken enough reform. What is "enough" is obviously in the eyes of the beholder, but this claim seems to me to be grossly unfair to the scores of leaders in Latin America and Africa who have spent considerable political capital in pursuit of Washington Consensus–style reforms. The weakness of the claim is also evident from the ease with which temporary successes in these countries have been ascribed to the reforms being implemented. Remember, for example, Argentina in the first half of the 1990s and how the growth spurt there was broadcast as evidence that "reform pays off."

A second counterargument is that "the check is in the mail" (to use my colleague Ricardo Hausmann's evocative caricature of this position). That is, the payoffs from reform have yet to appear, but will surely do so if we do not give up. The trouble is that this is entirely inconsistent with everything we know about the empirics of reform and growth. Growth follows rather immediately when the right things are done; there is no evidence to suggest that the returns to reform tend to be delayed a decade or more.

A third, somewhat related counterargument is that the first- and second-generation reforms were not enough, and that much more needs to be done to ensure growth will follow. Once again, this position is inconsistent with the evidence. The countries that performed well, for the most part, are not those that undertook ambitious reform agendas—quite to the contrary.

A fourth counterargument is that the poor performance in the reforming countries was due to external circumstances, for example, the overall slowdown in industrial country growth. This is not convincing because other developing countries managed rapid growth in the same economic environment. In any case, economic convergence ought to be a function of the convergence gap—the difference with the *level* of income prevailing in rich countries—which actually had grown larger in the case of Latin America and Africa by the early 1990s compared to the 1970s.

Finally, there is the counterargument that the contrast I have drawn above is false insofar as countries that did well were those in fact that did follow conventional advice. China did turn to markets and sought to integrate itself with the world economy. India did liberalize. Both of these countries, the argument goes, reformed at the maximum speed that their complicated politics allowed, and reaped the benefits. So what is the problem? For one thing, this line of thought overlooks the unconventional elements in these countries' successes (just as the focus on Korea's and Taiwan's outward orientation often obscured their active use of industrial policy). China did not simply liberalize and open up; it did so by grafting a market track on top of a plan track, by relying on TVEs rather than private enterprise, and through special economic zones rather than across-the-board trade liberalization. Moreover, implicit (and sometimes explicit) in this line of argument is that the partial, heterodox reform efforts in these countries would have yielded even more fruit had they been more by the book. One commonly hears that India, for example, would have grown faster had its government been able to reform more comprehensively and rapidly. The trouble is that one looks in vain for countries that did in fact reform more comprehensively and rapidly than India did and ended up with higher growth.

Nonetheless, the fact that there is enough in the successful heterodox approaches to give some comfort to the adherents of the orthodox agenda does indicate something. What it shows is that there are indeed broad principles to which all successful countries have adhered. Hence, all high-performing economies have managed to maintain macroeconomic stability, relied on market forces to varying extents and sought to integrate into the world economy, protected property rights of investors and entrepreneurs to some extent and enforced contracts, maintained a semblance of social cohesion and political stability, ensured adequate standards of prudential regulation and avoided financial crises, maintained productive dynamism and encouraged economic diversification, and done perhaps a bit more. Note, however, that these commonalities can be articulated only at a sufficiently high level of generality, and in a manner that yields scant guidelines for operationalization.

Take, for example, the objective of integration into the world economy. What is missing from the list is identification of what specific policies would best serve that objective. It is tempting to say that the requisite policies are low barriers to foreign trade and investment, but then again the evidence hardly points to a straightforward relationship between trade or capital-account liberalization and economic growth. The countries that most successfully integrated into the world economy (Korea and Taiwan in the 1960s and 1970s; China and Vietnam in the 1980s and 1990s) had highly protected home markets, and achieved integration through other means (export subsidies in the former, and special economic zones in the latter). The bottom line is that these common elements do not map into unique, well-defined policy recommendations.

One conclusion to take from this history is that our ability as economists to design growth strategies is extremely limited. Basically, anything goes, and it is up to imaginative politicians to come up with recipes that will work. We have very limited advice to give them ex ante, even though we are in the possession of many tools to evaluate the consequences of their policy decisions ex post.

We can do better than adopt this kind of nihilistic attitude toward advice on policy. If the original Washington Consensus erred in being too detailed and specific, and in assuming that the same set of policies works the same everywhere, nihilism goes too far in undervaluing the benefit of economic reasoning. Building on the analysis in the preceding chapters, I will outline here a way of thinking about growth strategies that avoids these two extremes. The approach consists of three elements. (*a*) diagnostic analysis, (*b*) policy design, and (*c*) institutionalization. First, we need to undertake a *diagnostic analysis* to figure out where the most significant constraints on economic growth are. Second, we need creative and imaginative *policy design* to target the identified constraints appropriately. Third, we need to *institutionalize* the process of diagnosis and policy response to ensure that the economy remains dynamic and growth does not peter out.

STEP 1: GROWTH DIAGNOSTICS

An important reason why the Washington Consensus, and its subsequent variant, second-generation reforms, have failed to produce the desired outcome is that they were never targeted on what may have been the most important constraints blocking economic growth. The fact that poor economies are poor indicates that they suffer from a variety of afflictions: they are poorly endowed with human capital, make ineffective use of capital and other resources, have poor institutions, have unstable fiscal and monetary policies, provide inadequate private incentives for investment and technology adoption, have poor access to credit, are cut off from world markets, and so on. To say that one has to overcome all these disadvantages in order to develop is at once a tautology and quite unhelpful. If Chad did not have these problems, it would look like Sweden, and it would not need to ask how a country can rise out of poverty. The trick is to find those areas where reform will yield the greatest return, or where we can get the biggest bang for the reform buck. What we need to know, in other words, is where the most binding constraint on growth lies. Otherwise, we are condemned to a spray-gun approach: we shoot our reform at as many targets as possible, hoping that some will turn out to be the real live ones. That is in effect what the augmented Washington Consensus does. While there is nothing wrong in principle with any of the recommendations on this laundry list of reforms, there is also no guarantee that the really serious constraints are the priority targets. A successful growth strategy, by contrast, begins by identifying the most binding constraints.

But can this be done? Is it possible to identify the most binding constraints? The analysis in the preceding chapter suggests a positive answer.

We begin with a basic but powerful taxonomy. In a low-income economy, economic activity must be constrained by at least one of the following three factors: the cost of financing economic activity may be too high, the economic (social) return to economic activity may be too low, or the private appropriability of the (social) returns may be too low. The first step in the diagnostic analysis is to figure out which of these conditions more accurately characterizes the economy in question. At first sight, this may seem like a hopeless task. But fortunately, it is possible to make progress because each of these syndromes throws out different sets of diagnostic signals or generates different patterns of co-movements in economic variables. For example, in an economy that is constrained by cost of finance, we expect real interest rates to be high, borrowers to be chasing lenders, the current account deficit to be as high as foreign borrowing constraints will allow, and entrepreneurs to be full of investment ideas. In such an economy, an exogenous increase in investible funds, such as foreign aid and remittances, will spur primarily investment and other productive economic activities rather than consumption or investment in real estate. This description comes pretty close to capturing the situation of Brazil, for example. By contrast, in an economy where economic activity is constrained by low private returns, interest rates will be low, banks will be flush in liquidity, lenders will be chasing after borrowers, the current account will be near balance or in surplus, and entrepreneurs will be more interested in putting their money in Miami or Geneva than in investing it at home. An increase in foreign aid or remittances will finance consumption, housing, or capital flight. These in turn are the circumstances of El Salvador.

When we identify low private returns as the culprit, we will next want to know whether the source is low *social* returns or low private appropriability. Low social returns can be due to poor human capital, lousy infrastructure, bad geography, or other similar reasons. Once again, we need to be on the lookout for diagnostic signals. If human capital (either because of low levels of education or because of disease) is a serious constraint, we expect the returns to education or the skill premium to be comparatively high. If infrastructure is the problem, we would observe the bottlenecks in transport or energy, private firms stepping in to supply the needed services, and so on. In the case of El Salvador, none of these circumstances seems to pose serious problems. Hence we infer that the constraint lies on the side of private appropriability.

Appropriability problems can in turn arise under two sets of circumstances. One possibility has to do with the policy or institutional environment: taxes may be too high, property rights may be protected poorly, high inflation may generate macro risk, labor-capital conflicts may depress production incentives, and so on. Alternatively, the fault may lie with the operation of markets insofar as markets cannot deal adequately with technological spillovers, coordination failures, and problems of economic "self-discovery" (see Chapter 4). As usual, we look for the telltale signs of each of these possibilities. Sometimes the diagnostic analysis proceeds down a particular path not because of direct evidence but because the other paths have been ruled out. So in the case of El Salvador one can conclude that lack of self-discovery is an important and binding constraint in part because there is little evidence in favor of the other traditional explanations.

It is possible to carry out this kind of analysis at a much finer level of disaggregation, and indeed any real-world application has to be considerably more detailed than the one I have offered here. What I hope I have offered is a glimpse of a type of analysis that is both doable and more productive than the conventional approach, which typically lacks a diagnostic component.

Step 2: Policy Design

Once the key problems have been identified, we need to think about the appropriate policy response. Here, conventional welfare economics becomes invaluable. The key in this step is to focus on the market failures and distortions associated with the constraint identified in the previous step. The principle of policy targeting offers a simple message: target the response as closely as possible on the source of the distortion. Hence if credit constraints are the main constraint, and the problem is the result of lack of competition and large bank spreads, the appropriate response is to reduce impediments to competition in the banking sector. If economic activity is held back because of high taxes at the margin, the solution is to lower them. If self-discovery externalities or coordination is at the root of stagnation, the solution is to internalize them through government programs or private-sector coordination.

Simple as it may be, this first-best logic often does not work, and indeed can be even counterproductive. The reason is that we are necessarily operating in a second-best environment because of other distortions or administrative and political constraints. In designing policy, we have to be on the lookout for unforeseen complications and unexpected consequences. Let me review and elaborate on some illustrations I mentioned in chapter 1.

Any economist visiting China in 1978 would have guessed that the most significant constraint holding the economy back was the lack of incentives in agriculture, caused by the state purchase system and the communal ownership of land. The recommendation to abolish obligatory deliveries to the state at controlled prices and to privatize land would have followed naturally. After all, these are the first-best solutions to the problems at hand. However, a more detailed consideration of the situation reveals that these policies would have been fraught with danger. Abolishing the state purchase system would have wiped out a significant source of fiscal revenue for the central government, since the difference between the purchase and sale prices of crops constituted part of the tax base. Since the government used its crop supply to subsidize food prices in urban areas, it would also have implied a rise in food prices in urban areas, leading to demands for higher wages. Privatization of land in turn would have brought in its wake severe legal and administrative difficulties. Therefore, agricultural price liberalization and land privatization look considerably less desirable once their attendant costs in the form of macro instability, social strife in urban areas, and legal and administrative chaos are factored in.

Of course, this is not an argument for abandoning reform. It is instead an argument for being creative and imaginative in designing responses that are sensitive to these second-best interactions. That, in any case, is the lesson of the Chinese reforms. For China neither abolished the state purchase system nor privatized land. The incentive problems were solved instead through the two-track pricing system—which involved grafting a market system on top of the state-order system—and the household responsibility system—which effectively made households the residual claimants of output without giving them ownership rights. Under these reforms, households were required to deliver their quotas to the state at controlled prices, but were free to sell any of their surplus produce at free market prices. As long as the state quotas remain inframarginal, efficiency in agriculture is increased. The beauty of this arrangement, easier to appreciate in hindsight, is that it delinks the provision of supply incentives from its fiscal and distributive consequences. Therefore, it avoids the second-best minefields that the more direct reforms would have stepped into.

A second illustration comes from another Chinese institutional innovation: township and village enterprises (TVEs). As we saw in chapter 1, the TVEs were the growth engine of China until the mid-1990s, with their share in industrial value added rising to more than 50 percent by the early 1990s. TVEs were owned by local communities (townships or villages). From the lens of first-best reform, these enterprises are problematic, since if our objective is to spur private investment and entrepreneurship, it would be far preferable to institute private property rights (as Russia and other East European transition economies did). Here again, the first-best logic runs into trouble. A private property system relies on an effective judiciary for the enforcement of property rights and contracts. In the absence of such a legal system, formal property rights are not worth much, as minority shareholders in Russia soon discovered. And it takes time to establish honest, competent courts. In the meantime, perhaps it makes more sense to make virtue out of necessity and force entrepreneurs into partnership with their most likely expropriators, the local state authorities. That is exactly what the TVEs did. The result was a much greater stimulus to private entrepreneurship and investment than would likely have been the case under conventional property-rights reform.

Or consider the case of achieving integration into the world economy. Leaders in countries such as South Korea and Taiwan in the early 1960s and China in the late 1970s had decided that enhancing their countries' participation in world markets was a key objective. For a Western economist, the most direct route would have been to reduce or eliminate barriers to imports and foreign investment. Instead, these countries achieved the same ends (i.e., reduce the antitrade bias of their economic policies) through unconventional means. South Korea and Taiwan employed export targets and export subsidies for their firms. China carved out special economic zones where foreign investors had access to a free-trade regime. These and other countries that opened up successfully but in an unconventional manner—Malaysia, Mauritius, and many others—presumably did so because their approach created fewer adjustment costs and put less stress on established social bargains.

Let me offer as a final illustration the case of a saving-constrained economy. Saving constraints can arise because households are in some sense shortsighted or do not fully internalize the high rate of returns that prevail in the real sector, in which case the first-best response would be to subsidize saving (say by offering favorable tax treatment of saving). Or they could arise because financial intermediation is not working properly, in which case the first-best response is to enhance the legal and supervisory apparatus that governs the financial markets. These solutions are impractical or take a long time to implement in low-income economies. A second-best solution is a moderate amount of financial repression—what Hellman, Murdock, and Stiglitz (1997) call "financial restraint." This entails controls on bank entry and ceilings on deposit rates, which generate rents for incumbent banks. Paradoxically, these rents induce banks to expand efforts to mobilize deposits (since there are rents to be earned on them). Both the quality and the level of financial intermediation can be higher than under financial liberalization.

The bottom line is that while the first-best is an obvious place to start, the lesson of successful countries is that desired objectives—supply incentives, effective property rights, integration into the world economy, saving mobilization—can be achieved in a variety of ways, often taking unconventional forms. As I argued in chapter 1, functions that institutions perform do not map into unique institutional forms. Poor countries suffer from market failures and institutional weaknesses that cannot all be removed in short order. This is an invitation to think of policy innovations that are explicitly second-best or that minimize the second-best complications. That is the essence of the illustrations just discussed. We need to be imaginative, look for homegrown solutions, and be prepared to experiment.

STEP 3: INSTITUTIONALIZING REFORM

It is in the very nature of the growth-diagnostics approach I have outlined that the identity of the binding constraint will change over time. Schooling may not be a binding constraint at present in a country, but if the strategy works and investment and entrepreneurship are stimulated, it is likely to become one unless the quality and quantity of schools increase over time. The poor quality of the judiciary may not have high cost at present, but legal shortcomings are likely to loom larger when the economy develops and becomes more sophisticated. Poor financial regulation may not be an issue when financial intermediation is rudimentary, but can prove to be explosive when the economy begins to boom.

Chapter 2 illustrated this shift in constraints with the example of the Dominican Republic. This country was able to spur growth with a number of sector-specific reforms that stimulated investment in tourism and maquilas. But it neglected the institutional investments required to lend resilience and robustness to economic growth—especially in the area of financial market regulation and supervision. When September 11 led to the drying up of tourism, the country paid a big price. A Ponzi scheme that had developed in the banking sector collapsed, and cleaning up the mess cost the government 20 percentage points of GDP and led the economy into a downward spiral. It turned out that the economy had outgrown its weak institutional underpinnings. The same can be said of Indonesia, where the financial crisis of 1997–98 led to total economic and political collapse. It may yet turn out to be case also of China, unless this country manages to strengthen the rule of law and enhance democratic participation.

Sustaining economic growth may be even harder than stimulating it. This was the clear message of the research that Ricardo Hausmann, Lant Pritchett, and I undertook on growth accelerations (Hausmann, Pritchett, and Rodrik 2005). We found that while growth accelerations are a frequent occurrence—on average a country has a one in four chance of experiencing a growth acceleration in any given decade—sustained growth is rare. Very few of the 83 accelerations we uncovered turned into sustained convergence with the living standards of the rich countries.

What is needed to sustain growth? I would emphasize two forms of institutional reforms in particular. First, there is the need to maintain productive dynamism over time. Natural resource discoveries, garment exports from maquilas, or a free-trade agreement may spur growth for a limited of time. Policies must ensure that this momentum is maintained with ongoing diversification into new areas of tradables. Otherwise, growth will simply peter out. What stands out in the performance of East Asian countries is their continued focus on the needs of the real economy and the ongoing encouragement of technology adoption and diversification. Market forces are not necessarily enough to generate this dynamism, and need to be complemented with proactive public strategies. The institutional implications of this will be discussed in the next chapter.

The second area that needs attention is the strengthening of domestic institutions of conflict management. The most frequent cause for the collapse in growth is the inability to deal with the consequences of external shocks—that is, terms-of-trade declines or reversals in capital flows. Resilience against such shocks requires strengthening the rule of law, solidifying (or putting in place) democratic institutions, establishing participatory mechanisms, and erecting social safety nets. When such institutions are in place, the macroeconomic and other adjustments needed to deal with adverse shocks can be undertaken relatively smoothly. When they are not, the result is distributive conflict and economic collapse. The contrasting experiences of South Korea and Indonesia in the immediate aftermath of the Asian financial crisis are quite instructive in this regard. I will have more to say on the important role of democracy as a shock absorber and as a "metainstitution" in chapter 5.

CONCLUDING REMARKS

I have offered here not a policy reform agenda, but a way of thinking about such an agenda that has more potential than the Washington Consensus in any of its variants. I have tried to show that a diagnostic approach *can* be implemented, has the advantage of providing country-specific solutions, and is by its very nature sensitive to political and administrative constraints. This approach is inherently bottom-up: it empowers countries to do their own diagnostic analyses. It warns multilateral organizations against uniformity and excessive restrictions on "policy space." Even when it does not yield clear-cut identification of the binding constraint, it provides a useful framework for discussing what should be done and why.

Furthermore, the diagnostic approach embeds all major existing strategic approaches to growth, and clarifies the conditions under which they are relevant. Hence, a substantial rise in foreign aid will work in countries that are saving-constrained. Industrial policy will work when private returns are low because of informational and coordination failures. Reducing trade barriers will work when such barriers are the main determinant of the gap between private and social returns to entrepreneurial activity. And so on.

Finally, the diagnostic approach has the advantage that it employs economists in their proper capacity: as evaluators of trade-offs instead of as advocates. Paraphrasing Oscar Wilde, Carlos Díaz-Alejandro once quipped that an economist is someone who knows the shadow price of everything but the value of nothing. The diagnostic approach makes a virtue of this occupational hazard: it asks economists for estimates of shadow prices (of various constraints associated with economic growth) and not for their value judgments.

PART B

Institutions

4
Industrial Policy for the Twenty-First Century

ONCE UPON a time, economists believed the developing world was full of market failures, and the only way in which poor countries could escape from their poverty traps was through forceful government interventions. Then there came a time when economists started to believe government failure was by far the bigger evil, and that the best thing that government could do was to give up any pretense of steering the economy. Reality has not been kind to either set of expectations. Import substitution, planning, and state ownership did produce some successes, but where they were entrenched and ossified over time, they led to colossal failures and crises. Economic liberalization and opening up benefited export activities, financial interests, and skilled workers, but more often than not, they resulted in economy-wide growth rates (in labor and total factor productivity) that fell far short of those experienced under the bad old policies of the past.

Few people seriously believe any more that state planning and public investment can act as the driving force of economic development. Even economists of the Left share a healthy respect for the power of market forces and private initiative. At the same time, it is increasingly recognized that developing societies need to embed private initiative in a framework of public action that encourages restructuring, diversification, and technological dynamism beyond what market forces on their own would generate. Perhaps not surprisingly, this recognition is now particularly evident in those parts of the world where market-oriented reforms were taken the farthest and the disappointment about the outcomes is correspondingly the greatest—notably in Latin America.[1]

Therefore we now confront a rare historic opportunity. The softening of convictions on both sides presents an opening to fashion an

---

[1] See, for example, de Ferranti et al. 2002. This is a report put out by the Latin America and Caribbean department of the World Bank. It is cognizant of the need to adopt some kind of industrial policies in order to generate technological dynamism in the region.

agenda for economic policies that takes an intelligent intermediate stand between the two extremes cited above. Market forces and private entrepreneurship would be in the driving seat of this agenda, but governments would also perform a strategic and coordinating role in the productive sphere beyond simply ensuring property rights, contract enforcement, and macroeconomic stability.

This chapter is a contribution to one component of such an agenda, focusing on policies for economic restructuring. Such policies have been called in the past "industrial policies," and for lack of a better term, I will continue to call them such. I will use the term to apply to restructuring policies in favor of more dynamic activities generally, regardless of whether they are located within industry or manufacturing per se. Indeed, many of the specific illustrations in this chapter concern nontraditional activities in agriculture or services. There is no evidence that the types of market failures that call for industrial policy are located predominantly in industry, and there is no such presumption in this chapter.

The nature of industrial policies is that they complement—opponents would say "distort"—market forces: they reinforce or counteract the allocative effects that the existing markets would otherwise produce. The objective of the chapter is to develop a framework for conducting industrial policy that maximizes its potential to contribute to economic growth while minimizing the risk that it will generate waste and rent-seeking.

I shall argue that in order to achieve this objective we need to think of industrial policy in a somewhat different light than is standard in the literature. The conventional approach to industrial policy consists of enumerating technological and other externalities and then targeting policy interventions on these market failures. The discussion then revolves around the administrative and fiscal feasibility of these policy interventions, their informational requirements, their political-economy consequences, and so on. I start also from generic market failures, but then I take it as a given that the location and magnitude of these market failures is highly uncertain. A central argument of the chapter is that the task of industrial policy is as much about eliciting information from the private sector on significant externalities and their remedies as it is about implementing appropriate policies. The right model for industrial policy is not that of an autonomous government applying Pigovian taxes or subsidies, but of strategic collaboration between the private sector and the government with the aim of uncovering the most significant obstacles to restructuring and determining what interventions are most likely to remove them. Correspondingly, the analysis of industrial policy needs to focus not on the policy *outcomes*—which are inherently unknowable ex ante—but on getting the policy *process* right. We need to worry about how we design a setting in which private and public actors come together to solve problems in the productive sphere, each side learning about the opportunities and constraints faced by the other. Deciding whether the right tool for industrial policy is, say, directed credit or R&D subsidies, or whether to promote the steel industry or the software industry comes later, as a by-product of this process.

Hence, the right way of thinking of industrial policy is as a discovery process—one where firms and the government learn about underlying costs and opportunities and engage in strategic coordination. The traditional arguments against industrial policy lose much of their force when we view industrial policy in these terms. For example, the typical riposte about governments' inability to pick winners becomes irrelevant. Yes, the government has imperfect information, but as I shall argue, so does the private sector. It is the information externalities generated by ignorance in the private sector that creates a useful public role—even when the public sector has worse information than the private sector. Similarly, the idea that governments need to keep private firms at arm's length to minimize corruption and rent-seeking gets turned on its head. Yes, the government needs to maintain its autonomy from private interests. But it can elicit useful information from the private sector only when it is engaged in an ongoing relationship with it—a situation that has been termed "embedded autonomy" by the sociologist Peter Evans (1995).

It is innovation that enables restructuring and productivity growth. A second key theme of this chapter is that innovation in the developing world is constrained not on the supply side but on the demand side. That is, it is not the lack of trained scientists and engineers, absence of R&D labs, or inadequate protection of intellectual property that restricts the innovations that are needed to restructure low-income economies. Innovation is undercut instead by lack of demand from its potential users in the real economy—the entrepreneurs. And the demand for innovation is low in turn because entrepreneurs perceive new activities to be of low profitability.

I will discuss the reasons for this conjecture in greater detail in the next section, but a useful analogy to keep in mind is with education and human capital. For quite a while, policymakers thought that the solution to poor human capital lay in improving the infrastructure of schooling—more schools, more teachers, more textbooks, and more access to all three. These interventions did increase the supply of schooling, but when the results were in, it became evident that the increase in schooling did not produce the productivity gains that were anticipated (Pritchett 2004). The reason is simple. The real constraint was the low *demand* for schooling—that is, the low propensity to acquire learning—in environments where the absence of economic opportunities depress the return to education. Similarly, an expansion of an economy's scientific and technological capacity will not endow it with the needed productive dynamism unless there is adequate demand for innovation by the business sector.

The chapter is organized as follows. In the next section, I review the main arguments in favor of industrial policy, emphasizing the pervasive role of market failures that result in the underprovision of entrepreneurship in pursuit of structural change. The standard rationale for industrial policy is technological externalities, either static or dynamic in the form of learning-by-doing that is external to firms. I will emphasize two other market failures that I believe are far more rampant: information externalities entailed in discovering the cost structure of an economy, and coordination externalities in the presence of scale economies. In the third section, "Institutional Arrangements for Industrial Policy," I turn to the institutional requirements for an effective industrial policy. I will argue here that getting the institutional setting right, with an adequate balance between autonomy and embeddedness on the part of government officials, is far more important than worrying about the precise instruments to be deployed. I will also provide some architectural and design guidelines for institutionalizing industrial policies and describe an illustrative range of programs.

In the fourth section, "The Exaggerated Rumors of Industrial Policy's Death," I discuss existing industrial policy programs and evaluate them in light of the foregoing discussion. Unlike what is commonly believed, the last two decades have not seen the twilight of industrial policy. Instead, incentives and subsidies have been refocused on exports and direct foreign investment, in the belief (largely unfounded, as it turns out) that these activities are the source of significant positive spillovers. Therefore, the challenge in most developing countries is not to rediscover industrial policy, but to redeploy it in a more effective manner. Finally, the fifth section asks whether the practice of industrial policy remains feasible under today's international rules of the game. I discuss the range of constraints that are embodied in multilateral, regional, and bilateral agreements. I emphasize that most of these constraints—with the significant exception of the WTO Agreements on Subsidies and TRIPS (Trade Related Intellectual Property Rights)—are either voluntary or do not bind in a significant way. What stands in the way of coherent industrial policy is the willingness of governments to deploy it, not their ability to do so.

WHY INDUSTRIAL POLICY?

In an important article published in the *American Economic Review*, Jean Imbs and Romain Wacziarg (2003) examined the patterns of sectoral concentration and diversification in a large cross-section of countries. They uncovered a striking regularity in their data. As poor countries get richer, sectoral production and employment become less concentrated and more diversified. And this diversification goes on until relatively late in the process of development. It is only after countries reach roughly the level of Ireland's income that production patterns start to become more concentrated. If sectoral concentration is graphed against income per capita, one therefore obtains a U-shaped curve. Imbs and Wacziarg stress the robustness of their finding:

"In fact, our result is an extremely robust feature of the data. The nonmonotonicity holds above and beyond the well-known shift of factors of production from agriculture to manufacturing and on to services—in particular, the U-shaped pattern is present when focusing only on manufactured goods. It is valid whether a sector's size is measured by its share in total employment or whether it is measured by shares in value added. It holds within countries through time as well as in a pure cross-section, for a variety of levels of disaggregation and data sources. The estimated turnaround point occurs quite late in the development process and at a surprisingly robust level of income per capita. Thus, increased sectoral specialization, although a significant development, applies only to high-income economies. Countries diversify over most of their development path" (Imbs and Wacziarg 2003, 64).

What is significant about this finding from our standpoint is that it goes against the standard intuition flowing from the principle of comparative advantage. The logic of comparative advantage is one of specialization. It is specialization that raises overall productivity in an economy that is open to trade. Those who associate underdevelopment with inadequate exposure to international markets generally imply—although this is often left unstated—that specialization according to comparative advantage is an essential ingredient of development.

Imbs and Wacziargs's findings suggest otherwise. Whatever it is that serves as the driving force of economic development, it cannot be the forces of comparative advantage as conventionally understood. The trick seems to be to acquire mastery over a broader range of activities, instead of concentrating on what one does best. This point is further underscored by the detailed analysis of export data by Klinger and Lederman (2006), who show that the number of new export products also follows an inverted U-curve in income.

The next question is what determines why some countries are better able to develop this mastery than others. Why do some economies find it easier to diversify from traditional to nontraditional products and keep the progression rolling along? We get a better handle on this question by turning it on its head and asking why diversification is not a natural process and how it can be easily derailed.

Imagine an economy with a well-behaved government that has done its Washington Consensus homework. Macroeconomic instability is not a problem, market interventions are minimal, trade restrictions are few, property rights are protected, and contracts are enforced. Will the type of entrepreneurship required to build up nontraditional activities be amply supplied? There are good reasons to believe that the answer is no. Most fundamentally, market prices cannot reveal the profitability of resource allocations that do not yet exist. (In general equilibrium theory, this is finessed by assuming that markets are "complete" and there is a price for everything.) The returns from investing in nontraditional activities are therefore hazy at best. It is possible to state this difficulty in the language of conventional economics, and in what follows I will discuss two key "externalities" that blunt the incentives for productive diversification: information externalities and coordination externalities. Both are reasons to believe that diversification is unlikely to take place without direct government intervention or other public action.

Consider a recent example taken from the pages of the *New York Times*. Taiwan has traditionally grown and exported sugar, an industry that has recently fallen into hard times because of low international prices, among other reasons. What should now be grown in the fields to replace the sugarcane that is the source of income for many farmers? In many countries, the result would have been a depressed rural sector, increasingly indebted farm households, and a drag on the economy. In Taiwan, the response has been a $65 million government investment program to develop a world-class orchid industry. The government pays for a genetics laboratory, quarantine site, shipping and packing areas, new roads, water and electrical hookups for privately owned greenhouses, and an exposition hall—in fact everything except the cost of the greenhouses. It also provides low-interest credit to farmers to help them build the greenhouses.[2]

This is admittedly an extreme example, and the Taiwanese experiment with orchids may yet turn out to be an expensive flop. But I will suggest below that this vignette illustrates a general principle rather than an exception. Most significant instances of productive diversification are indeed the result of concerted government action and of public-private collaboration. This is as true of Latin America as it is of East Asia.

Information Externalities

Diversification of the productive structure requires "discovery" of an economy's cost structure—that is, discovery of which new activities can

---

[2] This information is taken from *New York Times*, August 24, 2004, A1.

be produced at low enough cost to be profitable. Entrepreneurs must experiment with new product lines. They must tinker with technologies from established producers abroad and adapt them to local conditions. This is the process that Ricardo Hausmann and I called "self-discovery" (Hausmann and Rodrik 2003), and which seems integral to the stylized facts about development uncovered by Imbs and Wacziarg (2003).

When we put ourselves in the shoes of an entrepreneur engaged in cost discovery, we immediately see the key problem: this is an activity that has great social value and yet is very poorly remunerated. If the entrepreneur fails in his venture, he bears the full cost of his failure. If he is successful, he has to share the value of his discovery with other producers who can follow his example and flock into the new activity. In the limit, with free entry, entrepreneurship of this kind produces private costs and social gains. It is no great surprise that low-income countries are not teeming with entrepreneurs engaged in self-discovery.

Note that the kind of discovery that matters in this context differs from innovation and R&D as these terms are commonly understood. What is involved is not coming up with new products or processes, but "discovering" that a certain good, already well established in world markets, can be produced at home at low cost. This may involve some technological tinkering to adapt foreign technology to domestic conditions, but this tinkering rarely is patentable and therefore monopolizable. The entrepreneurs who figured out that Colombia was good terrain for cut flowers, Bangladesh for T-shirts, Pakistan for soccer balls, and India for software generated large social gains for their economies, but could keep very few of these gains to themselves. The policy regimes in developing countries have no analogues to the patent system that protects innovation in the advanced countries.

In Hausmann and Rodrik (2003) we provided some informal evidence to suggest that these features are endemic to the process of economic development. We showed that countries with nearly identical resource and factor endowments specialize in very different types of products, once one looks beyond very broad aggregates such as labor-intensive commodities. Bangladesh exports millions of dollars worth of hats, while Pakistan exports virtually none. Conversely, Pakistan exports tons of soccer balls, while Bangladesh lacks a significant soccer ball industry. At a different level of income, Korea is a world power in microwave ovens and barely exports any bicycles, while the pattern is reversed in Taiwan. It is impossible to ascribe these patterns of specialization to comparative advantage. They are more likely the result of random self-discovery attempts, followed by imitative entry. Indeed, we showed how whole industries often arise out of the experimental efforts of lone entrepreneurs. Garments in Bangladesh, cut flowers in Colombia, IT in India, and salmon in Chile (with a state entity acting as the entrepreneur in the last case) are some of the better-documented cases. In each one of these cases, imitative entry through managerial and labor turnover was the key mechanism that enabled industry growth (while undercutting the rents of incumbent entrepreneurs). The orchid case in Taiwan provides an example in the earlier stages of development. It is unlikely that a private farmer would have had the incentive to invest in orchids in the absence of good information that the effort would be profitable. Once the industry is established by the state, the number of private greenhouses will surely take off if the early investments pay off.

Klinger and Lederman (2006) have recently provided more systematic evidence on the market failures that restrict self-discovery. These authors show that their measure of self-discovery in a country (the number of new products being exported) is positively associated with the height of entry barriers: the more costly are government regulations that impede business formation, the higher the rate of self-discovery in exports. This somewhat counterintuitive result can only be understood in terms of the ideas considered here: ease of entry facilitates imitation, undercuts the rents to entrepreneurship in self-discovery, and therefore reduces the level of self-discovery.

The first-best policy response to the informational externalities that restrict self-discovery is to subsidize investments in new, nontraditional industries. As a practical matter, it is difficult to implement such a subsidy. The difficulty in monitoring the use to which the subsidy is put—an investor might as well use it for purposes that provide direct consumption benefits—renders the first-best policy intervention largely of theoretical interest.[3] In Hausmann and Rodrik (2003), we recommend generically a carrot-and-stick strategy. Since self-discovery requires rents to be provided to entrepreneurs, one side of the policy has to take the form of a carrot. This can be a subsidy of some kind, trade protection, or the provision of venture capital. Note that the logic of the problem requires that the rents be provided only to the initial investor, not to copycats. To ensure that mistakes are not perpetuated and bad projects are phased out, these rents must in turn be subject either to performance requirements (for example, a requirement to export), or to close monitoring of the uses to which they are put. In other words, there has to be a stick to discipline opportunistic action by the recipient of the subsidy. East Asian industrial policies have typically had both elements (see the classic discussions in Amsden 1989 and Wade 1990). Latin American industrial policies typically have used too much of the carrot, and too little of the stick, which explains why Latin

---

[3] The situation is somewhat analogous with respect to technological externalities that flow from R&D. In this case, the first-best is an R&D subsidy. But advanced countries provide patent protection, which is second-best, to stimulate R&D.

America has ended up with much inefficiency alongside some world-class industries.

A subtle but important point here is that that even under the optimal incentive program, some of the investments that are promoted will turn out to be failures. This is because optimal cost discovery requires equating the social marginal cost of investment funds to the *expected* return of projects in new areas. The realized return on some of the projects will necessarily be low or negative, to be compensated by the high return on the successes. The stunning success that Fundación Chile—a public agency—achieved with salmon can pay for many subsequent mistakes.[4] In fact, if there are no or few failures, this could even be interpreted as a sign that the program is not aggressive or generous enough. However, a good industrial policy will prevent such failures from gobbling up the economy's resources indefinitely, and it will ensure that they are phased out. The trick for the government is not to pick winners, but to know when it has a loser.

Coordination Externalities

Many projects require simultaneous, large-scale investments to be made in order to become profitable. Return, for example, to the orchid case in Taiwan. An individual producer contemplating whether to invest in a greenhouse needs to know that there is an electrical grid he can access nearby, irrigation is available, the logistics and transport networks are in place, quarantine and other public health measures have been taken to protect his plants from his neighbors' pests, and his country has been marketed abroad as a dependable supplier of high-quality orchids. All of these services have high fixed costs, and are unlikely to be provided by private entities unless they have an assurance that there will be enough greenhouses to demand their services in the first place. This is a classic coordination problem. Profitable new industries can fail to develop unless upstream and downstream investments are coaxed simultaneously. The Taiwanese government's investments upstream aim precisely to overcome this obstacle.

More generally, coordination failures can arise whenever new industries exhibit scale economies and some of the inputs are nontradable (or require geographic proximity) (Rodrik 1996b). Big-push models of

---

[4] Fundación Chile is a public agency that was created by funds donated by ITT. It began experimenting with salmon in the second half of the 1970s and set up a firm in the early 1980s using a technology adapted from Norway and Scotland. The company was eventually sold to a Japanese fishing company. Before Fundación Chile's efforts, Chile exported barely any salmon. The country is now one of the world's biggest salmon exporters. See Agosin 1999.

development are based on the idea that such features are predominant in low-income environments. The cluster approach to development represents a narrower version of the same idea, focusing on the development of specific sectors such as tourism, pharmaceuticals, or biotech. In all these versions, the coordination failure model places a premium on the ability to coordinate the investment and production decisions of different entrepreneurs. Sometimes, when the industry in question is highly organized and the benefits of the needed investments can be localized, this coordination can be achieved within the private sector, without the government playing a specific role. But more commonly, with a nascent industry and a private sector that has yet to be organized, a government role will be required.

An interesting but often neglected aspect of coordination failures is that they do not necessitate subsidization, and overcoming them need not be costly to the government budget. In this respect, coordination externalities differ from the information externalities discussed above that do necessitate subsidies of some sort. It is the logic of coordination failures that once the simultaneous investments are made, all of them end up profitable. Therefore, none of the investors needs to be subsidized ex post, unless there is an additional reason (i.e., a nonpecuniary externality) that such subsidization is required. The trick is to get these investments made in the first place. That can be achieved either by true coordination—"Firm A will make this investment if Firm B makes this other investment"—or by designing ex ante subsidies that do not need to be paid ex post. An implicit bailout, or an investment guarantee, is an example of such an ex ante subsidy. Suppose the government guarantees that the investor will be made whole if the project fails. This induces the investor to proceed with the investment. If the project succeeds, the investor does not need any cash transfer from the government, and no subsidies are paid out. This is one way in which some industries got started out in South Korea, as the regime of President Park gave implicit investment guarantees to leading *chaebols* that invested in new areas. On the other hand, this type of policy is obviously open to moral hazard and abuse; for a while it was common to blame the Asian financial crisis on the "cronyism" engendered by these implicit bailout guarantees.

As Andrés Rodríguez-Clare (2004) has recently stressed, all industries in principle have the characteristics that could produce clusters. Moreover, many industries can in principle operate at some level *in the absence* of clusters. This suggests that what needs support is not specific sectors per se, but the type of technologies that have scale or agglomeration economies and would fail to catch on in the absence of support. Simply providing trade protection to a particular sector may not overcome the coordination failure that prevents the adoption of a modern technology, since it increases the profitability of operating without that technology as well. The appropriate policy intervention is focused not on industries or sectors, but on the activity or technology that produces the characteristics of a coordination failure.

Hence, the policies that overcome coordination failure share an important characteristic with those focused on information externalities. Both sets of interventions need to be targeted on activities (a new technology, a particular kind of training, a new good or service), rather than on sectors per se. It is activities that are new to the economy that need support, not those that are already established.

Back to Reality

When viewed from the perspective of the discussion above, it is not surprising to observe that industrial restructuring rarely takes place without significant government assistance. Scratch the surface of nontraditional export success stories from anywhere around the world, and you will more often than not find industrial policies, public R&D, sectoral support, export subsidies, preferential tariff arrangements, and other similar interventions lurking beneath the surface. The role played by such policies in East Asia is well known. What is less well appreciated is their role in Latin America.

By way of illustration, table 4.1 lists the top five export items (to the United States) of three leading Latin American economies: Brazil, Chile, and Mexico. When one leaves aside traditional commodity exports such as copper and crude oil, it is striking how each of the products has been the beneficiary of preferential support policies. In the case of Brazil, the steel, aircraft, and (to an important extent) shoe industries are all the creation of import substitution policies of the past. High levels of protection (steel and shoes) and public ownership, public R&D, and subsidized credit (aircraft) were deliberately used to generate rents for entrepreneurs investing in new areas and to build up industrial clusters. In the case of Chile, industrial policies played a huge role in grapes, forestry, and salmon. The role of Fundación Chile in getting the salmon industry off the ground has been already mentioned. In grapes, there was significant public R&D in the 1960s that transformed an industry that was primarily oriented to the local market into a global powerhouse (Jarvis 1994). And in forestry, there is a history of at least 60 years of subsidizing plantations (see Clapp 1995) as well as a big push since 1974 to turn the wood, pulp and paper, and furniture cluster into a major export industry (Agosin 1999). Productive diversification in Chile is hardly the result of letting markets run free. In Mexico, the motor vehicles and computer industries are the creation of import-substitution policies (initially), followed by preferential tariff

TABLE 4.1
Top Five Export Items (HS4) to the United States from Brazil, Chile, and Mexico in 2000

Item	Value ($ millions)
Brazil	
Aircraft	1,435
Shoes	1,069
Noncrude petroleum	689
Steel	485
Chemical wood-pulp	465
Chile	
Copper	457
Grapes	396
Fish	377
Lumber	144
Wood	142
Mexico	
Motor vehicles	15,771
Crude oil	11,977
Computers and peripherals	6,411
Ignition wiring sets	5,576
Trucks	4,853

policies under NAFTA. None of these is the result of hands-off policies, or of level playing fields and unadulterated market forces.

Hence the difference between East Asia and Latin America is not that industrial transformation has been state-driven in one and market-driven in the other. It is that industrial policy has not been as concerted and coherent in Latin America as it has been in East Asia, with the consequence that the transformation has been less deeply rooted in the former than it is in the latter.

INSTITUTIONAL ARRANGEMENTS FOR INDUSTRIAL POLICY

In the previous discussion I have linked the need for industrial policy to two key market failures that weaken the entrepreneurial drive to restructure and diversify low-income economies. One has to do with the informational spillovers involved in discovering the cost structure of an economy, and the other has to do with the coordination of investment activities with scale economies. It is tempting to go on to discuss the list of policy instruments, first-best and second-best, that can overcome these difficulties. But this would overlook two key issues that bedevil the conduct of industrial policy.

First, the public sector is not omniscient, and indeed typically has even less information than the private sector about the location and nature of the market failures that block diversification. Governments may not even know what it is they do not know. Consequently, the policy setting has to be one in which public officials are able to elicit information from the business sector on an ongoing basis about the constraints that exist and the opportunities that are available. It cannot be one in which the private sector is kept at arm's length and autonomous bureaucrats issue directives. To use Peter Evans's terminology, industrial policymaking has to be embedded within a network of linkages with private groups.

Second, industrial policy is open to corruption and rent-seeking. Any system of incentives designed to help private investors venture into new activities can end up as a mechanism of rent transfer to unscrupulous businessmen and self-interested bureaucrats. The natural response is to insulate policymaking and implementation from private interests, and to shield public officials from close interaction with businessmen. Note how this impulse—"keep bureaucrats and businessmen distant from each other"—is diametrically opposed to the previous one arising from the need for information flows.

The critical institutional challenge, therefore, is to find an intermediate position between full autonomy and full embeddedness. Too much autonomy for the bureaucrats and you have a system that minimizes corruption, but fails to provide the incentives that the private sector really needs.[5] Too much embeddedness for the bureaucrats and they end up in bed with (and in the pockets of) business interests. Moreover, we would like the process to be democratically accountable and to carry public legitimacy.

Getting this balance right is so important that it overshadows, in my view, all other elements of policy design. In particular, once the institutional setting is "right," we need to worry considerably less about appropriate policy choice. A first-best policy in the wrong institutional setting will do considerably less good than a second-best policy in an appropriate institutional setting. Put differently, when it comes to industrial policy, specifying the process is more important than specifying the outcome.

[5] Some years ago, I compared the effectiveness of six different export subsidy programs around the world, and found, somewhat to my surprise, that the programs with the clearest rules and least opportunity for manipulation by the private sector were not the most effective on the ground. The best-functioning programs were those in places like Brazil and South Korea where the bureaucrats were in close interaction with the exporters they were subsidizing. See Rodrik 1995a.

Thinking of industrial policy as a "process" has the added benefit that it leaves open the possibility that the actual obstacles to diversification may differ significantly from those hypothesized above. Listening to businesspeople without getting captured may reveal that the real problems are not the government's errors of omission (e.g., externalities that have not been internalized), but its errors of commission (e.g., misguided interventions that have increased the cost of doing business). Occasionally, the problems lie in unexpected areas—for example, a quirk in the tax code or a piece of otherwise innocuous legislation. Policy recommendations based on ex ante reasoning would get it badly wrong in such cases.

These ideas have much in common with the recent literature on institutional innovation, which emphasizes the shortcomings of the hierarchical, principal-agent model of governance in environments of volatility and deep uncertainty (see in particular Sabel 2004a, 2004b). Solving the problems outlined in the previous section involves social learning—discovering where the information and coordination externalities lie and therefore what the objectives of industrial policy ought to be and how it is to be targeted. In this setting, the principal-agent model, with the government as the principal, the firms as its agent, and an optimal policy that aligns the agents' behavior with the principal's objectives at least cost, does not work very well. What is needed instead is a more flexible form of strategic collaboration between public and private sectors, designed to elicit information about objectives, distribute responsibilities for solutions, and evaluate outcomes as they appear. An ideal industrial policy process operates in an institutional setting of this form.

As Charles Sabel emphasizes, institutions of learning have to be experimentalist by their nature. Just as discovering underlying costs requires entrepreneurial experimentation, discovering the appropriate ways in which restructuring bottlenecks can be overcome needs a trial-and-error approach to policymaking.

These ideas need to be operationalized in order to become useful in practice. The challenge in a general analysis like the present one is to give a flavor of how this can be done without falling into the trap of misplaced concreteness and appearing to recommend a one-size-fits-all institutional strategy. I proceed in two steps. First, I will discuss some generically desirable architectural features of institutions of industrial policy. Next, I will enumerate some design principles that should inform the formulation of industrial policy. These suggestions occupy an intermediate position between the more abstract ideas discussed above and concrete recommendations on institutional design.[6]

---

[6] These ideas draw on work done in El Salvador and reported in Hausmann and Rodrik (2005). See also Sabel and Reddy (n.d.) for some suggestions on the architecture of industrial policymaking.

Elements of an Institutional Architecture

POLITICAL LEADERSHIP AT THE TOP

The success of industrial policy often depends on the presence of high-level political support. Fiscal prudence has a champion in the person of a finance minister and sound money has a champion in the person of a central bank governor. Economic restructuring also needs a political advocate who has the ear of the president or prime minister and can stand as equals with other members of the economic cabinet. This serves several purposes. First, it raises the profile of industrial policies and enables problems of economic transformation to receive a hearing at the highest levels of the government. Second, it provides coordination, oversight, and monitoring for the bureaucrats and the agencies entrusted with carrying out industrial policies. If the bureaucrats are to have autonomy, it is critical that their performance be systematically monitored by such a high-level official. Third, it identifies a clear political principal as accountable for the consequences of industrial policies. This political advocate could be a cabinet-level minister, the vice president (in presidential systems), or even the president himself (as was the case in South Korea under President Park).

COORDINATION AND DELIBERATION COUNCIL(S)

While institutional choices naturally differ from setting to setting, depending on initial conditions, there is a generic need for coordination or deliberation councils within which the information exchange and social learning, as discussed above, can take place. These are private-public bodies that ought to include relevant groups or their representatives. To avoid the biases of incumbents and insiders, these should go beyond the typical "peak" organizations that include only well-organized groups and business associations. They would be the setting in which private-sector interests would communicate their requests for assistance to the government, and the latter would goad the former into new investment efforts. These councils would seek out and gather information (from the private sector and elsewhere) on investment ideas, achieve coordination among different state agencies when needed, push for changes in legislation and regulation to eliminate unnecessary transaction costs or other impediments, generate subsidies and financial backing for new activities when needed, and credibly bundle these different elements of support along with appropriate conditionalities. They can be created both at the national and at subnational or sectoral levels. Preferably, the larger of these councils would have their staff of technocrats.

MECHANISMS OF TRANSPARENCY AND ACCOUNTABILITY

Industrial policies need to be viewed by society at large as part of a growth strategy that is geared to expand opportunities for all, rather than as giveaways to already privileged sections of the economy. This is particularly important since proactive policies of the type discussed in this chapter can sometimes be partial to bigger firms and entrepreneurs (unlike microcredit programs, say, or support of small and medium-sized enterprises). Hence, promotion activities need to be undertaken in a transparent and accountable manner. The operation of the deliberation and coordination councils should be published and their decisions announced. There should be full accounting of public resources spent in support of new activities.

Ten Design Principles for Industrial Policy

For reasons explained earlier, it is impossible (and undesirable) to specify ex ante the policy outputs that the type of architecture discussed above will yield. All depends on the opportunities and constraints that will be identified through the deliberative process. One country may choose to develop a services cluster around the expansion of the national port. Another may decide to set up public venture capital funds targeted at biotech and computer software. A third may go for tax breaks to encourage downstream processing of forestry products. A fourth may find that excessive red tape and bureaucratic regulations inhibit entrepreneurship in new activities. Nonetheless, it is possible to list some general "design principles" that can inform the formulation of the resulting industrial policies.

1. *Incentives should be provided only to "new" activities.* The main purpose of industrial policy is to diversify the economy and generate new areas of comparative advantage. It follows that incentives ought to focus on economic activities that are new to the domestic economy. "New" refers to both products that are new to the local economy and to new technologies for producing an existing product. Many countries provide tax incentives for new investments without sufficiently discriminating between investments that expand the range of capabilities of the home economy and those that do not. Note also that this focus differs substantially from the tendency of many incentive programs to subsidize small and medium-sized enterprises. Such policies are based on the criterion of size—not on whether the activity in question has the potential to spawn new areas of specialization. It is the latter that produces economic growth.

2. *There should be clear benchmarks or criteria for success and failure.* As I have already emphasized, industrial policy is a necessarily experimental process. It is the nature of entrepreneurship that not all investments in new activities will pay off. And not all promotion efforts will

be successful. In Korea, Taiwan, and Chile, successes have more than paid for the mistakes. But in the absence of a clear idea of what constitutes success and observable criteria for monitoring it, failures can get entrenched. Recipients of subsidies can game public agencies and continue to receive support despite poor outcomes. Bureaucrats administering incentives can claim success and keep their programs running. Ideally, the criteria for success should depend on productivity—both its rate of increase and its absolute level—and not on employment or output. While productivity can be notoriously difficult to measure, project audits by business and technical consultants can provide useful indications. So can benchmarking, using the experience of similar industries in neighboring countries. Performance in international markets (i.e., export levels) is also a good indicator, as it provides a quick-and-dirty way of gauging how the industry is doing relative to world-class competitors.

3. *There must be a built-in sunset clause.* One way to ensure that resources (both financial and human) do not remain tied up for a long time in activities that are not paying off is to phase out support by default. Hence, every publicly supported project needs to have not only a clear statement ex ante of what constitutes success and failure, but also an automatic sunset clause for withdrawing support after an appropriate amount of time has elapsed.

4. *Public support must target activities, not sectors.* It is common for investment promotion agencies to specify their priorities in terms of sectors or industries—for example, tourism, call centers, or biotech. This leads to the misdirection of industrial promotion efforts. The targets of public support should be viewed not as sectors but as activities. This facilitates structuring the support as a corrective to specific market failures instead of generic support for this or that sector. Rather than providing investment incentives, say, for tourism or call centers, government programs should subsidize bilingual training, feasibility reports for nontraditional agriculture, infrastructure investment, adaptation of foreign technology to local conditions, risk and venture capital, and so on. Cross-cutting programs such as these have the advantage that they span several sectors at once and are targeted at market failures directly.

5. *Activities that are subsidized must have the clear potential of providing spillovers and demonstration effects.* There is no reason to provide public support to an activity unless that activity has the potential to crowd in other, complementary investments or generate informational or technological spillovers. Public support must be contingent on an analysis of this sort. Moreover, activities that are supported should be structured in such a way as to maximize the spillovers to subsequent entrants and rivals.

6. *The authority for carrying out industrial policies must be vested in agencies with demonstrated competence.* It is common to complain about

incompetence and corruption in government bureaucracies. But bureaucratic competence varies greatly among different agencies within the same country, and most countries have some pockets of bureaucratic competence. It is preferable to lodge promotion activities in such agencies instead of creating new agencies from scratch or using existing ones with poor track records. This will have an implication about the tools of industrial policy that can be used. If the development bank is in good shape but tax administration is a mess, promotion may need to be done through directed credit rather than tax incentives. Note that this principle may conflict with the requirement that policy tools be targeted as closely as possible to the source of a market failure. The location of competence may predetermine the tools used. But this is a necessary compromise: when administrative and human resources are scarce, it is better to employ second-best instrument effectively than to use first-best instruments badly.

7. *The implementing agencies must be monitored closely by a principal with a clear stake in the outcomes who has political authority at the highest level.* As we have seen, effective industrial policy requires a certain degree of autonomy for the bureaucratic agencies implementing it. But autonomy does not and should not mean lack of accountability. Close monitoring (and coordination) of the promotion activities by a cabinet-level politician, a "principal" who has internalized the agenda of economic restructuring and shoulders the main responsibility for it, is essential. Such monitoring guards not only against self-interested behavior on the part of the agencies, but also helps protect the agencies from capture by private interests. As suggested above, this principal could be a cabinet-level minister, a vice president, or even the president (or prime minister).

8. *The agencies carrying out promotion must maintain channels of communication with the private sector.* Autonomy and insulation do not mean that bureaucrats must maintain arm's-length relationships with entrepreneurs and investors. In fact, ongoing contacts and communication are important in providing public officials with good information on business realities, without which sound decision-making would be impossible.

9. *Mistakes that result in "picking the losers" will occur.* Public strategies of the sort advocated here are often derided because they can lead to picking the losers rather than the winners. It is important, of course, to build safeguards against this, as outlined above. But an optimal strategy of discovering the productive potential of a country entails mistakes. Some promoted activities will fail. The objective should not be to minimize the chance that a mistake will occur—which would result in *no* self-discovery—but to minimize the costs of mistakes when they occur. If governments make no mistakes, they are not trying hard enough.

10. *Activities need to have the capacity to renew themselves, so that the cycle of discovery becomes an ongoing one.* Just as there is no single

blueprint for undertaking promotion, the needs and circumstances of productive discovery are likely to change over time. This requires that the agencies carrying out policies have the capacity to refashion themselves. Over time, some of the key tasks of industrial policy will have to be phased out, while new ones are taken on.

An Illustrative Range of Incentive Programs

As I have argued, industrial policy should not be thought of as a generic range of incentive programs. It is instead a process designed to find areas where policy actions are most likely to make a difference. The output of such a process—the type of policies and approaches used—will depend critically on a country's own circumstances. Nonetheless, it may be useful to discuss briefly a number of illustrative programs in order to provide a more concrete sense of what industrial policies will entail.

1. *Subsidizing costs of "self-discovery."* As I discussed above, uncertainty about what new products can be profitably produced constitutes a key obstacle to economic restructuring. The resolution of this uncertainty typically requires some upfront investments, as well as productive tinkering to get imported technologies to work well under local conditions. Since both of these areas are rife with externalities (successes can be easily emulated), the economic case for subsidizing them is strong. Therefore, governments will generally need a facility to defray the costs of the early stages of the cost discovery process. This can be envisaged as a "contest" whereby private-sector entrepreneurs would bid for public resources by bringing forth preinvestment proposals. The criteria for financing such studies would be that (a) they relate to substantially new activities; (b) they have the potential to provide learning spillovers to others in the economy; and (c) the private sector entities are willing to submit themselves to oversight and performance audits.

2. *Developing mechanisms for higher-risk finance.* Going from the preinvestment phase of a project to the investment stage requires a more sizable expenditure of resources, which must be financed somehow. Commercial banks are typically not good at this: they intermediate deposits and must remain liquid for prudential reasons. Business development and self-discovery require longer-term and riskier forms of financial intermediation. Other forms of risk finance, such as corporate debt markets, equity markets, or private venture capital funds, are also typically conspicuous by their absence. Hence, governments will need alternative sources of finance. This may come in several different forms, depending on the available fiscal and bureaucratic resources. Some examples are development banks, publicly funded (but professionally managed) venture funds,

public guarantees for longer-term commercial bank lending, or special vehicles that direct a share of public pension fund assets to a portfolio of higher-risk investments.

3. *Internalizing coordination externalities.* Coordination externalities are highly specific to each activity and are essentially impossible to make concrete ex ante. The needs of tourism are very different from the needs of call centers. What this means is that governments need to have the capacity to identify these coordination failures and attempt to resolve them. The coordination and deliberation councils discussed above are one mechanism for instituting and developing such a capacity. But it is clear that these efforts need to be undertaken at multiple levels—at the national level as well as the regional and sectoral levels. In all this, chambers of commerce and industry and farmer and labor associations can play a constructive role. As discussed above, the government's relationships with these private-sector entities need to be socially legitimized through mechanisms of accountability and transparency. Proposals need to be made public, formally analyzed and evaluated by technocrats, and their fiscal impact costed out. The goal is to identify coordination opportunities while constraining inconvenient rent-seeking behavior.

4. *Public R&D.* Technology cannot be acquired from advanced countries in an off-the-shelf manner. Whether it is table grapes in Chile or information technology in Taiwan, many new industries have required publicly funded R&D efforts to identify, adapt, and transfer technology from abroad. The trick is to ensure that these efforts are well integrated with private sector activities and are targeted to their needs. Programs that work best are likely to be those that are responsive to private sector demands.

5. *Subsidizing general technical training.* New activities will eventually encounter a shortage of adequately trained personnel, even if this is not a binding constraint at the outset. Innovating firms will fear that labor turnover will reduce the returns to on-the-job training and will thus under-provide training. This will inevitably delay the process of self-discovery. So there is a strong case to be made for subsidizing training for vocational, technical, and language skills. In general, public training facilities have a lousy reputation in developing countries, as they seem rarely targeted on the real needs of the private sector. Therefore, it may be preferable to offer subsidies or matching grants to private firms or institutes to co-finance their training efforts.

6. *Taking advantage of nationals abroad.* Many if not most developing countries have sizable numbers of migrant workers in the advanced countries. These workers tend to be among the most entrepreneurial in society, and often have higher skills than the workers at home (see Kapur and McHale 2005). Most governments look at these expatriate workers

almost exclusively as a source of remittance income. But given their entre-preneurialism, skills, and exposure to business in the developed world, as well as the desire of many of them to return home (under the right set of circumstances), they may well be far more valuable as a source of self-discovery at home. Governments can actively court them, encourage their return, and use them to spawn new domestic economic activities, as Taiwan has done so successfully in support of its computer industry (see Saxenian 2002). If even a fraction of the tax incentives used to attract foreign invest-ment is targeted at nationals abroad, the benefits could well be sizable.

THE EXAGGERATED RUMORS OF INDUSTRIAL POLICY'S DEATH

An agenda of the sort laid out above may seem overly ambitious and too big a departure from today's accepted policy practice. After all, industrial policies are supposed to have been confined to the trash bin of history in modern and modernizing economies, along with other out-moded policies like central planning and trade protection. The reality is that industrial policies have run rampant during the last two decades—and nowhere more than in those economies that have steadfastly adopted the agenda of orthodox reform. If this fact has escaped attention, it is only because the preferential policies in question have privileged *exports* and *foreign investment*—the two fetishes of the Washington Consensus era—and because their advocates have called them strategies of "outward orienta-tion" and other similar sounding names instead of industrial policies. Anytime a government consciously favors some economic activities over others, it is conducting industrial policy. And by this standard, the recent past has seen more than its share of industrial policies.

While exports have been supported in a number of different ways, export-processing zones (EPZs) are the most visible form of discrimination in their favor. There are close to 1,000 EPZs around the world, and it is rare to find a country without one. Firms that locate in EPZs get favored treatment in a number of ways: they are allowed unlimited duty-free access on all their imports (provided they export their output); they receive tax holidays on cor-porate, property, and income taxes; they are generally sheltered from bureau-cratic regulations that other firms have to contend with; they are provided with superior infrastructure and communication services; they are often exempt from labor legislation that applies to other firms (Madani 1998).

Incentives offered to foreign direct investment are, if anything, more common. Practically all countries in the world have a government agency charged with attracting foreign investment and a program of tax holidays and other subsidies directed at foreign firms. In addition to these tax subsidies, foreign investors are offered one-stop shopping services, receive help in navigating through domestic regulatory requirements, sometimes receive trade protection in return for their investment, and often receive privileged legal status. For example, unlike domestic firms, foreign investors frequently have the option of submitting domestic legal disputes to international arbitration. Developing countries actively compete with each other to provide generous incentives to attract foreign firms, even though such incentives tend to play at best a marginal role in the location decisions of multinational firms.

The driving force behind the incentives in favor of exports and foreign investment has been the belief that these economic activities are particularly prone to positive externalities and spillovers. Exports and foreign direct investment are supposed to generate technological and learning spillovers for other activities. Hence, despite the decisive turn to markets during the last two decades, the dominant view among policymakers—revealed at least through their actions—has been that particular externalities remain rampant and need to be corrected through the deployment of generous subsidies. What stands out with this brand of industrial policy is the strong presumption that the important externalities reside in exports and direct foreign investment.

Economic research provides little support for this presumption. It has been known for a while that exporting firms tend to be more productive and technologically more dynamic than firms that sell mainly to the home market. As a general rule, the cause is not benefits that accrue from the activity of exporting per se, but selection effects: It is better firms (in all respects) that are able to or choose to export (see Tybout 2000 for a survey). Consequently, subsidizing exporting can do very little to enhance overall productive or technological capacity. Similarly, careful studies have found very little systematic evidence of technological and other externalities from foreign direct investment, some even finding negative spillovers (see Hanson 2001 for a discussion of the issues). In these circumstances, subsidizing foreign investors is a silly policy, as it transfers income from poor-country taxpayers to the pockets of shareholders in rich countries, with no compensating benefit.

Export-processing zones and incentives for direct foreign investment are the most noticeable elements of industrial policy in developing countries, but they are not the only ones. Most countries have maintained industrial policies of different types, some of which are the vestiges of import-substitution policies of the past, while others are ad hoc responses to perceived shortcomings of existing policy setups. This is not adequately appreciated, so I present in table 4.2 an illustrative list of credit and tax incentives for domestic investment and production in a range of developing countries. The table is based on Melo 2001, which was confined to countries in South America, but expands Melo's compilation to countries in other parts of the world using national and international sources.[7] As the table shows, credit facilities and tax incentives for favored sectors have been extremely widespread, in Latin America no less than in Asia and Africa. In Latin America, the incentives tend to be focused on tourism, mining, forestry, and agribusiness. Elsewhere, selected manufacturing and service industries also tend to be promoted.

The lesson from this survey of current practice is that industrial policy has far from disappeared. In most countries, the challenge is not to reinstitute industrial policy, but to redeploy the machinery already in place in a more productive manner. As we have just seen, much of today's industrial policy takes a presumptive stand on where the externalities are— exports and direct foreign investment—and is formulated in sectoral terms. The institutional architecture is rarely adequate to engage in the kind of discovery that I have advocated here. The overarching vision that informs the design of policy is hardly ever articulated. Consequently, what is needed is not more industrial policy, but better industrial policy. Indeed, it would not be surprising if in many countries industrial policies could be

---

[7] Sources for table 4.2 are Melo 2001 for Central and South American countries, and for the others: India: (1): http://www.idbi.com/; (2): http://www.idbi.com/; (4): http://www.idbi.com/; http://www.finance.indiamart.com/exports_imports/incentives/index.html; (5): http://www.finance.indiamart.com/exports_imports/incentives/index.html; (6): EIU; (7): http://www.finance.indiamart.com/exports_imports/incentives/general_tax_incentives .html and EIU; (8): http://www.techno-preneur.net/timeis/haryana/incentive.html. China: (1): EIU (general incentives); (2): EIU (general incentives); (5): http://english1.peopledaily .com.cn/english/200005/18/eng20000518_41146.html; (7): http://www.ey.com/GLOBAL/ content.nsf/China_E/Tax_-_Tax_Insight_-_2003_July_31; (8): http://www.hsbc.com.hk/hk/ corp/aoc/businf.htm. Malaysia: (1): http://www.smidec.gov.my/detailpage.jsp?section= financialassistance&subsection=loan&detail=bankindustri3&level=4; (2): http://www.smidec .gov.my/detailpage.jsp?section=financialassistance&subsection=loan&detail=bankindustri3& level=4;(4):http://www.smidec.gov.my/detailpage.jsp?section=financialassistance&subsec tion=loan&detail=bankindustri3&level=4;(5):EIU;(7):http://e-directory.com.my/ web/sw-investorinfo-incentive.htm; (8): http://www.mida.gov.my. Thailand: (1): http://www .ifct.co.th/database/index.asp?l=eng and ; (2): Industrial Finance Corporation of Thailand; (3): http://www.ifct.co.th/database/index.asp?mid=7&sid=15&cid=54; (7): http://www.del tha.cec.eu.int/bic/doing_business_thailand/incentive_investment_promotion_act.htm; (8) http://www.deltha.cec.eu.int/bic/doing_business_thailand/incentive_investment_promotion _act.htm. Nigeria: (1): http://www.nigeriabusinessinfo.com/ifcfinance-nigeria2002.htm; (2): http://www.nigeriabusinessinfo.com/ifcfinance-nigeria2002.htm; (4): http://www.nipc;nigeria .org/dfi.htm; Nigerian Industrial Development Bank (NIDB); (5): EIU; (7): http://www.nigeria .gov.ng/business/incentives.htm; (8): http://www.nigeria.gov.ng/business/incentives.htm. Ghana: (1): The National Investment Bank is an industrial development bank providing financial assistance to manufacturing and processing industries, including agro-industrial projects. (no web site); (4): http://www.ghana-embassy.org/financial_intitutions.htm; (7): http://www

rendered more effective by actually *reducing* their scope (and targeting them better).[8]

Is Industrial Policy Still Feasible?

Developing countries operate today in a global policy environment that is quite different from the one two or three decades ago. In particular, there has been a tendency to discipline national economic policies through multilateral, regional, or bilateral agreements. These disciplines impose restrictions on the ability of developing countries to conduct certain types of industrial policies. But while it is true developing countries have a somewhat narrower room for policy autonomy today, it is easy to exaggerate the significance of the restrictions. There remains much scope for coherent industrial policy of the type I have outlined above, especially if countries do not give up policy autonomy *voluntarily* by signing up for bilateral agreements with the United States or for restrictive international codes. Few of the illustrative programs described above in the section "Institutional Arrangements for Industrial Policy" would come under international disciplines. What constrains sensible industrial policy today is largely the willingness to adopt it, not the ability to do so.

Restrictions on industrial policy come in different guises.[9] I present a more detailed view of them in table 4.3, and point to some general features here. Foremost in the hierarchy are the rules of the WTO, which are more far-reaching and intrusive than those under the old GATT system. Previously, membership in the world trading system had few or no entry requirements for poor countries. The balance-of-payments and infant-industry exceptions were liberal enough to allow countries to adopt any and all industrial policies. Under the WTO, there are several restrictions. Export subsidies are now illegal (for all but least-developed countries), as are domestic content requirements and other performance requirements on enterprises that are linked to trade, quantitative restrictions on imports,

---

.gipc.org.gh/IPA_Information.asp?hdnGroupID=3&hdnLevelID=3; (8): http://www.gipc.org
.gh/IPA_Information.asp?hdnGroupID=3&hdnLevelID=3. Uganda: (1): http://www.bou.or.ug/
DevFIN.htm; (2): http://www.bou.or.ug/DevFIN.htm; (4): http://www.bou.or.ug/DevFIN.htm;
(7): http://www.unctad.org/en/docs//iteipcmisc3_en.pdf; (8): http://www.ugandainvest.com/
incentives.htm.

[8] For example, Uruguay has a generous tax holiday program for new investments that does not discriminate between investments that are likely to generate the informational and coordination spillovers that I focused on above and those that are not. As a consequence, the program ends up financing projects such as the renovation of a hippodrome (which apparently was the largest project that has benefited from tax incentives so far).

[9] See also Lall 2004 for a discussion of existing constraints.

TABLE 4.2
Illustrative List of Industrial Policies in Support of Production and Investment

	Loans for Working Capital (1)	Loans for Fixed Assets and/or Investment Projects (2)	Equity Investment (3)	Loans to Specific Sectors (4)	Credit Programs for Particular Regions (5)	Horizontal Tax Incentives (6)	Tax Incentives to Specific Sectors (7)	Tax Incentives to Particular Regions (8)
Central and South American Countries								
Argentina	X	X		X	X		Mining, forestry	
Bahamas						X	Hotels, financial services, spirits and beer	
Barbados						X	Financial services, insurance, information technology	
Belize						X	Mining	
Bolivia							Mining	
Brazil	X	X	X	Oil, natural gas, shipping, power sector, telecom, software, motion picture industry	X			X

TABLE 4.2 (cont.)

	Loans for Working Capital (1)	Loans for Fixed Assets and/or Investment Projects (2)	Equity Investment (3)	Loans to Specific Sectors (4)	Credit Programs for Particular Regions (5)	Horizontal Tax Incentives (6)	Tax Incentives to Specific Sectors (7)	Tax Incentives to Particular Regions (8)
Chile	X	X			X	X	Forestry, oil, nuclear materials	X
Colombia	X	X	X	Motion picture industry	X			X
Costa Rica	X						Forestry, tourism	
Dominican Republic							Tourism, agribusiness	
Ecuador	X	X	X				Mining, tourism	
El Salvador	X	X		Mining, services sector				
Guatemala								
Guyana							Agribusiness	
Haiti						X		
Honduras	X	X		Transport sector, shrimp				

Country		Motion picture industry			Industries
Jamaica	X				Motion picture industry, tourism, bauxite, aluminum, factory construction
Mexico	X	X	X		Forestry, motion picture industry, air and maritime transportation, publishing industry
Nicaragua	X				Tourism
Panama	X				Tourism, forestry
Paraguay	X		X	X	Tourism,
Peru	X		X	X	mining, oil
Surinam			X		
Trinidad & Tobago			X		Hotels, construction

TABLE 4.2 (cont.)

	Loans for Working Capital (1)	Loans for Fixed Assets and/or Investment Projects (2)	Equity Investment (3)	Loans to Specific Sectors (4)	Credit Programs for Particular Regions (5)	Horizontal Tax Incentives (6)	Tax Incentives to Specific Sectors (7)	Tax Incentives to Particular Regions (8)
Uruguay	X	X				X	Hydrocarbons, printing, shipping, forestry, military industry, airlines, newspapers, broadcasters, theaters, motion picture industry	
Venezuela	X	X				X	Hydrocarbons and other primary sectors	

Other countries						
India	X	X	?	X	X	Motion picture industry, jute textiles, tea plantations	X	Infrastructure facilities, power projects, new industries in electronic hardware/software parks, airports, ports, inland ports and waterways, and industrial parks; for hotels, cold-storage firms and manufacturers of priority items
China	X	X	?	X	?	Software	X	High-tech IC manufacturers and software development enterprises that source production equipment made domestically in China

TABLE 4.2 (cont.)

	Loans for Working Capital (1)	Loans for Fixed Assets and/or Investment Projects (2)	Equity Investment (3)	Loans to Specific Sectors (4)	Credit Programs for Particular Regions (5)	Horizontal Tax Incentives (6)	Tax Incentives to Specific Sectors (7)	Tax Incentives to Particular Regions (8)
Malaysia	X	X	?	Shipping industry, shipyard industry, and maritime-related activities	X	?	Manufacturing sector, technology industries, agricultural sector, tourism industry, research and development, software, computers and ICT	X
Thailand	X	X	X	?	?	?	Agriculture and agricultural products, direct involvement in technological and human resource development, public utilities	X

Nigeria	X	?	Agriculture	X	?	Agriculture, oil, and gas sectors, minerals such as barites, gypsum, kaolin and marble, energy sector
						X
						and infrastructure, environmental protection and conservation, and targeted industries
Ghana	X	?	Manufacturing and processing industries, including agro-industrial, fishing and agricultural sectors (food production, livestock breeding, poultry farming and processing of agricultural produce)	X	?	Nontraditional export, hotels, real estate, rural banks, agriculture and agro-industry, waste processing, free zones for enterprise or development
						X

TABLE 4.2 (cont.)

	Loans for Working Capital (1)	Loans for Fixed Assets and/or Investment Projects (2)	Equity Investment (3)	Loans to Specific Sectors (4)	Credit Programs for Particular Regions (5)	Horizontal Tax Incentives (6)	Tax Incentives to Specific Sectors (7)	Tax Incentives to Particular Regions (8)
Uganda	X	X	?	Agriculture, forestry, animal husbandry including pisciculture, agro-industries including manufacturing and distribution of agricultural inputs	?	?	Plants, machinery, and construction materials	X

Sources: See note 7 to the text.

TABLE 4.3
Restrictions Imposed by International Agreements on the Ability of Countries to Undertake Industrial Policies

Restriction	How Restriction is Defined	Under What Conditions it Applies
WTO		
Most favored nation (MFN) rule	A product made in one member country must be treated no less favorably than a "like" good that originates in another country.	It applies unconditionally, although exceptions are made for the formation of free trade areas or custom unions and for preferential treatment of developing countries.
National treatment	Foreign goods, once they have satisfied whatever bordermeasures are applied, must be treated no less favorably, in terms of internal taxation, than like or directly competitive domestically produced goods.	The obligation applies whether or not a specific tariff commitment was made, and it covers taxes and other policies, which must be applied in a nondiscriminatory fashion to like domestic and foreign products.
Reciprocity	Mutual or correspondent concessions of advantages or privileges in the commercial relations between two countries.	The developed contracting parties do not expect reciprocity for commitments made by them in trade negotiations to reduce or remove tariffs and the barriers to the trade of less developed contracting parties (yet this condition is not legally binding).
Safeguard actions	A WTO member may take a "safeguard" action (i.e., restrict imports of a product temporarily) to protect a specific domestic industry from an increase in imports of any product that is causing, or that is threatening to cause, serious injury to the industry.	(a) For public health or national security, not for economic objectives (b) to ensure fair competition (antidumping measures, etc.) (c) for economic reasons (serious balance-of-payment deficits or desire of the government to support infant industries).
Antidumping agreement	Impose discipline on the use of antidumping by countries; one of the main safeguard instruments used among developing countries.	Contains provisions aimed at reducing the extent to which antidumping can be used against developing countries that are trying to develop their exports.

TABLE 4.3 (*cont.*)

Restriction	How Restriction is Defined	Under What Conditions it Applies
Agreement on Subsidies and Countervailing Measures (SCM)	Prohibits exports subsidies by countries with incomes per capita above US$ 1,000 and lays out rules for the use of countervailing measures to offset injury to domestic industries caused by foreign production subsidies.	Provision related to developing countries: if the subsidy is less than 2% of the per unit value of the product exported, developing countries are exempt from countervailing measures (whereas this figure is 1% when a product from and industrial country is under investigation).
Agreement on Trade-Related Investment Measures	Prohibits the use of investment performance-related measures that have an effect on trade: local content and trade-balancing requirements.	The agreement requires mandatory notification of all nonconforming TRIMs and their elimination within two years for developed countries, within five years for developing countries, and within seven years for least-developed countries.
TRIPS Agreement	The IP areas covered are patents and the protection of plant varieties; copyrights and related rights, undisclosed information, trademarks, geographical indications, industrial designs, and the layout of designs of integrated circuits. Generally, IP gives creators exclusive rights over the use of their creations for a fixed duration of time. In some cases however, the intellectual property rights (IPR) are valid indefinitely.	The required strengthening of protection IPR has implications for industrial policy. In the case of domestic firms, it implies both a need, and greater incentives, to innovate and compete dynamically; reverse engineering and imitations becomes less feasible. For foreign firms it means that market access through a commercial presence may become more attractive as IPR protection improves. TRIPS Article 66.2 requires industrial countries to support technology transfer to least-developed countries.

International Financial Codes and Standards

| | | These principles are voluntary, but compliance with them is frequently checked in the context of World Bank or IMF programs. |

Basel Core Principles for Effective Banking Supervision

| Directed lending and connected lending | Bank supervisors must set prudential limits to restrict bank exposures to single borrowers or groups of related borrowers; they must have in place requirements that banks lend to related companies and individuals on an arm's-length basis, that such extensions of credit be effectively monitored, and that other appropriate steps be taken to control or mitigate the risks. | These principles are voluntary, but compliance with them is frequently checked in the context of World Bank or IMF programs. |

Code of Good Practices on Transparency in Monetary and Financial Policies

| Transparency of financial practices in support of government policies. | Requires transparency in the conduct of central banking and financial operations, inter alia, when those operations are undertaken in support of government economic policies. | These principles are voluntary, but compliance with them is frequently checked in the context of World Bank or IMF programs. |

Code of Good Practices on Fiscal transparency

| Nondiscrimination in government regulation. | Government involvement in the private sector (e.g., through regulation and equity ownership) should be conducted in an open and public manner, and on the basis of clear rules and procedures that are applied in a nondiscriminatory way. | These principles are voluntary, but compliance with them is frequently checked in the context of World Bank or IMF programs. |

TABLE 4.3 (*cont.*)

Restriction	How Restriction is Defined	Under What Conditions it Applies
Regional trade agreements		
NAFTA		
Tariff elimination	Except as otherwise provided in the agreement, no party may increase any existing customs duty, or adopt any customs duty, on an originating good.	Each party may adopt or maintain import measures to allocate in-quota imports, provided that such measures do not have trade restrictive effects on imports additional to those caused by the imposition of the tariff rate quota.
Restriction on drawback and duty deferral programs	(1) No party may refund the amount of customs duties paid, or waive or reduce the amount of customs duties owed, on a good imported into its territory. (2) No party may, on condition of export, refund, waive or reduce an antidumping or countervailing duty that is applied pursuant to a party's domestic law.	This article does not apply to: (*a*) a good entered under bond for transportation and exportation to the territory of another party; (*b*) a good exported to the territory of another party in the same condition as when imported into the territory of the party from which the good was exported (processes such as testing, cleaning, repacking, or inspecting the good, or preserving it in its same condition, are not be considered to change a good's condition). (*c*) a refund of customs duties by a party on a particular good imported into its territory and subsequently exported to the territory of another party.
Waiver of customs duties	No party may adopt any new waiver of customs duties, or expand with respect to existing recipients or extend to any new recipient the application of an	This article does not apply to measures subject to Article 303 (Restriction on Drawbacks and Duty Deferral Programs).

Investment: performance requirements

existing waiver of customs duties, where the waiver is conditioned, explicitly or implicitly, on the fulfillment of a performance requirement.

No party may impose or enforce any of the following requirements, to an investment or an investor of a party or of a nonparty in its territory: (*a*) to export a given level or percentage of goods or services; (*b*) to achieve a given level or percentage of domestic content; (*c*) to purchase, use, or accord a preference to goods produced or services provided in its territory, or to purchase goods or services from persons in its territory; (*d*) to relate in any way the volume or value of imports to the volume or value of exports or to the amount of foreign exchange inflows associated with such investment;

(*e*) to restrict sales of goods or services in its territory that such investment produces or provides by relating such sales in any way to the volume or value of its exports or foreign exchange earnings; (*f*) to transfer technology; or (*g*) to act as the exclusive supplier of the goods it produces or services it provides to a specific region or world market.

Provided that such measures are not applied in an arbitrary or unjustifiable manner, or do not constitute a disguised restriction on international trade or investment, the restriction does not prevent any party from adopting or maintaining measures, including environmental measures: (*a*) necessary to secure compliance with laws and regulations that are not inconsistent with the provisions of the agreement; (*b*) necessary to protect human, animal, or plant life or health; or (*c*) necessary for the conservation of living or nonliving exhaustible natural resources.

TABLE 4.3 (*cont.*)

Restriction	How Restriction is Defined	Under What Conditions it Applies
Import and export restrictions	Except as otherwise provided in the agreement, no party may adopt or maintain any prohibition or restriction on the importation of any good of another party or on the exportation or sale for export of any good destined for the territory of another party.	Applies under all conditions except in accordance with Article XI of the GATT, including its interpretative notes, and to this end Article XI of the GATT and its interpretative notes, or any equivalent provision of a successor agreement to which all parties are party, are incorporated into and made a part of the agreement.
EU		
Freedom of movement for goods	It follows from the abolition, in intra-Community trade, of customs duties and charges having equivalent effect in addition to quantitative restrictions in trade and measures having equivalent effect. In both cases, the dismantling of barriers is based on the standstill concept, according to which member states are not authorized to restore such instruments between themselves.	It applies unconditionally.
Freedom of movement for services	The concept of the freedom to perform services is closely linked to the right of establishment. In both cases, the nonnational or Community business in question must be given national treatment, i.e., the conditions applied to them must not be different from those applied to nationals or national businesses.	Certain limits have been set by the treaty, which excludes services linked to the civil service and which stipulates that restrictions on the freedom to perform services can be justified on grounds of public policy, public security, and public health. In addition, certain sectors such as transport, banking, and insurance also have their own systems. These sectors have usually been subject to substantial

		regulation in the member states, and the application of the freedom of movement for services could not easily be achieved simply through mutual recognition of standards.
Freedom of movement for capital	In connection with the free movement of capital, the treaty prohibits all restrictions on capital movements (investments) and all restrictions on payments (payment for goods or services).	Member states are authorized to take any measure justified by the wish to prevent infringements of their own legislation, specifically relating to fiscal provisions or prudential supervision of financial institutions. Moreover, member states may lay down procedures for declaring capital movements for administrative or statistical information purposes in addition to measures associated with public policy or public security. However, these measures and procedures must not be a means of arbitrary discrimination or a disguised restriction on the free movement of capital and payments.
EU-Morocco Freedom of movement of goods	No new customs duties on imports nor charges having equivalent effect may be introduced in trade between the Community and Morocco. Customs duties and charges having equivalent effect applicable on import into Morocco of products originating in the Community are abolished upon the entry into force of the agreement.	Some products are exempt of this restriction (those listed in Annexes 3, 4, 5 and 6). Also, exceptional measures of limited duration may be taken by Morocco in the form of an increase or reintroduction of customs duties. These measures may only concern infant industries, or certain sectors undergoing restructuring or facing serious difficulties, particularly where these difficulties produce major social problems.

TABLE 4.3 (cont.)

Restriction	How Restriction is Defined	Under What Conditions it Applies
	Products originating in Morocco may be imported into the Community free of customs duties and charges having equivalent effect. No new quantitative restriction on imports or measure having equivalent effect may be introduced in trade between the Community and Morocco. The two parties must refrain from any measures or practice of an internal fiscal nature establishing, whether directly or indirectly, discrimination between the products of one party and like products originating in the territory of the other party.	
EU-Tunisia Freedom of movement of goods	No new customs duties on imports nor charges having equivalent effect may be introduced in trade between the Community and Tunisia. Products originating in Tunisia are imported into the Community free of customs duties and charges having equivalent effect and without quantitative restrictions or measures having equivalent effect.	This does not preclude the retention by the Community of an agricultural component on imports of certain goods originating in Tunisia (listed in Annex 1). The agricultural component must reflect differences between the price on the Community market of the agricultural products considered as being used in the production of such goods and the price of imports from third countries where the total cost of the said basic products is higher in the Community. The agricultural component may take the form of a fixed

amount or an ad valorem duty. Such differences must be replaced, where appropriate, by specific duties based on tariffication of the agricultural component or by ad valorem duties. Exceptional measures of limited duration which derogate from the provisions of Article 11 may be taken by Tunisia in the form of an increase or reintroduction of customs duties. These measures may only concern infant industries, or certain sectors undergoing restructuring.

The Community and Tunisia are committed to gradually implementing greater liberalization of their reciprocal trade in agricultural and fishery products. Without prejudice to the provisions of the GATT: (a) no new quantitative restriction on imports or measure having equivalent effect may be introduced in trade between the Community and Tunisia; (b) quantitative restrictions on imports and measures having equivalent effect in trade between Tunisia and the Community must be abolished upon the entry into force of the agreement; (c) the Community and Tunisia must apply to the other's exports customs neither duties or charges having equivalent effect nor quantitative restrictions or measures of equivalent effect.

Where any product is being imported in increased quantities and under such conditions as to cause or threaten to cause: (a) serious injury to domestic producers of like or directly competitive products in the territory of one of the contracting parties, or (b) serious disturbances in any sector of the economy or difficulties that could bring about serious deterioration in the economic situation of a region, the Community or Tunisia may take appropriate measures under the conditions and in accordance with the procedures laid down in Article 27. "The safeguard measures shall be immediately notified to the Association Committee by the party concerned

TABLE 4.3 (*cont.*)

Restriction	How Restriction is Defined	Under What Conditions it Applies
		and shall be the subject of periodic consultations, particularly with a view to their abolition as soon as circumstances permit."
	1. The two parties must refrain from any measures or practice of an internal fiscal nature establishing, whether directly or indirectly, discrimination between the products of one party and like products originating in the territory of the other party. 2. Products exported to the territory of one of the parties may not benefit from repayment of indirect internal taxation in excess of the amount of indirect taxation imposed on them directly or indirectly.	
US-Jordan Tariffs	The FTA eliminates all tariff barriers on virtually all goods traded between the United States and Jordan within ten years.	Not every export of the United States or Jordan will qualify for this duty-free treatment. The United States and Jordan have agreed to eliminate existing tariffs only on "originating goods of the other Party." Goods must qualify under the Rules of Origin in order to take advantage of the FTA. Also, products under special staging categories including certain alcohol and textile products, generalized system of preference (GSP) exports, agriculture quota-class goods, poultry, apples, and cars will experience either an accelerated reduction of tariffs or a delay in redution.

Intellectual property	Jordan has agreed to accede to Articles 1–14 of the World Intellectual Property Organization's (WIPO) Copyright Treaty; Articles 1–23 of the WIPO Performances and Phonographs Treaty; Articles 1–22 of the International Convention for the Protection of New Varieties of Plants; Articles 1–6 of the Joint Recommendation Concerning Provisions on the Protection of Well-Known Marks; Patent Cooperation Treaty (1984); Protocol Relating to the Madrid Agreement Concerning the International Registrations of Marks (1989).	The United States and Jordan have agreed to take measures related to certain regulated products, particularly in the area of "approving the marketing of pharmaceuticals or agricultural chemical products that utilize new chemical entities" and protecting the information against disclosure and unfair commercial use.
Services	Liberalization of bilateral trade in services between the United States and Jordan. With the liberalization, U.S. companies will have greater access to Jordanian service industries, especially tourism, transportation, health, financial, education, environmental, business, communications, distribution, and recreational/ cultural services.	
Rules of origin	The FTA defines originating goods as having three components: a qualitative definition of origin (the "wholly obtained"/"substantial transformation" tests), a quantitative definition of origin (the 35% domestic content requirement), and a direct transport requirement.	The direct transport requirement and permitted exceptions are discussed in chapter 9 of the Rules of Origin.

TABLE 4.3 (cont.)

Restriction	How Restriction is Defined	Under What Conditions it Applies
US-Chile Tariffs eliminations	Neither party may increase any existing customs duty, or adopt any customs duty, on an originating good. Each party shall progressively eliminate its customs duties on originating goods. The United States must eliminate customs duties on any nonagricultural originating goods that, after the date of entry into force of the agreement, are designated as articles eligible for duty-free treatment under the U.S. Generalized System of Preferences, effective from the date of such designation.	A party may (a) raise a customs duty back to the level established in its Schedule to Annex 3.3 following a unilateral reduction; or (b) maintain or increase a customs duty as authorized by the Dispute Settlement Body of the WTO.
Drawback and duty deferral programs	Neither party may refund the amount of customs duties paid, or waive or reduce the amount of customs duties owed, on a good imported into its territory. Neither party may, on condition of export, refund, waive, or reduce: (a) an antidumping or countervailing duty; (b) a premium offered or collected on an imported good arising out of any tendering system in respect of the administration of quantitative import restrictions, tariff rate quotas, or tariff preference levels; or (c) customs duties paid or owed on a good imported into its territory	This applies on condition that the good is (a) subsequently exported to the territory of the other party; (b) used as a material in the production of another good that is subsequently exported to the territory of the other party; or (c) substituted by an identical or similar good used as a material in the production of another good that is subsequently exported to the territory of the other party.

	and substituted by an identical or similar good that is subsequently exported to the territory of the other party.	This prohibits any country from adopting (a) export and import price requirements, except as permitted in enforcement of countervailing and antidumping orders and undertakings; (b) import licensing conditioned on the fulfillment of a performance requirement; or (c) voluntary export restraints not consistent with Article VI of GATT 1994, as implemented under Article 18 of the SCM Agreement and Article 8.1 of the AD Agreement.
Import and export restrictions	Neither party may adopt or maintain any prohibition or restriction on the importation of any good of the other party or on the exportation or sale for export of any good destined for the territory of the other party	
Export taxes	Neither party may adopt or maintain any duty, tax, or other charge on the export of any good to the territory of the other party.	Applies always, unless such duty, tax, or charge is adopted or maintained on any such good when destined for domestic consumption
Textiles and apparel	If, as a result of the elimination of a duty provided for in the agreement, a textile or apparel good benefiting from preferential tariff treatment under the agreement is being imported into the territory of a party in such increased quantities, in absolute terms or relative to the domestic market for that good, and under such conditions as to cause serious damage, or actual threat thereof, to a domestic industry producing a like or directly competitive good, the importing party may, to the extent and for such time as may be necessary to prevent or remedy such damage and to facilitate adjustment, take	The importing party may take an emergency action under this article only following an investigation by its competent authorities. Also, (a) no emergency action may be maintained for a period exceeding three years; (b) no emergency action may be taken or maintained beyond the period ending eight years after duties on a good have been eliminated pursuant to the agreement; (c) no emergency action may be taken by an importing party against any particular good of the other party more than once; and (d) on termination of the action, the good returns to duty-free status.

TABLE 4.3 (*cont.*)

Restriction	How Restriction is Defined	Under What Conditions it Applies
	emergency action, consisting of an increase in the rate of duty on the good to a level not to exceed the lesser of (*a*) the MFN applied rate of duty in effect at the time the action is taken; and (*b*) the MFN applied rate of duty in effect on the date of entry into force of the agreement.	
Intellectual property	Both parties need to accede or ratify to a series of patent and intellectual property treaties.	Each party may, but shall not be obliged to, implement in its domestic law more extensive protection than is required by the agreement provided that such protection does not contravene the provisions of the agreement.
IMF (structural conditionality)		
Trade policy (general)	Complete equalization of excises on all domestic, imported goods and eliminate reference prices for all imports and remove exchange controls.	
Indonesia Stand-By Agreement 1998	Eliminate all restrictions on foreign investment in palm oil plantations, retail and wholesale trade and establish a level playing field in the import and distribution of essential food items between BULOG and private sector participants.	

Eliminate subsidies on sugar, wheat flour, corn, soybean meal, and fishmeal. Phase out local content program for motor vehicles and abolish local content regulations on dairy products. Discontinue budgetary and extra budgetary support and privileges to IPTN (Nusantara Aircraft Industry) projects. Reduce by 5 percentage points tariffs on items currently subject to tariffs of 15 to 25 percent. Tariff reduction on nonfood agricultural, chemical, steel-metal, and fishery products. Phase out remaining quantitative import restrictions and other nontariff barriers. Abolish export taxes on leather, cork, ores and waste aluminum products and reduce export taxes on logs, sawn timber, rattan and minerals. Eliminate all other export restrictions. Take effective action to allow free competition in (*a*) importation of wheat, wheat flour, soybeans, and garlic; (*b*) sale or distribution of flour; and (*c*) importation and marketing of sugar.

TABLE 4.3 (cont.)

Restriction	How Restriction is Defined	Under What Conditions it Applies
Korea		
Stand-By Arrangement December 5, 1997, Economic Program	(1) Eliminate trade-related subsidies; (2) eliminate restrictive import licensing; (3) eliminate the import diversification program; and (4) streamline and improve the transparency of the import certification procedures.	
Turkey		
Stand-By Arrangement with the International Monetary Fund, 2001	Agriculture reform program: removal of credit subsidies from state banks, reform sugar market, and liberalization of the tobacco sector.	
Ethiopia		
Letter of Intent, Memorandum of Economic and Financial Policies, and Technical Memorandum of Understanding, 2001	Cease price verification on all nonagricultural commodity exports and noncoffee agricultural exports for which verifiable international prices are not readily available. For other agricultural exports, except coffee, replace ex ante price verification with ex post audit, and, for coffee, replace the verification of a single point price with the verification of a range of prices for each variety; reduce import tariffs and liberalize the payments and exchange regulations for foreign trade in goods and services. (1) Remove restrictions on foreign suppliers'/partners' credit	

and on importing inputs without payment from foreign collaborators, as well as on other implicit forms of credit not involving formal loan agreements; (2) allow all exporters of manufactures (including of agro-processed products) to obtain foreign commercial borrowing; (3) ease the constraints on debt-equity ratios for exporters by allowing the NBE to authorize exporters to exceed the limit of 60/40 that currently obtains; and (4) allow banks to open import letters of credit for exporters with confirmed letters. Eliminate price and quality preferences for domestic input suppliers and further improve the duty drawback and exemption schemes.

Mozambique
Enhanced
Structural
Adjustment
Facility
1998–2000

Rationalize import tariffs. Lower the top import tariff rate from 35 percent to at least 30 percent. Reduce export tax exemptions.

Sources: WTO: World Bank 2002. NAFTA: http://www.nafta-sec-alena.org/DefaultSite/home/index_e.aspx. EU: http://europa.eu.int/pol/comm/ index_en.htm. EU-Morocco: http://europa.eu.int/eur-lex/pri/en/oj/dat/2000/l_070/l_07020000318en00020190.pdf. EU-Tunisia: http://europa .eu.int/eur-lex/pri/en/oj/dat/1998/l_097/l_09719980330en00020174.pdf. US-Jordan: http://www.jordanusfta.com/. US-Chile: http://www.ustr.gov/ new/fta/Chile/final/03.market%20access.PDF. IMF: http://www.imf.org/external/np/pdr/cond/2001/eng/trade/index.htm; http://www.imf.org/external/ np/pdr/cond/2001/eng/trade/index.htm. Indonesia: http://www.imf.org/external/np/loi/041098.pdf. Korea: http://www.imf.org/external/np/oth/ korea.htm; http://www.imf.org/external/np/loi/122497.htm#box5. Turkey: http://www.imf.org/external/np/loi/2001/tur/02/index.htm; Letter of Intent, May 2001. Ethiopia: http://www.imf.org/external/np/pfp/eth/etp.htm; http://www.imf.org/external/pubs/ft/scr/1999/cr9998.pdf. Mozambique: http://www.imf.org/external/np/pfp/mozam/moztap.htm.

and patent laws that fall short of international standards. All of these had been part of the arsenal of industrial policies utilized by South Korea and Taiwan during the 1960s and 1970s. Moreover, countries that are not yet members of the WTO are often hit with more restrictive demands as part of their accession negotiations.

Regional or bilateral agreements typically expand the range of disciplines beyond those that are found in the WTO. In particular, the United States has pushed for tighter restrictions in the areas of investment regulations, intellectual property protection, and capital account whenever it negotiates a free-trade agreement with a developing country (see illustrations in table 4.3). On the financial side, a number of international codes and standards have clauses that can be interpreted as restricting the use of industrial policy (see table 4.3). And IMF conditionality often goes beyond narrow monetary and fiscal matters to prescribe policies on trade and industrial policy (so-called structural conditionality). The pinnacle of IMF structural conditionality was reached during the Asian financial crisis. While the IMF's official line has veered away from structural conditionality since then, IMF programs typically still contain many detailed requirements on trade and industrial policies (see table 4.3 for illustrations from Turkey and Ethiopia).

It is important to emphasize that not all international disciplines are necessarily harmful. For example, the principle of *transparency* that is enshrined in international trade agreements and in international financial codes and standards is fully consistent with the industrial-policy architecture recommended above, and hence is hard to find fault with. Moreover, when designed appropriately, regional trade agreements can be a useful vehicle for industrial policy programs. For example, both Morocco and Tunisia put in place ambitious industrial upgrading (*mise à niveau*) programs in conjunction with their free-trade agreements with the EU, and obtained EU and World Bank funds to pay for them. Mercosur had a special regime for the automotive sector that gave a big boost to auto and components industries in Argentina and Uruguay. Governments with a strategic sense of their economic priorities can generally put such international agreements to good use, and transform potential constraint into opportunity.

Among existing international disciplines, probably the most significant is the one that constrains the use of export subsidies. The WTO's Agreement on Subsidies essentially renders illegal all free trade zones of the type discussed previously (as well as other fiscal and credit incentives geared toward exports) for countries above the $1,000 per capita income level. How much of a real loss this is remains unclear. As I discussed in the previous section, at present existing policies in many countries are probably too biased toward exporting as it is. There is nothing in the empirical literature to suggest that exports generate the kind of positive externalities that would justify their subsidization as a general rule. On the other hand, conditioning subsidies on exports has the valuable feature that it ensures the incentives are reaped by winners (i.e., those that are able to compete in international markets) rather than the losers. As such, export subsidies are a nice example of performance-based incentive policies (which makes them consistent with the design principles enunciated above). The success in East Asia with export subsidies has much to do with this carrot-and-stick feature: you get the subsidy, but only so long as you perform in world markets. On balance, therefore, the Agreement on Subsidies must be judged to have made a significant dent in the ability of developing countries to employ intelligently designed industrial policies.[10]

A second area where international rules may have some bite is in intellectual property. As Richard Nelson (2004) has stressed, the ability to copy technologies developed in advanced countries has been historically one of the most important elements determining the ability of lagging nations to catch up. The WTO's TRIPS Agreement and its more restrictive versions in bilateral or regional trade agreements make it virtually impossible to employ a strategy of reverse engineering and copying. The developmental costs of TRIPS have so far received attention mainly in regard to public health and access to essential medicines. Its adverse effects on technological capacity have yet to receive commensurate attention.

In light of this, it is encouraging that discussions of the multilateral trade regime are increasingly paying attention (or at least lip service) to the question of "policy space" for developing countries (see Hoekman 2005). There is growing recognition that the pendulum between policy autonomy and international rules may have swung too far in the direction of the latter in recent trade rounds. The attempt in the Doha Round to extend multilateral disciplines to national competition and investment policies has gone nowhere. And many consider the "single undertaking" model of trade negotiations adopted since the Uruguay Round, under which all nations, regardless of their levels of development and needs, sign on to the same text, to be all but dead. This is all good news from the perspective developed in this chapter. Developing nations should push hard for "policy space" in future trade negotiations. In the past they compromised on that issue in return for greater access in rich country markets. This has turned out to be a bad bargain. The purpose of international rules should not be to impose common

---

[10] Note that a prohibition on export subsidies cannot be justified using the traditional beggar-thy-neighbor arguments. Unlike, say, the use of import tariffs by a large country, the use of export subsidies produces a net benefit to the rest of the world since it lowers the world market price of the subsidized commodity and improves the external terms of trade of the rest of the world.

rules on countries with different regulatory systems, but to accept these differences and regulate the interface between them so as to reduce adverse spillovers. I will discuss this issue at greater length when I turn to global economic governance (chapters 7 and 8).

CONCLUDING REMARKS

Markets can malfunction both when governments interfere too much and when they interfere too little. Development policies of the last two decades have been obsessed with the first category of mistakes—governments' errors of commission. Hence the efforts to reduce or eliminate regulations, trade restrictions, financial repression, and public ownership.

Governments' errors of omission—needed interventions that were not supplied—were de-emphasized, in part as a reaction to the strong emphasis placed on them by earlier policies of import substitution. Recently governments around the world have begun to seek a more balanced strategy as liberalization and privatization have failed to deliver the expected performance. I have argued in this chapter that properly formulated industrial policies have an important role to play in such strategies.

There is no shortage of arguments against industrial policy. A less than comprehensive list of such arguments would include the following.

- Governments cannot pick winners.
- Developing countries lack the competent bureaucracies to render it effective.
- Industrial interventions are prone to political capture and corruption.
- There is little evidence that industrial policies work.
- What is needed is not industrial policy, but across-the-board support for R&D and intellectual protection.
- And in any case international rules no longer leave scope for industrial policy interventions.

There is more than a grain of truth in each of these claims. Yet, as we have seen, there are also good counterarguments in each case.

- Yes, the government cannot pick winners, but effective industrial policy is predicated less on the ability to pick winners than on the ability to cut losses short once mistakes have been made. In fact, making mistakes ("picking wrong industries") is part and parcel of good industrial policy when cost discovery is at issue.
- Competent bureaucracies are a scarce resource in most developing countries, but most countries do have (or can build) pockets of bureaucratic competence. In any case, it is not clear what the counterfactual is. The standard

market-oriented package hardly economizes on bureaucratic competence. As we have discovered during the last decade, and as the expansion of the Washington Consensus agenda into governance and institutional areas indicates, running a market economy puts a significant premium on regulatory capacity. Industrial policy is no different.

  • Industrial policies can be captured by the interests whose behavior they aim to alter. But once again, this is little different from any other area of policy. In many countries, privatization has turned out to be a boon for insiders or government cronies.

  • It is not true that there is a shortage of evidence on the benefits of industrial policy. To the contrary, as I have illustrated above with reference to Latin America, it is difficult to come up with real winners in the developing world that are not a product of industrial policies of some sort.

  • Supply-side innovation policies may have a role, but what constrains productive restructuring is a more fundamental feature of low-income environments: entrepreneurship in new activities has high social returns but low private returns.

  • There is plenty of scope for industrial policies in the present international economic environment. In fact, contrary to general belief, the last two decades have seen a tremendous amount of industrial policy.

I have taken the view in this chapter that industrial policy is a process of economic self-discovery in the broader sense. The right image to carry in one's head is not of omniscient planners who can intervene with the first-best Pigovian subsidies to internalize any and all externalities, but of an interactive process of strategic cooperation between the private and public sectors that, on the one hand, serves to elicit information on business opportunities and constraints and, on the other hand, generates policy initiatives in response.

It is impossible to specify the results of such a process ex ante: the point is to discover where action is needed and what type of action can bring forth the greatest response. It is pointless to obsess, as is common in many discussions of industrial policy, about policy instruments and modalities of interventions. What is much more important is to have a process in place that helps reveal areas of desirable interventions. Governments that understand this will be constantly on the lookout for ways in which they can facilitate structural change and collaboration with the private sector. As such, industrial policy is a state of mind more than anything else.

I close by making two points that relate the discussion here to the broader policy agenda that faces developing countries. The first point is that much of industrial policy, as discussed here, is concerned with the provision of public goods for the productive sector. Public labs and public R&D, health and infrastructural facilities, sanitary and phytosanitary standards, infrastructure, vocational and technical training can all be viewed as public goods required for enhancing technological capabilities. From this perspective, industrial policy is just good economic policy of the type that traditional, orthodox approaches prescribe. Second, the capacity to provide these public goods effectively is an important part of the social capabilities needed to generate development. That in turn requires good institutions, with the key features that I have discussed. Such institutional development is at the core of today's orthodox development agenda.[11] In both senses, then, the agenda of industrial policy laid out in this chapter not only does not greatly differ from today's broader, conventional agenda of development, it is part and parcel of it.

[11] Paradoxically, as Ocampo (2003, 28) has rightly emphasized, the "suboptimal development of institutions in the area of productive development has . . . become a direct institutional deficiency affecting economic growth, which is generally ignored in the call to strengthen institutional development."

5

Institutions for High-Quality Growth

THE comparative experience with economic growth over the last few decades has taught us a number of lessons. One of the more important of these is the need for private initiative and incentives. All instances of successful development are ultimately the collective result of individual decisions by entrepreneurs to invest in risky new ventures and try out new things. The good news here is that we have found *homo economicus* to be alive and well in the tropics and other poor lands. The idea of "elasticity pessimism"—the notion that the private sectors in developing countries would fail to respond quickly to price incentives and other lures to investment—has been put to rest by the accumulating evidence. We find time and again that investment decisions, agricultural production, and exports turn out to be quite sensitive to price incentives, as long as these are perceived to have some predictability.

The discovery that relative prices matter a lot, and that therefore neoclassical economic analysis has much to contribute to development policy, led for a while to what was perhaps an excessive focus on relative prices. Price reforms—in external trade, in product and labor markets, in finance, and in taxation—were the rallying cry of the reformers of the 1980s, along with macroeconomic stability and privatization. By the 1990s, the shortcomings of the focus on price reform were increasingly evident. The encounter between neoclassical economics and developing societies revealed the institutional underpinnings of market economies. A clearly delineated system of property rights; a regulatory apparatus curbing the worst forms of fraud, anticompetitive behavior, and moral hazard; a moderately cohesive society exhibiting trust and social cooperation; social and political institutions that mitigate risk and manage social conflicts; the rule of law and clean government—these are social arrangements that economists usually take for granted, but which are conspicuous by their absence in poor countries.

Hence it became clear that incentives would not work or would generate perverse results in the absence of adequate institutions. Some of the implications of this insight were recognized early on, for example in discussions on rent-seeking in the context of trade policy (where corruption was the main issue) or in the discussions on common-property resources (where lack of adequately defined property rights was the problem). But the broader point that markets need to be supported by nonmarket institutions in order to perform well took a while to sink in. Three sets of disparate developments conspired to put institutions squarely on the agenda of reformers. One of them was the dismal failure in Russia of price reform and privatization in the absence of a supportive legal, regulatory, and political apparatus. A second is the lingering dissatisfaction with market-oriented reforms in Latin America and the growing realization that these reforms have paid too little attention to mechanisms of social insurance and to safety nets. The third was the Asian financial crisis, which has shown that allowing financial liberalization to run ahead of financial regulation is an invitation to disaster.

The question before policymakers, therefore, is no longer, "Do institutions matter?"[1] but, "Which institutions matter and how does one acquire them?" Following Lin and Nugent (1995, 2306–7), it is useful to think of institutions broadly as "a set of humanly devised behavioral rules that govern and shape the interactions of human beings, in part by helping them to form expectations of what other people will do." I begin this chapter with a discussion of the types of institutions that allow markets to perform adequately. These institutions are needed because markets are not self-creating, self-regulating, self-stabilizing, or self-legitimizing. While we can identify in broad terms the nature of the institutional remedies required, there is no unique mapping between markets and the nonmarket institutions that underpin them (as I argued in chapter 1). The plausible variation in institutional setups is larger than is usually presupposed.[2]

I then turn to the more difficult question of how one thinks about appropriate strategies for institution building. I emphasize the importance of "local knowledge," and argue that a strategy of institution building must

---

[1] See Lin and Nugent 1995 for an excellent review of the huge literature on institutions as it relates to economic development specifically. This literature has been enriched recently by a growing body of empirical cross-national work that quantifies the growth-promoting effects of superior institutions. See Hall and Jones 1999 on "social infrastructure"; Knack and Keefer 1995, 1997, on bureaucratic quality and social capital; Temple and Johnson 1998 on "social capability"; Rodrik 1999b on institutions of conflict management; and Acemoglu, Johnson, and Robinson 2003 on the role played by institutions bequeathed by colonists. Work by Kaufmann, Kraay, and Zoido-Lobatón (1999) has developed aggregate indicators of six different aspects of governance-voice and accountability, political instability and violence, government effectiveness, regulatory burden, rule of law, and graft-showing that all of these are significantly associated with income levels in the expected manner.

[2] I refer the reader to Unger 1998 for a broader discussion of this point and of its implications. I have benefited greatly from talking with Roberto Unger on some of these issues.

not overemphasize best-practice "blueprints" at the expense of local experimentation. I make the case that participatory and decentralized political systems are the most effective ones we have for processing and aggregating local knowledge. We can think of democracy as a metainstitution for building good institutions.

The penultimate section of the chapter provides a range of evidence indicating that participatory democracies enable higher-quality growth: they allow greater predictability and stability, are more resilient to shocks, and deliver superior distributional outcomes. The concluding section offers some implications for the design of conditionality.

WHICH INSTITUTIONS MATTER?

Institutions do not figure prominently in the training of economists. The standard Arrow-Debreu model with a full set of complete and contingent markets extending indefinitely into the future seems to require no assistance from nonmarket institutions. But of course this absence of institutions is quite misleading even in the context of that model. The standard model assumes a well-defined set of property rights. It also assumes that contracts are signed with no fear that they will be revoked when it suits one of the parties. So in the background there exist institutions that establish and protect property rights and enforce contracts. We must, in other words, have a system of laws and courts to make even "perfect" markets function.

Laws in turn have to be written and they have to be backed up by the use of sanctioned force. That implies a legislator and a police force. The legislator's authority may derive from religion, family lineage, or access to superior violence, but in each case she needs to ensure that she provides her subjects with the right mix of "ideology" (a belief system) and threat of violence to forestall rebellion from below. Or the authority may derive from the legitimacy provided by popular support, in which case she needs to be responsive to her constituency's (voters') needs. In either case, we have the beginnings of a governmental structure that goes well beyond the narrow needs of the market.

One implication of all this is that the market economy is necessarily "embedded" in a set of nonmarket institutions. Another is that not all of these institutions are there to serve the needs of the market economy first and foremost, even if their presence is required by the internal logic of private property and contract enforcement. The fact that a governance structure is needed to ensure that markets can do their work does not imply that the governance structure serves only that end. Nonmarket institutions will sometimes produce outcomes that are socially undesirable, such as the use of public office for private gain. They may also produce outcomes that restrict the free play of market forces in pursuit of a larger goal, such as social stability and cohesiveness.

Markets require institutions because they are not self-creating, self-regulating, self-stabilizing, or self-legitimizing. The rest of this section discusses five types of market-supporting institutions, each responding to one of these failures: property rights; regulatory institutions; institutions for macroeconomic stabilization; institutions for social insurance; and institutions of conflict management.

Property Rights

While it is possible to envisage a thriving *socialist* market economy in theory, as Oskar Lange established in the famous debates of the 1920s, today's prosperous economies have all been built on the basis of private property. As North and Thomas (1973) and North and Weingast (1989), among many others, have argued, the establishment of secure and stable property rights has been a key element in the rise of the West and the onset of modern economic growth. It stands to reason that entrepreneurs do not have the incentive to accumulate and innovate unless they have adequate *control* over the return to the assets that are thereby produced or improved.

Note that the key word is "control" rather than "ownership." Formal property rights do not count for much if they do not confer control rights. By the same token, sufficiently strong control rights may do the trick even in the absence of formal property rights. Russia during much of the 1990s represented a case where shareholders had property rights but often lacked effective control over enterprises and their managers. Township and village enterprises (TVEs) in China are an example where control rights have spurred entrepreneurial activity despite the absence of clearly defined property rights. As these instances illustrate, establishing "property rights" is rarely a matter of just passing a piece of legislation. Legislation in itself is neither necessary nor sufficient for the provision of the secure control rights. In practice, control rights are upheld by a combination of legislation, private *and* public enforcement, and custom and tradition. They may be distributed more narrowly or more diffusely than property rights. Stakeholders can matter as much as shareholders.

Moreover, property rights are rarely absolute, even when set formally in the law. The right to keep my neighbor out of my orchard does not normally extend to my right to shoot him if he enters it. Other laws or norms—such as those against murder—may trump property rights. Each society decides for itself the scope of allowable property rights and the acceptable restrictions on their exercise. Intellectual property rights are protected assiduously in the United States and most advanced societies, but not in many developing countries. On the other hand, zoning and environmental legislation restricts the ability of households and enterprises in the rich countries to do as they please with their "property" to a much greater extent than is the case in developing countries. All societies recognize that private property rights can be curbed if doing so serves a greater public purpose. It is the definition of what constitutes "greater public purpose" that varies.

Regulatory Institutions

Markets fail when participants engage in fraudulent or anticompetitive behavior. They fail when transaction costs prevent the internalizing of technological and other nonpecuniary externalities (as discussed in the previous chapter). And they fail when incomplete information results in moral hazard and adverse selection. Economists recognize these failures and have developed the analytical tools required to think systematically about their consequences and possible remedies. Theories of the second best, imperfect competition, agency, mechanism design, and many others offer an almost embarrassing choice of regulatory instruments to counter market failures. Theories of political economy and public choice offer cautions against unqualified reliance on these instruments.

In practice, every successful market economy is overseen by a panoply of regulatory institutions, regulating conduct in goods, services, labor, assets, and financial markets. A few acronyms from the United States will suffice to give a sense of the range of institutions involved: FTC, FDIC, FCC, FAA, OSHA, SEC, EPA, and so on. In fact, the freer are the markets, the greater is the burden on the regulatory institutions. It is not a coincidence that the United States has the world's freest markets as well its toughest antitrust enforcement. It is hard to envisage in any country other than the United States a hugely successful high-tech company like Microsoft being dragged through the courts for alleged anticompetitive practices. The lesson that market freedom requires regulatory vigilance has been driven home by the experience in East Asia during the Asian financial crisis. In South Korea and Thailand, as in so many other developing countries, financial liberalization and capital-account opening led to financial crises precisely because of inadequate prudential regulation and supervision.[3]

[3] See Mishkin 2006 for a recent account. See also the paper by Johnson and Shleifer (1999), which attributes the more impressive development of equity markets in Poland, as compared to the Czech Republic, to the stronger regulations in the former country upholding minority shareholder rights and guarding against fraud.

It is important to recognize that regulatory institutions may need to extend beyond the standard list covering antitrust, financial supervision, securities regulation, and a few others. As discussed in the previous chapter, this is true especially in developing countries, where market failures may be more pervasive and the requisite market regulations more extensive. Recent models of coordination failure and capital market imperfections[4] make it clear that strategic government interventions may often be required to get out of low-level traps and elicit desirable private investment responses. The experience of South Korea and Taiwan in the 1960s and 1970s can be interpreted in that light. The extensive subsidization and government-led coordination of private investment in these two economies played a crucial role in setting the stage for self-sustaining growth (Rodrik 1995a). It is clear that many other countries have tried and failed to replicate these institutional arrangements. And even South Korea may have taken a good thing too far by maintaining the cozy institutional linkages between the government and *chaebol* well into the 1990s, at which point they may have become dysfunctional. Once again, the lesson is that desirable institutional arrangements vary, not only across countries but within countries over time.

Institutions for Macroeconomic Stabilization

Since Keynes, we have come to a better understanding of the reality that capitalist economies are not necessarily self-stabilizing. Keynes and his followers worried about shortfalls in aggregate demand and the resulting unemployment. More recent views of macroeconomic instability stress the inherent instability of financial markets and its transmission to the real economy. All advanced economies have come to acquire fiscal and monetary institutions that perform stabilizing functions, having learned the hard way about the consequences of not having them. Probably most important among these institutions is a lender of last resort—typically the central bank—which guards against self-fulfilling banking crises.

There is a strong current within macroeconomic thought, represented in its theoretically most sophisticated version by the real business cycles (RBC) approach—that disputes the possibility or effectiveness of stabilizing the macroeconomy through monetary and fiscal policies. There is also a sense in policy circles, particularly in Latin America, that fiscal and monetary institutions—as currently configured—have added to macroeconomic instability, rather than reduced it, by following procyclical rather than anticyclical policies (Hausmann and Gavin 1996). These

---

[4] See Hoff and Stiglitz 2001 for a useful survey and discussion.

developments have spurred the trend toward central bank independence, and helped open a new debate on designing more robust fiscal institutions.

Some countries (Argentina being the most significant example in the 1990s) have given up on a domestic lender-of-last-resort function by making their central bank function like a currency board. The Argentine calculation was that having a central bank that can *occasionally* stabilize the economy is not worth running the risk that the central bank will *mostly* destabilize it. Perhaps Argentine history gives plenty of reason to think that this is not a bad bet. But can the same be said for Mexico or Brazil, or for that matter, Turkey or Indonesia? What may work for Argentina may not work for the others. And even in Argentina, the currency board system worked only for a while (and collapsed spectacularly in 2001 for reasons that I will discuss in chapter 7). The debate over currency boards and dollarization illustrates the obvious, but occasionally neglected fact that the institutions needed by a country are not independent of that country's history.

Institutions for Social Insurance

A modern market economy is one where change is constant and idiosyncratic (i.e., individual-specific) risk to incomes and employment is pervasive. Modern economic growth entails a transition from a static economy to a dynamic one where the tasks that workers perform are in constant evolution, and movement up and down in the income scale is frequent. One of the liberating effects of a dynamic market economy is that it frees individuals from their traditional entanglements—the kin group, the church, the village hierarchy. The flip side is that it uproots them from traditional support systems and risk-sharing institutions. Gift exchanges, the fiesta, and kinship ties—to cite just a few of the social arrangements for equalizing the distribution of resources in traditional societies—lose much of their social insurance functions. And the risks that have to be insured against become much less manageable in the traditional manner as markets spread.

The huge expansion of publicly provided social insurance programs during the twentieth century is one of the most remarkable features of the evolution of advanced market economies. In the United States, it was the trauma of the Great Depression that paved the way for the major institutional innovations in this area: Social Security, unemployment compensation, public works, public ownership, deposit insurance, and legislation favoring unions (see Bordo, Goldin, and White 1998, 6). As Jacoby (1998) notes, prior to the Great Depression the middle classes were generally able to self-insure or buy insurance from private intermediaries. As these private forms of insurance collapsed, the middle classes threw their considerable political weight behind the extension of social insurance and the creation of what would later be called the welfare state. In Europe, the roots of the welfare state reached in some cases to the tail end of the nineteenth century. But the striking expansion of social insurance programs, particularly in the smaller economies most open to foreign trade, was a post—World War II phenomenon (Rodrik 1998a). Despite a considerable political backlash against the welfare state since the 1980s, neither the United States nor Europe has significantly scaled back these programs.

Social insurance need not always take the form of transfer programs paid out of fiscal resources. The East Asian model, represented well by Japan, is one where social insurance is provided through a combination of enterprise practices (such as lifetime employment and enterprise-provided social benefits), sheltered and regulated sectors (mom-and-pop stores), and an incremental approach to liberalization and external opening. Certain aspects of Japanese society that seem inefficient to outside observers—such as the preference for small-scale retail stores or extensive regulation of product markets—can be viewed as substitutes for the transfer programs that would otherwise have to be provided (as they are in most European nations) by a welfare state. Such complementarities among different institutional arrangements within a society have the important implication that it is very difficult to alter national systems in a piecemeal fashion. One cannot (or should not) ask the Japanese to get rid of their lifetime employment practices or inefficient retail arrangements without ensuring that alternative safety nets are in place. Another implication is that substantial institutional changes come only in the aftermath of large dislocations, such as those created by the Great Depression or World War II.

Social insurance legitimizes a market economy by rendering it compatible with social stability and social cohesion. At the same time, the existing welfare states in western Europe and the United States engender a number of economic and social costs—mounting fiscal outlays, an "entitlement" culture, long-term unemployment—which have become increasingly apparent. Partly because of that, developing countries, such as those in Latin America that adopted the market-oriented model following the debt crisis of the 1980s, have not paid sufficient attention to creating institutions of social insurance (Rodrik 2001a). The upshot has been economic insecurity and a backlash against the reforms. How these countries will maintain social cohesion in the face of large inequalities and volatile outcomes, both of which are being aggravated by the growing reliance on market forces, is a question without an obvious answer. But if Latin America and the other developing regions are to carve a different path in social insurance than that followed by Europe or North America, they will have to develop their own vision—and their own institutional innovations—to bridge the tension between market forces and the yearning for economic security.

Institutions of Conflict Management

Societies differ in their cleavages. Some are made up of an ethnically and linguistically homogeneous population marked by a relatively egalitarian distribution of resources (Finland). Others are characterized by deep cleavages along ethnic or income lines (Nigeria). These divisions, when not bridged adequately, can hamper social cooperation and prevent the undertaking of mutually beneficial projects. Social conflict is harmful both because it diverts resources from economically productive activities and because it discourages such activities by the uncertainty it generates. Economists have used models of social conflict to shed light on questions such as the following: Why do governments delay stabilizations when delay imposes costs on all groups (Alesina and Drazen 1991)? Why do countries rich in natural resources often do worse than countries that are resource-poor (Tornell and Lane 1999)? Why do external shocks often lead to protracted economic crises that are out of proportion to the direct costs of the shocks themselves (Rodrik 1999b)?

All of these circumstances can be thought of as instances of a failure by social factions to coordinate on outcomes that would be of mutual benefit. Healthy societies have a range of institutions that make such colossal coordination failures less likely. The rule of law, a high-quality judiciary, representative political institutions, free elections, independent trade unions, social partnerships, institutionalized representation of minority groups, and social insurance are examples of such institutions. These arrangements function as institutions of conflict management because they entail a double "commitment technology": they warn the potential "winners" of social conflict that their gains will be limited, and assure the "losers" that they will not be expropriated. They tend to increase the incentives for social groups to cooperate by reducing the payoff to socially uncooperative strategies.

HOW ARE "GOOD" INSTITUTIONS ACQUIRED?

As I argued in the preceding section, a market economy relies on a wide array of nonmarket institutions that perform regulatory, stabilizing, and legitimizing functions. Once these institutions are accepted as part and parcel of a market-based economy, traditional dichotomies between market and state or laissez-faire and intervention begin to make less sense. These alternatives are not competing ways of organizing a society's economic affairs; they are complementary elements that render the system sustainable. Every well-functioning market economy is a mix of state and market, laissez-faire and intervention.

Accepting Institutional Diversity

A second major implication of the discussion is that the institutional basis for a market economy is not uniquely determined. Formally, there is no single mapping between the market and the set of nonmarket institutions required to sustain it. This finds reflection in the wide variety of regulatory, stabilizing, and legitimizing institutions that we observe in today's advanced industrial societies. The American style of capitalism is very different from the Japanese style of capitalism. Both differ from the European style. And even within Europe, there are large differences between the institutional arrangements in, say, Sweden and Germany. Few would disagree about the existence of such differences. Yet much of institutional reform in developing countries is predicated on the assumption that there is a single set of institutions worth emulating.

The view that one set of institutional arrangements necessarily outperforms others is a common journalistic error. Hence the fads of each decade: with its low unemployment, high growth, and thriving culture, Europe was the continent to emulate throughout much of the 1970s; during the trade-conscious 1980s, Japan became the exemplar of choice; and the 1990s were the decade of U.S.-style freewheeling capitalism. It is anybody's guess which countries will capture the imagination next. Back to Sweden perhaps?

The point about institutional diversity has in fact a more fundamental implication. The institutional arrangements that we observe in operation today, varied as they are, themselves constitute a *subset* of the full range of potential institutional possibilities. This point has been forcefully and usefully argued by Roberto Unger (1998). There is no reason to suppose that modern societies have already managed to exhaust all the useful institutional variations that could underpin healthy and vibrant economies. Even if we accept that market-based economies require certain types of institutions, as listed in the previous section,

> such imperatives do not select from a closed list of institutional possibilities. The possibilities do not come in the form of indivisible systems, standing or falling together. There are always alternative sets of arrangements capable of meeting the same practical tests. (Unger 1998, 24–25)

We need to maintain a healthy skepticism toward the idea that a specific type of institution—a particular mode of corporate governance, social security system, or labor market legislation, for example—is the only type that is compatible with a well-functioning market economy.

Two Modes of Acquiring Institutions

How does a developing society acquire functional institutions—functional in the sense of supporting a healthy, sustainable market-based system? An analogy with *technology transfer* is helpful. Think of the acquisition or building of institutions as the adoption of a new technology that allows society to transform its primary endowments (land, raw labor, natural resources) into a larger bundle of outputs. Let us call this new technology a "market economy," where we understand that the term encompasses all of the nonmarket institutional complements discussed previously. Adoption of a market economy in this broad sense makes higher production possible, and in that sense is equivalent to technical progress, in economists' parlance.

But what kind of a technology is a market economy? To oversimplify, consider two possibilities. One possibility is that the new technology is a general purpose one, that it is codified, and that it is readily available on world markets. In this case, it can be adopted by simply importing a *blueprint* from the more advanced economies. The transition to a market economy, in this vision, consists of getting a manual with the title *How to Build a Market Economy* (a.k.a. the "Washington Consensus") and following the directions: remove price distortions, privatize enterprises, harden budget constraints, enact legal codes, and so on.

A different possibility is that the requisite technology is highly specific to local conditions and that it contains a high degree of tacitness. Specificity implies that the institutional repertoire available in the advanced countries may be inappropriate to the needs of the society in question—just as different relative factor prices in LDC agriculture require more appropriate techniques than those available in the rich countries. Tacitness implies that much of the knowledge that is required is in fact not written down, leaving the blueprints highly incomplete.[5] For both sets of reasons,

---

[5] An example from South Korea's history with technology acquisition nicely illustrates the tacitness of technology. The Korean shipbuilder Hyundai started out by importing its basic design from a Scottish firm. But it soon found out that this design was not working out. It relied on building the ship in two halves, because the original manufacturer had enough capacity to build only half a ship at a time. When Hyundai followed the same course, it could not get the two halves to fit. Subsequent designs imported from European consulting firms also had problems in that the firms would not guarantee the rated capacity, leading to costly delays. In the end, Hyundai was forced to rely on in-house design engineers. This case is discussed in Amsden 1989, 278–89.

imported blueprints are useless. Institutions need to be developed locally, relying on hands-on experience, local knowledge, and experimentation.

The two scenarios are of course only caricatures. Neither the *blueprint* nor the *local-knowledge* perspective captures the whole story on its own. Even under the best possible circumstances, an imported blueprint requires domestic expertise for successful implementation. Alternatively, when local conditions differ greatly, it would be unwise to deny the possible relevance of institutional examples from elsewhere. But the dichotomy— whether one emphasizes the blueprint or the local knowledge—clarifies some key issues in institution building and sheds light on important debates about institutional development. Consider the debate on Chinese gradualism.

One perspective, represented forcefully by Sachs and Woo (2000), underplays Chinese particularism by arguing that the successes of the economy are not due to any special aspects of the Chinese transition to a market economy, but instead are largely due to a convergence of Chinese institutions to those in nonsocialist economies. In this view, the faster the convergence, the better the outcomes. "[F]avorable outcomes have emerged not because of gradualism, but despite gradualism" (Sachs and Woo 1997, 3). The policy message that follows is that China should focus not on institutional experimentation but on harmonizing its institutions with those abroad. (To be fair to these authors, the harmonization that Sachs and Woo (1997) foresee seems to be with the institutions in the rest of East Asia, not those of the United States or western Europe.)

The alternative perspective, perhaps best developed in work by Qian and Roland, is that the peculiarities of the Chinese model represent solutions to particular political or informational problems for which no blueprint-style solution exists. Hence, Lau, Qian, and Roland (1997) interpret the dual-track approach to liberalization as a way of implementing Pareto-efficient reforms: an alteration in the planned economy that improves incentives at the margin, enhances efficiency in resource allocation, and yet leaves none of the plan beneficiaries worse off. Qian, Roland, and Xu (1999) interpret Chinese-style decentralization as allowing the development of superior institutions of coordination: when economic activity requires products with matched attributes,[6] local experimentation is a more effective way of processing and using local knowledge.

Sachs, Woo, and other members of the convergence school worry about the costs of Chinese-style experimentalism because they seem to say, "Well, we already know what a market economy looks like: it is one with private property and a unified system of prices—just get on with it." Qian

---

[6] Think again of the problem of fitting the two halves of a ship described in the preceding note.

et al., on the other hand, think the system generates the right incentives for developing the tacit knowledge required to build and sustain a market economy, and therefore are unbothered by some of the economic inefficiencies generated along the way. These two contrasting visions of the transition to a market economy have pervaded our discussions of policy and have shaped our preference for gradualism and experimentalism or for shock therapy.

Although my sympathies in this debate are with the experimentalists, I can also see dangers with experimentalism. First, one needs to distinguish self-conscious experimentalism from delay and gradualism designed to serve privileged interests. The dithering, two-steps-forward, one-step-backward style that prevails in much of the former Soviet Union and sub-Saharan Africa is driven not so much by a desire to build better institutions as by aversion to reform. This has to be distinguished from a programmatic effort to acquire and process local knowledge to better serve local needs. The gradualism that countries like Mauritius[7] or South Korea[8] have exhibited over their recent history is very different from the "gradualism" of Nigeria or of Ukraine in the 1990s.

Second, it is obviously costly—in terms of time and resources—to build institutions from scratch when imported blueprints can serve just as well. Costs in this context have to be evaluated carefully, since forgoing experimentalism can have opportunity costs as well, insofar as it forecloses certain paths of *future* institutional development. Nonetheless, experimentalism can backfire if it overlooks opportunities for institutional arbitrage. Much of the legislation establishing a SEC-like watchdog agency for securities markets, for example, can be borrowed wholesale from those countries that have already learned how to regulate these markets the hard way—by their own trial and error. The same goes perhaps for an antitrust agency, a financial supervisory agency, a central bank, and many other governmental functions.[9] One can always learn from the institutional arrangements prevailing elsewhere, even if they are inappropriate or cannot be transplanted. Some societies can go further by adopting institutions that cut deeper—in social insurance, labor markets, fiscal institutions. Perhaps one reason that

[7] See Wellisz and Saw 1993; Rodrik 1999a, chap. 3; and the discussion in the next subsection on two-track reforms in Mauritius.

[8] South Korea is often portrayed as a case where autonomous and insulated technocrats took a series of decisions without local input. Evans (1995) has usefully emphasized the "embedded" nature of bureaucratic autonomy in Korea, in particular the dense network of interactions between the bureaucracy and segments of the private sector that allowed for the exchange of information, the negotiation and renegotiation of policies, and the setting of priorities.

[9] But even in the financial arena, molding regulatory institutions to local realities is important for effective governance (Mishkin 2006).

a "big bang" worked for Poland is that it had already defined its future: it wanted to be a "normal" European society, with full membership in the European Union. Adopting European institutions wholesale was not only a means to an end; it was also the ultimate objective.

The difficult questions, and the trade-offs between the blueprint and the experimentalist approaches, arise when the attainable objectives are not so clear. What kind of a society do the Chinese want for themselves, and realistically hope to achieve? How about the Brazilians, Indians, or Turks? Local knowledge matters greatly in answering these questions. Blueprints, best practices, international codes and standards, harmonization can do the trick for some of the narrowly "technical" issues. But large-scale institutional development by and large requires a process of discovery about local needs and capabilities.

Participatory Politics as a Metainstitution

The blueprint approach is largely top-down, relying on expertise on the part of technocrats and foreign advisors. The local-knowledge approach, by contrast, is bottom-up and relies on mechanisms for eliciting and aggregating local information. In principle, these mechanisms can be as diverse as the institutions that they help create. But I would argue that the most reliable forms of such mechanisms are participatory political institutions. Indeed, it is helpful to think of participatory political institutions as *metainstitutions* that elicit and aggregate local knowledge and thereby help build better institutions.

It is certainly true that nondemocratic forms of government have often succeeded admirably in the task of institution building using alternative devices. The previously mentioned examples of South Korea (with its "embedded" bureaucratic autonomy) and China (with its decentralization and experimentalism) come immediately to mind. But the broad, cross-national evidence indicates that these are the exceptions rather than the rule. Nothing prevents authoritarian regimes from using local knowledge; the trouble is that nothing compels them to do so.

The case of Mauritius illustrates nicely how participatory democracy helps build better institutions that lay the foundation for sustainable economic growth. The initial conditions in Mauritius were inauspicious from a number of standpoints. The island was a monocrop economy in the early 1960s and faced a population explosion. A report prepared by James Meade in 1961 was quite pessimistic about the island's future, and argued that "unless resolute measures are taken to solve [the population problem], Mauritius will be faced with a catastrophic situation" (Meade et al. 1961, 37). Mauritius is also an ethnically and linguistically divided society, and its independence in 1968 was preceded by a series of riots between Muslims and Creoles.

Mauritius's superior economic performance has been built on a peculiar combination of orthodox and heterodox strategies. To an important extent, the economy's success was based on the creation of an export-processing zone (EPZ) operating under free-trade principles, which enabled an export boom in garments to European markets and an accompanying investment boom at home. Yet the island's economy has combined the EPZ with a domestic sector that was highly protected until the mid-1980s.[10] Mauritius has essentially followed a two-track strategy similar to that of China. This economic strategy was in turn underpinned by social and political arrangements that encouraged participation, representation, and coalition building. Rather than discouraging social organization, governments have encouraged it. In the words of Miles (1999), Mauritius is a "supercivil society," with a disproportionately large number of civil society associations per capita.

The circumstances under which the Mauritian EPZ was set up in 1970 are instructive, and highlight the manner in which participatory political systems help design creative strategies for building locally adapted institutions. Given the small size of the home market, it was evident that Mauritius would benefit from an outward-oriented strategy. But as in other developing countries, policymakers had to contend with the import-substituting industrialists who had been propped up by the restrictive commercial policies of the early 1960s prior to independence. These industrialists were naturally opposed to relaxing the trade regime.

A Washington economist would have advocated across-the-board liberalization, without regard to what that might do the precarious political and social balance of the island. Instead, the Mauritian authorities chose the two-track strategy. The EPZ scheme in fact provided a neat way around the political difficulties. The creation of the EPZ generated new opportunities of trade and of employment, without taking protection away from the import-substituting groups and from the male workers who dominated the established industries. The segmentation of labor markets early on between male and female workers—with the latter predominantly employed in the EPZ—was particularly crucial, as it prevented the expansion of the EPZ from driving wages up in the rest of the economy, thereby disadvantaging import-substituting industries. New profit opportunities were created at the margin, while leaving old opportunities undisturbed. There were no identifiable losers. This in turn paved the way for the more substantial liberalizations that took place in the mid-1980s and in the 1990s.

---

[10] Gulhati (1990, table 2.10) reports an average effective rate of protection in 1982 for manufacturing in Mauritius of 89 percent, with a range of −24 percent to 824 percent.

Mauritius found its own way to economic development because it created social and political institutions that encouraged participation, negotiation, and compromise. That it did so despite inauspicious beginings and following a path that diverged from orthodoxy speaks volumes about the importance of such institutions. A broadly parallel account of another African success story (Botswana) is provided by Acemoglu, Johnson, and Robinson (2003). These authors stress the role of participatory political institutions that restricted the ability of elites to adopt rent-extracting policies that have been all too common in Africa. The following section presents some cross-national evidence suggesting that democracy tends in fact to be a reliable mechanism for generating such desirable outcomes.

PARTICIPATORY POLITICAL REGIMES DELIVER HIGHER-QUALITY GROWTH

In policy circles, the discussion on the relationship between political regime type and economic performance inevitably gravitates toward the experience of a handful of economies in East and Southeast Asia, which (until recently at least) registered the world's highest growth rates under authoritarian regimes. These countries constitute the chief exhibit for the argument that economic development requires a strong hand from above. The deep economic reforms needed to embark on self-sustaining growth, this line of thought goes, cannot be undertaken in the messy push and pull of democratic politics. Chile under General Pinochet is usually exhibit number 2.

A systematic look at the evidence, however, yields a much more sanguine conclusion. While East Asian countries have prospered under authoritarianism, many more have seen their economies deteriorate—think of Zaire, Uganda, or Haiti. Recent empirical studies based on samples of more than 100 countries suggest that there is little reason to believe democracy is conducive to lower growth over long time spans.[11] Neither is it the case that economic reforms are typically associated with authoritarian

---

[11] Helliwell (1994) and Barro (1996) try to control for the endogeneity of democracy in estimating the effect of the latter on growth. Helliwell finds that democracy spurs education and investment, but has a negative (and insignificant) effect on growth when investment and education are controlled. On balance, he finds no "systematic net effects of democracy on subsequent economic growth." Barro finds a nonlinear relationship, with growth increasing at low levels of democracy and decreasing in democracy at higher levels. The turning point comes roughly at the levels of democracy existing in Malaysia and Mexico (in 1994), and somewhat above South Africa's level prior to its transition. A more recent paper by Chowdhurie-Aziz (1997) finds a positive association between the degree of nonelite participation in

regimes (Williamson 1994). Indeed, some of the most successful reforms of the 1980s and 1990s were implemented under newly elected democratic governments—think of the stabilizations in Bolivia (1985), Argentina (1991), and Brazil (1994), for example. Among former socialist economies, too, the most successful transitions have occurred in the most democratic countries.

In fact, the record is even more favorable to participatory regimes than is usually acknowledged. This section provides evidence in support of the following assertions:[12]

1. Democracies yield long-run growth rates that are more predictable.
2. Democracies produce greater short-term stability.
3. Democracies handle adverse shocks much better.
4. Democracies deliver better distributional outcomes.

The first of these implies that economic life is less of a crapshoot under democracy. The second suggests that, whatever the long-run growth level of an economy, there is less instability in economic outcomes under democratic regimes than under autocracies. The third finding indicates that political participation improves an economy's capacity to adjust to changes in the external environment. The final point suggests that democracies produce superior distributional outcomes.

Taken together, these results provide a clear message: participatory political regimes deliver higher-quality growth. I would contend that they do so because they produce superior institutions better suited to local conditions.

Democracy and Long-Term Performance

Figure 5.1 shows a scatter plot for a sample of 90 countries. The figure shows the *partial* relationship between a country's level of democracy and its growth rate of GDP per capita during the 1970–89 period, after initial income, education, and regional effects are controlled for. Democracy is measured on a scale of 0 to 1, using the Freedom House index of political rights and civil liberties. While the slope of the relationship is positive and statistically significant, this result is not very robust. As is clear

---

politics and economic growth. See also Tavares and Wacziarg 2001, which estimates a system of simultaneous equations and find a positive effect of democracy on growth through the channels of enhanced education, reduced inequality, and lower government consumption. The huge literature on the relationship between democracy and growth has continued to expand. For a recent analysis, see Persson and Tabellini 2006.

[12] Most of the evidence presented in this section comes from Rodrik 1997a, 1999b, and 1999c.

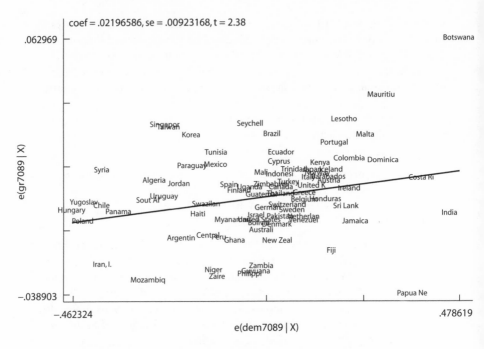

Fig. 5.1. Partial correlation between democracy and economic growth, 1970–89 (controlling for initial income, education, and regional dummies)

from the figure, removing Botswana—which is an important outlier—would make a big difference to the results. This is in line with existing results in the literature, which suggest that there is no strong, determinate relationship between political participation and average levels of long-run growth.

Looking at individual cases, it becomes quickly evident why this is so. Among high-growth countries, Taiwan, Singapore, and Korea rank low in terms of democracy (during the period covered by the regression), this being the source of the conventional wisdom among policymakers reported above. But some other countries, Botswana and Mauritius in particular, have done equally well or even better under fairly open political regimes. (Note that the rankings in this figure have to be interpreted relative to the benchmarks established by the presence of the other controls in the regression.) Poor performers can similarly be found at either end of the democracy spectrum: South Africa and Mozambique have done poorly under authoritarian regimes, Papua New Guinea and Jamaica under relatively democratic ones.

Hence *mean* long-run growth rates tend not to depend systematically on political regime type. But this is only part of the broader picture.

TABLE 5.1

Variance of Economic Performance under Different Political Regimes

	Coefficient of Variation of Long-Run Economic Growth Rates	
	Autocracies	Democracies
Unconditional	1.05	0.54
Conditional	0.70	0.48
	"Low Democracy"	"High Democracy"
Unconditional	1.02	0.61
Conditional	0.64	0.54

Note: See text for explanation.

A different question is whether democracy is the safer choice in the following sense: is the cross-national *variance* in long-run growth performance smaller under democracies than it is under autocracies? Since mean growth rates do not differ, a risk-averse individual would unambiguously prefer to live under the regime where expected long-run growth rates cluster more closely around the mean.

I first divide the country sample into two roughly equal-sized groups. I call those with values of the democracy index less than 0.5 "autocracies" ($n = 48$), and those with values greater or equal to 0.5 "democracies" ($n = 45$). The top panel in table 5.1 shows the coefficients of variation of long-run growth rates, computed across countries for the 1960–89 period, for the two samples. The first row shows the unconditional coefficients of variation, without any controls for determinants of growth rates. The second row displays the conditional version of the same, where the variation now refers to the unexplained component from a cross-national regression (separate for each sample) with the following control variables: initial GDP per capita, initial secondary school enrollment ratio, and regional dummies for Latin America, East Asia, and sub-Saharan Africa. I find that the coefficient of variation (whether conditional or unconditional) is substantially higher for autocracies than it is for democracies.

Since countries with authoritarian regimes tend to have lower incomes, perhaps this result reflects the greater randomness in the long-run growth rates of poor countries. To check against this possibility, I divided countries differently. First, I regressed the democracy index on income and secondary enrollment levels across countries ($R^2 = 0.57$). Then I regrouped my sample of countries according to whether their actual democracy levels stood below or above the regression line. Countries above (below) the regression line are those with greater (less) political participation than would be expected on the basis of their income and educational levels. In the bottom panel of table 5.1, these two groups are labeled "high democracy" ($n = 49$) and "low democracy" ($n = 44$) respectively. The coefficients of variation for long-term growth rates are then calculated for each group in the same way as before. Our results remain qualitatively unchanged, although the gap between the two groups shrinks somewhat: the coefficient of variation is smaller in countries with greater political participation (where "greater" now refers to the benchmark set by the cross-national regression relating participation levels to income and education).

The bottom line is that living under an authoritarian regime is a riskier gamble than living under a democracy.

Democracy and Short-Term Performance

A point similar, but not identical, to the one just discussed was anticipated by Sah (1991), who argued that decentralized political regimes (and democracies in particular) should be less prone to volatility. The rationale behind this idea is that the presence of a wider range of decision-makers results in greater diversification and hence less risk in an environment rife with imperfect information. This is a point similar to the one made above regarding the importance of local knowledge. Note that this specific argument is about short-term volatility in economic performance, and not about the dispersion in long-term growth rates that was the focus of the previous section.

To determine the relationship between regime type and volatility in short-run economic performance, I focus on three national-accounts aggregates: (a) real GDP, (b) real consumption, and (c) investment. (All data are from the Penn World Tables, Mark 5.6.) In each case, volatility is measured by calculating the standard deviation of annual growth rates of the relevant aggregate over the 1960–89 period (more accurately, by taking the standard deviation of the first differences in logs). Then each measure of volatility is regressed on a number of independent variables, including our measure of participation (democracy). The other independent variables included are log per capita GDP, log population, exposure to external risk, and dummies for Latin America, East Asia, sub-Saharan Africa, and OECD.

Table 5.2 shows the results. The estimated coefficient on the measure of democracy is negative and statistically significant in all cases. A movement from pure autocracy (democracy = 0) to pure democracy (= 1) is associated with reductions in the standard deviations of growth rates of GDP, consumption, and investment of 1.3, 2.3, and 4.4 percentage points, respectively. These effects are fairly sizable. Figure 5.2 shows a partial scatterplot that helps identify where different countries stand. Long-standing democracies such as India, Costa Rica, Malta, and Mauritius have

TABLE 5.2

Political Participation and Volatility of Economic Performance, by Dependent Variable (estimated coefficient on democracy from multiple regression)

	Standard Deviation of Growth Rate			
	Real GDP (OLS)	Consumption (OLS)	Investment (OLS)	Consumption (IV)
Democracy	−1.31*	−2.33*	−4.36**	−4.97*
	(0.60)	(1.09)	(1.61)	(2.10)
N	101	101	101	88

Note: Additional regressors (not shown): log per capita GDP, log population, a measure of exposure to external risk, dummies for Latin America, East Asia, sub-Saharan Africa, and OECD. Robust standard errors reported in parentheses. Secondary enrollment ratio used as instrument in IV estimation.

*$p < 05$. **$p < 01$.

experienced significantly less volatility than countries like Syria, Chile, or Iran, even after controlling for country size and external shocks.[13]

Moreover, as the last column of table 5.2 shows, causality seems to run directly from regime type to volatility (rather than vice versa). In this column I have used secondary enrollment ratio as an instrument for democracy (in addition to the other independent variables mentioned earlier). With democracy instrumented in this fashion, the estimated coefficient actually *doubles* in absolute value.

The evidence strongly suggests, therefore, that democracy is conducive to lower volatility in economic performance.

Democracy and Resilience in the Face of Economic Shocks

The late 1970s were a watershed for most developing economies. A succession of external shocks during this period left many of them in severe payment difficulties. In some cases, as in most of Latin America, it took almost a decade for macroeconomic balances to be restored and for growth to resume. The question I now pose is whether democratic and participatory institutions helped or hindered adjustment to these shocks of external origin.

The main thing I am interested in explaining is the extent of economic collapse following an external shock. In Rodrik 1999b I have explored how social cleavages and domestic institutions of conflict management

[13] Similar findings have also been reported in Chandra 1998; and Quinn and Woolley 1998.

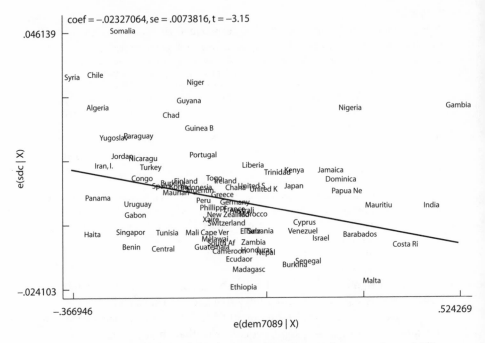

Fig. 5.2. Partial correlation between democracy and consumption volatility

mediate the effects of shocks on economic performance. Here I focus on the role of participatory institutions specifically.

In a review of the growth experience of developing countries, Pritchett (1997) looked for breaks in trend growth rates. These breaks tend to coalesce around the middle to late 1970s, with 1977 as the median break year. I use the difference in growth rates before and after the break as my dependent variable.

The basic story in Rodrik 1999b is that the adjustment to shocks will tend to be worse in countries with deep latent social conflicts and with poor institutions of conflict management. Consequently, such countries will experience larger declines in growth rates following shocks. These ideas are tested by regressing the *change* in growth on indicators of latent conflict and on proxies for institutions of conflict management (in addition to other variables).[14] Figure 5.3 displays a sample partial scatterplot, showing the relationship between ethnic cleavages and the growth decline. Controlling for other variables, there is a systematic relationship between these

[14] Each regression in this chapter includes the following variables on the right-hand side in addition to those specifically discussed: log GDP per capita in 1975, growth rate prior to break year, measure of external shocks during the 1970s, ethno-linguistic fragmentation (elf60), and regional dummies for Latin America, East Asia, and sub-Saharan Africa.

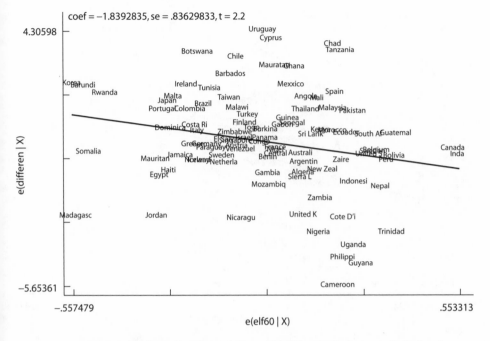

Fig. 5.3. Ethnic cleavages and growth differentials (pre- and postbreak year in trend growth)

two: countries with greater ethnic and linguistic fragmentation experienced larger declines in economic growth.[15]

Our interest in democratic institutions in this context derives from the idea that such institutions provide ways of regulating and managing social conflicts through participatory means and the rule of law, and hence dissipate the adverse consequences of external shocks. To test this hypothesis, we check to see whether our measure of democracy—this time restricted to the 1970s only, to avoid possible reverse-causality—is related to changes in growth rates subsequent to the shocks. The partial scatterplot shown in figure 5.4, covering 101 countries, suggests a clear affirmative answer. Countries with greater political freedoms during the 1970s experienced *lower* declines in economic growth when their trend growth rate changed. The relationship is highly significant in statistical terms; the

[15] A careful reader will notice that Rwanda—the scene of one of the most violent ethnic clashes in recent history—ranks at the low end of the ethnic fragmentation measure used here (elf60), which suggests that the measure in question leaves much to be desired. The reason for the ranking is that a single ethnic group constitutes the vast majority in Rwanda. I have not tried to adjust for apparent anomalies of this kind, so as not to introduce subjective biases to the analysis.

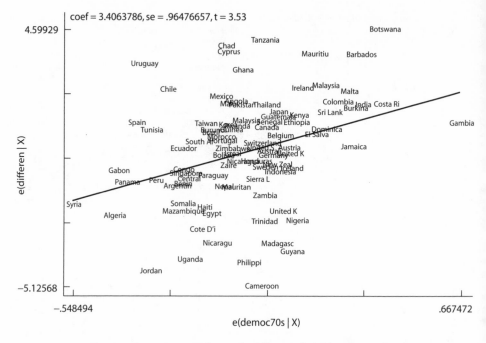

Fig. 5.4. Democracy and growth differentials (pre- and postbreak year in trend growth)

t-statistic on the estimated coefficient on democracy is 3.53, with a p-value of 0.001. Figure 5.5 shows the results when sub-Saharan African countries are excluded from the sample. They are excluded because of concern with data quality and the possibility that the relationship is driven by a few African countries with extreme values. But the relationship holds just as well in the restricted sample: the partial slope coefficient is virtually unchanged and the t-statistic is almost as high (3.32). As these two figures show, the hardest-hit countries tended to be those with few political liberties (relative to what would be expected of countries at their levels of income), such as Syria, Algeria, Panama, and Gabon. Countries with open political regimes, such as Costa Rica, Botswana, Barbados, and India, did much better.

These results are perhaps surprising in view of the common presumption that it takes strong, autonomous governments to undertake the policy adjustments required in the face of adversity. They are less surprising from the perspective articulated above: adjustment to shocks requires managing social conflicts, and democratic institutions are useful institutions of conflict management.

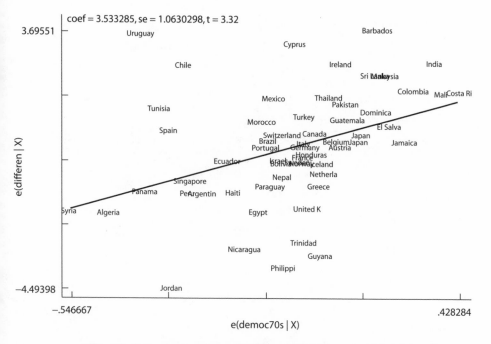

Fig. 5.5. Democracy and growth differentials (pre- and postbreak year in trend growth), excluding sub-Saharan African countries

To probe the issues more deeply, I investigate the relationship between declines in growth and three other aspects of political regime: (*a*) the degree of institutional (de jure) independence of the executive; (*b*) the degree of operational (de facto) independence of the executive; and (*c*) the degree to which nonelites can access political institutions. These three variables come originally from the Polity III data (see Jaggers and Gurr 1995), and have been recoded on a scale of 0 to 1 for the purposes of the current exercise. As before, I use the averages of the values reported for each country during the 1970s. Note that these three indicators are correlated with the Freedom House measure of democracy (which I have been using up to this point) in the expected manner: independence of the executive tends to be lower in democracies, and avenues of nonelite participation are larger. But there are interesting exceptions. The United States, for example, ranks highest not only on the democracy index, but also in the degree of *institutional* (de jure) independence of the executive. Other democracies with relatively autonomous executives (de jure) are France, Canada, and Costa Rica. By contrast, South Africa is coded as having had (during the 1970s) little democracy *and* little executive autonomy.

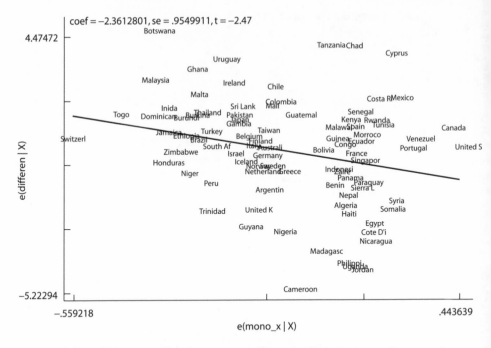

Fig. 5.6. Institutional (de jure) independence of the executive and growth differentials (pre- and postbreak year in trend growth)

A nagging question in the literature on political economy is whether an insulated and autonomous executive is necessary for the implementation of economic reforms.[16] This question is somewhat distinct from the question about democracy proper, since, as the examples just mentioned illustrate, one can conceive of democratic systems that nonetheless have well-insulated executives. Therefore the Polity indicators are particularly relevant.

The results shown in figures 5.6–5.8 are again somewhat surprising—at least when approached from the technocratic perspective. I find that more significant growth declines are associated with *greater* institutional and operational independence of the executive and *lower* levels of political access by nonelites.[17] The estimated coefficients are statistically highly significant in all cases. Therefore, not only do we not find that executive autonomy results in better economic management, the

[16] This literature is briefly surveyed and evaluated in Rodrik 1996a.

[17] Moreover, the estimated signs on these variables remain unchanged if the Freedom House index of democracy is entered separately in the regression.

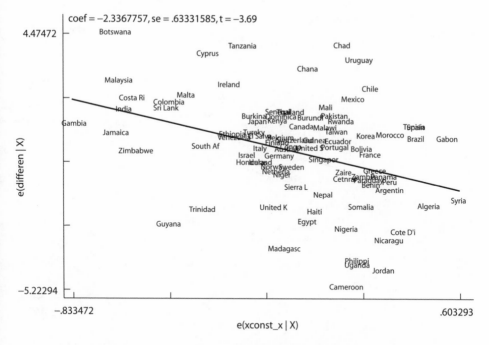

Fig. 5.7. Operational (de facto) independence of the executive and growth differentials (pre- and postbreak year in trend growth)

results strongly suggest the converse: political regimes with lower executive autonomy and more participatory institutions handle exogenous shocks better![18] This might be part of the explanation for why democracies experience less economic instability over the long run (as demonstrated in the previous subsection).

It is worth mentioning in passing that the recent experience in East Asia strongly validates these results. South Korea and Thailand, with more open and participatory political regimes, handled the Asian financial crisis significantly better than Indonesia. I have argued in Rodrik 1999a that democracy helped the first two countries manage the crisis for at least three reasons. First, it facilitated a smooth transfer of power from a discredited set of politicians to a new group of government leaders. Second, democracy imposed mechanisms of participation, consultation, and bargaining, enabling policymakers to fashion the consensus needed to undertake the necessary policy adjustments decisively. Third, because democracy

---

[18] The finding on political participation echoes the argument in Isham, Kaufmann, and Pritchett 1997 that more citizen voice results in projects with greater economic returns.

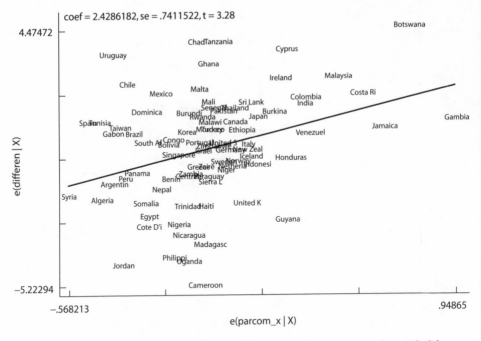

Fig. 5.8. Ability of nonelites to access political institutions and growth differentials (pre- and postbreak year in trend growth)

provides for institutionalized mechanisms of "voice," the Korean and Thai institutions obviated the need for riots, protests, and other kinds of disruptive actions by affected groups, as well as lowering the support for such behavior by other groups in society.

Democracy and Distribution

Finally, I turn to distributional issues. I have shown in Rodrik 1999c that democracy makes an important difference to the distribution of the enterprise surplus in the manufacturing sectors of national economies. In particular, there is a robust and statistically significant association between the extent of political participation and wages received by workers, controlling for labor productivity, income levels, and other possible determinants. The association exists both across countries and over time *within* countries (i.e., in panel regressions with fixed effects as well as in cross-section regressions). Countries with greater political participation than would have been predicted from their income levels, such as India, Israel, Malta, and Cyprus, also have correspondingly higher wages relative

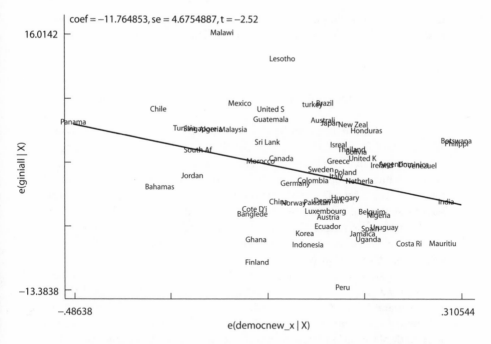

Fig. 5.9. Partial association between democracy and economy-wide inequality (Gini coefficient), 1985–89

to productivity. Some countries at the other end of the spectrum—lower-than-expected values for the democracy index and low wages—are Syria, Saudi Arabia, Turkey, and Mexico. Moving from Mexico's level of democracy to that of the United States is associated with an increase in wages of about 30 percent. Instrumental-variables and event-study evidence suggests strongly that the relationship is causal; that is, changes in political regime *cause* a redistribution of the enterprise surplus toward workers.

Figure 5.9 shows a different type of evidence relating to *economy-wide inequality.* One problem with the evidence on the functional distribution of income within manufacturing (discussed above) is that a prolabor distribution in manufacturing can go hand in hand with a more regressive distribution overall. This would be the case, for example, where prolabor policies create a "labor aristocracy" to the detriment of the informal and rural sector worker. Figure 5.9 is quite comforting on that score. It shows that the relationship between democracy and economy-wide inequality (measured by the Gini coefficent from the high-quality Deininger-Squire data set) is in fact negative. More participatory regimes produce greater equality not only within the modern (manufacturing) sector, but throughout the economy. And they do so—as the previous evidence indicates—without cost to economic growth and while producing greater stability and resilience overall.

CONCLUDING REMARKS

Institutional reform has become the buzzword of the day. Policy advisors and international financial institutions (IFIs) find it tempting to extend their advice and conditionality to a broad range of institutional areas, including monetary and fiscal institutions, corporate governance, financial and asset market supervision, labor-market practices, business-government relations, corruption, transparency, and social safety nets. While such efforts have the basic diagnosis right—the development of a market-based economy requires a heavy dose of institution building—they suffer from two weaknesses.

First, it is not clear whether the IFIs can overcome their bias toward a particular, "neoliberal" social-economic model—a model that is approximated, if not fully replicated, in the real world by the United States. It is telling that when South Korea came under IMF conditionality in the aftermath of the Asian financial crisis, the IMF asked the country to undertake an ambitious range of reforms in trade and capital accounts, government-business relations, and labor-market institutions that entailed remolding the Korean economy in the image of a Washington economist's idea of a free-market economy. This model is not only untested, it forecloses some development strategies that have worked in the past, and others that could work in the future. If Korea, a country with an exemplary development record, is subject to pressures of this kind, one can imagine what is in store for small countries with more checkered economic histories. As I have argued in this chapter, an approach that presumes the superiority of a particular model of a capitalist economy is quite restrictive in terms of the range of institutional variation that market economies can (and do) admit.

Second, even if the IFIs could shed their preference for the neoliberal model, there would remain an organizational bias toward providing similar, even if not identical, advice to client governments. It would be difficult for institutions like the World Bank and the IMF to adopt a "let a hundred flowers bloom" strategy, as it would appear that some countries are being treated more or less favorably. The result is likely to be at best unfriendly to institutional experimentation on the part of client governments.

To be sure, some institutional convergence can be useful and proper. No one can seriously oppose the introduction of proper accounting standards or improved prudential supervision of financial intermediaries. The more serious concern with regard to IFI conditionality is that such standards will act as the wedge with which a broader set of institutional preferences—friendly to open capital accounts, deregulated labor markets, arm's-length finance, and American-style corporate governance, and hostile to industrial policies—will be imposed on the recipient countries.

My focus on the importance of local knowledge, and on participatory democracy as a metainstitution for eliciting and aggregating it, suggests that conditionality is perhaps better targeted at basic political freedoms. I have shown in this chapter that democracies perform better on a number of dimensions: they produce less randomness and volatility, they are better at managing shocks, and they yield distributional outcomes that are more desirable. One interpretation of these results, and the one that I have emphasized throughout, is that democracy helps build better institutions. While I am a great believer in institutional diversity, I see no argument that would make it appropriate for some governments to deny their citizens basic political rights such as freedom of speech, the right to vote and stand for political office, or freedom of association.

6

Getting Institutions Right

THERE is now widespread agreement among economists study-ing economic growth that institutional quality holds the key to prevailing patterns of prosperity around the world. Rich countries are those where investors feel secure about their property rights, the rule of law prevails, private incentives are aligned with social objectives, monetary and fiscal policies are grounded in solid macroeconomic institutions, idiosyncratic risks are appropriately mediated through social insurance, and citizens have civil liberties and political representation. Poor countries are those where these arrangements are absent or ill-formed. Of course, high-quality institutions are perhaps as much a result of economic prosperity as they are its cause. But however important the reverse arrow of causality may be, a growing body of empirical research has shown that institutions exert a very strong determining effect on aggregate incomes.[1] Institutions are *causal* in the sense that a poor country that is able to revise the rules of the game in the direction of strengthening the property rights of entrepreneurs and investors is likely to experience a lasting increase in its productive capacity.

Much less well understood are the implications of this line of rea-soning. Indeed, the empirical finding that "institutions rule" has sometimes been interpreted as a form of property-rights reductionism—one that views the formal institutions of property rights protection as the end-all of development policy. In the academic literature, this has led to a tendency to oversimplify the issues at stake—for example by treating institutional development in a monocausal manner (i.e., linking it exclusively to colonial history) or by identifying "institutions" solely with the formal, legislated rules in existence. In the policy field, the new focus on institutions has led to an overly ambitious agenda of "governance" reforms aimed at reducing corruption, improving the regulatory apparatus, rendering monetary and fiscal institutions independent, strengthening corporate governance, en-hancing the functioning of the judiciary, and so on. Sometimes called

[1] See in particular Hall and Jones 1999; Acemoglu, Johnson, and Robinson 2001; Easterly and Levine 2003; and Rodrik, Subramanian, and Trebbi 2004. Glaeser et al. (2004) provide a dissenting perspective.

"second-generation reforms," these new reforms are meant to overcome the apparent inefficacy of the earlier wave of reforms relying heavily on liberalization, stabilization, and privatization. Simple policy changes are ineffective, the argument now goes, unless they are grounded strongly in institutional reforms.

In this chapter, I elaborate on these and some other issues. My own perspective is that the empirical literature on institutions and growth has pointed us in the right direction, but that one needs to be very careful in interpreting its central message appropriately. Many of the policy implications drawn from this literature are at best irrelevant and at worst misleading.

AN INSTRUMENT DOES NOT A THEORY MAKE

The empirical work on what one may call "macroinstitutions" received a big boost with Acemoglu, Johnson, and Robinson's (2001; AJR) important paper called "The Colonial Origins of Comparative Development." This mistitled (see below) paper came up with an ingenious solution to a dilemma that had long stymied serious empirical work in this arena.

The difficulty with the empirical analysis of institutional development has been that institutional quality is as endogenous to income levels as anything can possibly be. Our ability to disentangle the web of causality between prosperity and institutions is seriously limited. AJR proposed using colonial history to achieve econometric identification. Parts of the world that confronted would-be colonizers with greater health hazards, they argued, were less likely to be permanently settled by Europeans, who as a consequence were less likely to build institutions protecting property rights, limiting their efforts to pure extraction. Settler mortality rates three centuries ago could help identify which countries acquired good institutions and which did not, and plausibly help account for which countries grew rich and which remained poor. This encounter of ecology with history could be used to test for the causal impact of institutional quality on levels of development. Moreover, the fact that natives had immunity to the diseases to which settlers succumbed helped support the point that settler mortality (the instrumental variable) was not necessarily a stand-in for the local health environment. Using this strategy, AJR were able to show that a substantial part of the variation in today's income levels among former colonies can be explained by differences in investors' perceptions with regard to the likelihood of expropriation.

What AJR seemed to suggest with their title was that they had identified differing encounters with colonialism as the root of the variance in income levels around the world. But this is a problematic interpretation.

The variation in average income levels among countries that have never been colonized is almost as large as that in the colonized sample (Rodrik, Subramanian, and Trebbi 2004, RST). If the roots of underdevelopment lie in contrasting encounters with colonizers, how can we explain the fact that countries that have never been colonized by Europeans are among both the poorest and richest of today's economies? Consider for example countries such as Ethiopia and Afghanistan at one end of the spectrum and Japan at the other end, with middle-income countries such as Turkey and Thailand lying somewhere in between.

The correct interpretation of AJR, in my view, is that colonial experience—as captured by the settler mortality variable—simply provides a convenient "instrumental variable," without in itself holding much explanatory power for patterns of global inequality. Finding an appropriate econometric instrument is not the same as providing an adequate explanation—a distinction that is somewhat blurred in AJR. One should therefore not read too much into AJR with regard to the role played by colonialism in shaping today's contours of wealth and poverty.

GEOGRAPHY-BASED INSTRUMENTAL VARIABLES DO NOT IMPLY GEOGRAPHY-BASED EXPLANATIONS

Settler mortality was obviously a function of ecological conditions, and this raises the question of whether AJR unwittingly gave a starring role to geography. Indeed, since few things other than geography are exogenous in economics, most instruments for institutional quality are likely to have a significant geographical component (resource endowments, latitude, and so on). Indeed, there is a long and distinguished list of scholars who have pointed to the importance of geography. Jeffrey Sachs has forcefully argued that geography exerts a strong independent effect through its impact on the public health environment and on transport costs (Sachs 2003; Gallup, Sachs, and Mellinger 1998). Jared Diamond (1997) has shown how apparently innocuous accidents of geography (such as the alignment of continents) can have long-lasting effects on patterns of technological development and diffusion. So can these studies still effectively parse out the respective roles of geography and institutions in determining income levels?

The answer is yes. To see how this can be possible, consider a different, but analogous, exercise. Suppose we were interested in explaining differences in income levels among German *Länder* lying on both sides of the Berlin Wall prior to 1989. Suppose also that our hypothesis was that these differences were due primarily to differences in the degree of protection of private property rights. Cognizant of reverse causality, we might want to look for an instrumental variable—something that is correlated with institutions, but is not a determinant of income levels through another channel. Longitude provides such a variable, because *Länder* in the eastern part of the country were much more likely to fall under Soviet occupation and acquire Communist institutions. We might then use longitude as an instrument for the system of property rights and rightly conclude that the protection of private property rights is a superior means for generating wealth. The correct inference here would not be that geography (longitude) is the cause of income differences: geography, in interaction with history, simply provides a convenient source of exogenous variation to identify the role played by *institutions*.

Of course, geographic variables have to be given a fair chance to compete against institutions as ultimate explanators of income differences. In RST, we tried a large number of geographic variables and found their direct impact on income to be either insignificant or nonrobust. That led us to conclude that "institutions rule." Similar results were also reported in AJR and Easterly and Levine (2003). However, there are other studies that find a role for geographical determinants such as malaria ecology (Sachs 2003) or climate, latitude, and East-West orientation (Hibbs and Olsson 2004) even after controlling for institutional quality. It would be fair to say that scholarly opinion remains divided on the significance of geography as a direct determinant of income levels.

But the Centrality of Institutions Does Not Preclude an Important Indirect Role for Geography

At the same time, there is wider agreement on the *indirect* role played by geography. In particular, when one endogenizes institutional formation, one often finds geographical determinants to be an important part of the story. For example, Engerman and Sokoloff (1994) have linked the contrasting patterns of institutional development in North and South America to the differences in resource endowments: large-scale plantation agriculture is much more conducive, compared to smallholding, to inequality and autocratic institutions that repress nonelites. Sala-i-Martin and Subramanian (2003) have provided systematic evidence that shows abundance of natural resources and rents to be damaging to the quality of institutions. RST find that distance from equator is a significant (positive) contributor to institutional quality. This line of work suggests that even if geography and endowments do not exert an important independent impact on incomes, contra Sachs (2003), they may have a significant indirect impact *through* institutions.

The challenge for the empirical literature on institutions is to explore these patterns without falling into the trap of reductionism or of historical and geographical determinism. As I discussed in the preceding chapter, the process through which countries acquire "good" institutions is typically quite idiosyncratic and context-specific. Luck plays an important role, as does human agency.

INSTITUTIONAL QUALITY, AS IT IS TYPICALLY
MEASURED, REMAINS A NEBULOUS CONCEPT

The manner in which institutional quality is measured in the empirical literature discussed above leaves a lot of questions unanswered. The most commonly used indices of institutional quality are based on surveys of foreign and domestic investors, in which the respondents in a particular country are asked whether they consider their investments safe or how they rate the "rule of law" (see, for example, Kaufmann, Kraay, and Zoido-Lobatón 2002). So these indices capture investors' perceptions, rather than any of the formal aspects of the institutional setting. They measure how well the rules of the game with regard to property rights are perceived to operate, and not what those rules are. This in turn raises two difficulties, one more serious than the other.

The first difficulty is that these perceptions are likely to be shaped not just by the actual operation of the institutional environment, but also by many other aspects of the economic environment. Most importantly, investors are likely to rate institutional quality high when the economy is doing well, regardless of whether causality goes one way or another. But this is just another instance of endogeneity and reverse causation. If the researcher has a valid instrumentation strategy, it ought to take care of this problem too. So the fact that our measure of institutional quality is perception-based does not invalidate inferences drawn from its use (subject to the caveat below) as long as proper care is taken in econometric identification.

The more serious issue is that, even if causality is properly established, the results do not tell us what specific rules, legislation, or institutional design is actually responsible for the institutional outcome being measured. All that we can infer is that performance is superior when investors feel their property rights are protected (or the rule of law is upheld). The results are silent on what it is that makes investors feel that way.

To appreciate the significance of this, compare Russia and China. In Russia, an investor has in principle the full protection of a regime of private property rights enforced by an independent judiciary. In China, there is no such protection, since private property has not been (until very recently) legally recognized and the court system is certainly not independent. Yet during the middle to late 1990s, investors consistently gave China higher marks on the rule of law than they did Russia. They evidently felt better protected in China than they did in Russia. This is no surprise to anyone who has observed the evolution of the Russian legal system over the last decade. But the important point from the current perspective is the apparent disconnect between the perception of the rules and the actual rules.

Consequently, the empirical finding that effective property rights are critical yields very little operational guidance as to how they are established. As the Russia-China comparison nicely illustrates, it does not even imply that a legal system based on *private* property rights dominates one where property rights are held collectively! What matters is that investors feel safe, regardless of how that safety is achieved. The empirical literature does not tell us how that safety is attained, only that it matters a lot.

INSTITUTIONAL FUNCTIONS DO NOT MAP
INTO UNIQUE INSTITUTIONAL FORMS

So how is it that Chinese investors could feel more secure than Russian investors despite the absence of private property rights legislation in China? We do not know, but here is a plausible story.

To be effective, a formal legal regime protecting investors' rights requires a noncorrupt, independent judiciary with enforcement power. Let us posit, without doing great injustice to reality, that setting up such a judiciary is hard at low levels of income and takes time. So enhancing property rights by simply rewriting domestic legislation—changing the formal aspects of the institutional environment—is naturally of uncertain efficacy. That seems to have been the trap in which the Russian transition was caught up for some time.

How did China evade this trap? The largest boom in "private" investment in China took place (at least until the mid-1990s) in township and village enterprises (TVEs). These were firms in which ownership was typically held by local governments. Private entrepreneurs were effectively partners with the government. In a system where courts cannot be relied upon to protect property rights, letting the government hold residual rights in the enterprise may have been a second-best mechanism for avoiding expropriation. In such circumstances, the expectation of future profits can exert a stronger discipline on the public authority than fear of legal sanction by an independent third party. Private entrepreneurs felt secure not because the government was prevented from expropriating them, but because, sharing in the profits, it had no desire to expropriate them.

This is a specific illustration of a broader point, namely that there is no unique, non-context-specific way of achieving desirable institutional outcomes. China was able to provide a semblance of effective property rights *despite* the absence of private property rights. The Russian experience strongly suggests that the obvious alternative of legal reform would not have been nearly as effective. We can multiply the examples. As I have already discussed, China provided market incentives through two-track reform rather than across-the-board liberalization, which would have been the standard advice. Hence, in agriculture and industry, price efficiency was achieved not by abolishing quotas and planned allocations, but by allowing producers to trade at market prices *at the margin.* In international trade, openness was achieved not by reducing import protection, but by creating special economic zones with different rules than those that applied for domestic production.

The important point is that effective institutional outcomes do not map into unique institutional designs. And since there is no unique mapping from function to form, it is futile to look for uncontingent empirical regularities that link specific legal rules to economic outcomes. What works will depend on local constraints and opportunities. The best that we can do as analysts is to come up with contingent correlations—institutional prescriptions that are contingent on the prevailing characteristics of the local economy. At the moment we are very far from being able to do this for any but a few institutional areas.[2]

In the Short Run, Large-Scale Institutional Reform Is Rarely Necessary to Accelerate Growth

The bad news, as the foregoing discussion indicates, is that the literature on the institutional determinants of economic prosperity has yet to yield solid policy prescriptions. The good news is that everything that we know about economic growth suggests large-scale institutional transformation is hardly ever a *prerequisite* for getting growth going. It is true that sustained economic convergence eventually requires acquiring high-quality institutions (of the type discussed in the preceding chapter). That is the whole point of the empirical literature I have discussed above. But the initial spurt in growth can be achieved with minimal changes in institutional arrangements. In other words, we need to distinguish between

---

[2] One example where a fair amount of work has been done relates to the choice of an exchange-rate regime. The literature on the optimum currency area can be interpreted as the search for prescriptions that are sensitive to the structural characteristics of an economy.

stimulating economic growth and *sustaining* it. Solid institutions are much more important for the latter than for the former. Once growth is set into motion, it becomes easier to maintain a virtuous cycle, with high growth and institutional transformation feeding on each other.

Ricardo Hausmann, Lant Pritchett, and I recently examined growth accelerations in the period since about 1950 (Hausmann et al. 2005). We identified more than 80 such episodes, in which a country increased its growth rate by two percentage points or more for a period of at least seven years. The surprise was not only that there were so many cases of growth accelerations,[3] but that the vast majority of them seemed unrelated to major economic reforms of the conventional type—that is, economic liberalization and opening up. To the extent that we can identify triggers for growth, they seem to be related to the relaxation of specific constraints that were holding back private economic activity.

Even in the better-known cases, institutional changes at the outset of growth accelerations have been typically modest. I have already mentioned some of the gradual, experimental steps toward liberalization that China undertook in the late 1970s without recourse to systemwide transformation. South Korea's experience in the early 1960s was similar. The military government led by Park Chung Hee that took power in 1961 moved in a trial-and-error fashion, experimenting at first with various public investment projects. The hallmark reforms associated with the Korean miracle, the devaluation of the currency and the rise in interest rates, came in 1964 and fell far short of full liberalization of currency and financial markets. As these instances illustrate, an attitudinal change on the part of the top political leadership toward a more market-oriented, private-sector-friendly policy framework often plays as large a role as the scope of policy reform itself. Such an attitudinal change appears to have had a particularly important effect in one of the important growth miracles of the last quarter century—India since the early 1980s (Rodrik and Subramanian 2005).

This is good news because it suggests countries do not need an extensive set of institutional reforms in order to start growing. Instigating growth is a lot easier in practice than the standard Washington recipe, with its long list of institutional and governance reforms, would lead us to believe. This should not be surprising from the standpoint of growth theory. When a country is so far below its potential steady-state level of income, even moderate movements in the right direction can produce a big growth payoff. This is encouraging to policymakers, who are often

---

[3] Our filter almost certainly understates the true number of growth accelerations. We excluded very small countries, countries with less than two decades of data, cases where the pickup of growth represented a recovery from a crisis, and instances where growth stood at below 3.5 percent per annum even after the acceleration.

overwhelmed and paralyzed by the apparent need to undertake ambitious reforms on a wide and ever-expanding front.

The trick is to be able to identify the binding constraint on economic growth at the relevant moment in time—to undertake what I have called "growth diagnostics." In the South Korea of 1961, the major constraint probably was the large gap between the social and private return to investment. In the China of 1978, the constraint was obviously the absence of market-oriented incentives. In the India of 1980, it was a government that was perceived to be too hostile to the private sector. In the Chile of 1983, it was an overvalued exchange rate. Of course, it is much easier to determine these things ex post than it is to do it ex ante. But as we saw in chapter 2, it is not impossible.

PART C

Globalization

7

Governance of Economic Globalization

THE MIXED economy stands as the crowning economic achievement of the twentieth century. If it was the nineteenth century that unleashed capitalism in its full force, it was the twentieth century that tamed it and boosted its productivity by supplying the institutional underpinnings of market-based economies. Central banks to regulate credit and the supply of liquidity, fiscal policies to stabilize aggregate demand, antitrust and regulatory authorities to combat fraud and anticompetitive behavior, social insurance to reduce lifetime risk, political democracy to make the above institutions accountable to the citizenry—these were all innovations that firmly took root in today's rich countries only during the second half of the twentieth century. That the second half of the century was also a period of unprecedented prosperity for western Europe, the United States, Japan, and some other parts of East Asia is no coincidence. These institutional innovations greatly enhanced the efficiency and legitimacy of markets, and in turn drew strength from the material advancement unleashed by market forces.

Globalization[1]—by which I mean enhanced trade and financial integration—poses both opportunities and challenges to the mixed economy. On the plus side, the global expansion of markets promises greater prosperity through the channels of division of labor and specialization according to comparative advantage. This opportunity is of particular significance to developing countries, since it allows them access to state-of-the-art technology and cheap capital goods on world markets.

But globalization also undercuts the ability of nation-states to erect regulatory and redistributive institutions, and does so at the same time that it increases the premium on solid national institutions. Social safety nets become more difficult to finance just as the need for social insurance becomes greater; financial intermediaries increase their ability to evade national regulation just as prudential supervision becomes more

[1] See Keohane and Nye 1999 for a discussion of various aspects of globalization, as well as useful conceptual distinctions between some relevant terms: globalization, globalism, interdependence, sensitivity, connectivity, and vulnerability.

important; macroeconomic management becomes trickier just as the costs of policy mistakes are amplified. Once again, the stakes are greater for the developing countries, since they have weak institutions to begin with. The dilemma that we face in the early years of the twenty-first century is that markets are striving to become global while the institutions needed to support them remain by and large national. I will argue in this chapter that the implications of this discrepancy are twofold. On the one hand, the existence of jurisdictional boundaries, drawn largely along national lines, restricts economic integration. This inhibits efficiency. On the other hand, the desire by producers and investors to go global weakens the institutional base of national economies. This inhibits equity and legitimacy.

Taken together, the two processes drive us toward a no-man's world. Exporters, multinationals, and financiers complain about impediments to trade and capital flows. Labor advocates, environmentalists, and consumer safety activists decry the downward pressures on national standards and legislation. Broad sections of the populace treat globalization as a dirty word while happily devouring its fruits. And government officials vacillate, trying to please each group in turn while satisfying none.

In the long run, the way out of the dilemma is to envisage a world in which politics is as global as economics. This would be a world of global federalism, with the mixed economy reconstructed at the global level. In the short run, the continued existence of nation-states forces us toward more realistic and practical arrangements. I will argue that a sound intermediate architecture has to combine international harmonization and standard setting with generalized exit schemes, opt-outs, and escape clauses. This design allows most of the efficiency gains from integration to be reaped while still leaving room for a range of divergent national practices. This kind of architecture would reconstitute the "compromise of embedded liberalism"[2] for the realities of the early twenty-first-century economy.

How Global is the Global Economy?

A common view of today's world economy is that of a global marketplace in which goods, services, and assets flow across national boundaries without friction. This is the picture that one finds, for example, in the popular accounts of Greider (1997) and Friedman (1999)—two works that are divergent in all other respects. Both authors write about a seamless world market in which nation-states have been stripped of virtually all powers, while drawing very different conclusions about the desirability of this state of things.

---

[2] The term is due to John Ruggie. See below.

How global is the global economy in reality? The natural benchmark for thinking about economic globalization is to consider a world in which markets for goods, services, and factors of production are perfectly integrated. How far are we presently from such a world?

The answer is that we are quite far. Contrary to conventional wisdom and much punditry, international economic integration remains remarkably limited. This robust finding comes across in a wide range of studies, too numerous to cite here.[3] National borders (such as the U.S.-Canadian one) seem to have a significantly depressing effect on commerce, even in the absence of formal tariff or nontariff barriers, linguistic or cultural differences, exchange-rate uncertainty, and other economic obstacles. International price arbitrage in tradable commodities tends to occur very slowly. In a recent analysis, Anderson and van Wincoop (2004) estimate the ad valorem equivalent of trade costs (for goods) to be of the order of 170 percent for the representative advanced economy (of which 55 percent is local distribution cost, and 74 percent is international trade costs).[4] Formal trade barriers such as import tariffs, by contrast, are tiny, and in single digits.

Integration in asset markets remains also limited. Investment portfolios in the advanced industrial countries typically exhibit large amounts of "home bias": that is, people invest a higher proportion of assets in their own countries than the principles of asset diversification would seem to suggest. National investment rates remain highly correlated with and dependent on national saving rates. Even in periods of exuberance, capital flows between rich and poor nations fall considerably short of what theoretical models would predict. Real interest rates are not driven to equality even among advanced countries with integrated financial markets. Severe restrictions on the international mobility of labor are the rule rather than the exception. And even the Internet, the epitome of technology-driven internationalization, remains parochial in many ways: ask yourself, for example, why Amazon.com feels compelled to maintain a distinct British site, Amazon.co.uk, with different recommendations and sales rankings than its American parent.

While formal barriers to trade and capital flows have been substantially reduced over the last three decades, international markets for goods, services, and capital are not nearly as "thick" as they would be under complete integration. Why so much trade in goods and capital has gone missing is the subject of an active research agenda in international economics. The answers are not yet entirely clear. But whatever these may be, it is

---

[3] See in particular Feldstein and Horioka 1980, the results of which have been confirmed in numerous subsequent studies; Helliwell 1998; and the discussion in Frankel 2000b.

[4] These two numbers do not sum to 170 percent because the effect of price "wedges" is multiplicative: $1.7 = (1.55 \times 1.74) - 1$.

clear that economic globalization has far to go before the full efficiency benefits of economic integration are reaped.

THE INTERNATIONAL DIVISION OF LABOR IS LIMITED
BY THE SCOPE OF POLITICAL AND LEGAL JURISDICTIONS

At some level there is no mystery about the "border" effects noted above. National borders demarcate political and legal jurisdictions. Such demarcations serve to segment markets in much the same way that transport costs or border taxes do. This is because exchanges that cross national jurisdictions are subject to a wide array of transaction costs introduced by discontinuities in political and legal systems.

These transaction costs arise from various sources, but perhaps the most obvious relate to the problem of contract enforcement. When one of the parties reneges on a written contract, local courts may be unwilling—and international courts unable—to enforce a contract signed between residents of two different countries. National sovereignty interferes with contract enforcement, leaving international transactions hostage to an increased risk of opportunistic behavior. This problem is most severe in the case of capital flows, and has the implication that national borrowing opportunities are limited by the willingness of countries to service their obligations, rather than their ability to do so. But the problem exists generically for any commercial contract signed by entities belonging to two differing jurisdictions.[5]

When contracts are implicit rather than explicit, they require either repeated interaction or other side constraints to make them sustainable. These constraints are generally harder to achieve across national borders. In the domestic context, implicit contracts are often "embedded" in social networks, which provide sanctions against opportunistic behavior. One of the things that keeps businesspeople honest is fear of social ostracism. The role played by ethnic networks in fostering trade linkages, as in the case of the Chinese in Southeast Asia, is a clear indication of the importance of group ties in facilitating economic exchange.[6]

Ultimately, contracts are often neither explicit nor implicit; they simply remain incomplete. Laws, norms, and customs are some of the ways in which the problem of incompleteness of contracts is alleviated in the

---

[5] See Anderson and Marcouiller 2002 for empirical evidence suggesting that inadequate contract enforcement imposes severe costs on trade.

[6] Casella and Rauch (2002) were the first to emphasize the importance of group ties in international trade, using a model of differentiated products.

domestic sphere. To borrow an example from Tirole (1989, 113–14), what protects a consumer from the small likelihood that a soda-pop bottle might explode is not a contingent contract signed with the manufacturer, but the country's product liability laws. International law provides at best partial protection against incomplete contracts, and international norms and customs are hardly up to the task either.

The presence of separate national monetary regimes provides another example of trade-restricting transaction costs. Rose (1999) has recently found that countries that share the same currency trade with each other three times as much as countries that have separate currencies. Moreover, this effect is much larger than the effects of exchange-rate volatility per se. The trade consequences of the latter are comparatively minor. Hence, the jurisdictional discontinuity introduced by separate national currencies has a large negative effect on trade even when currency values are stable.

This line of argument has important implications for the question of how far international economic integration can go. If the depth of markets is limited by the reach of jurisdictional boundaries, does it not follow that national sovereignty imposes serious constraints on international economic integration? Can markets become international while politics remains local? Or, to ask a different but related question, what would politics look like in a world in which international markets had nothing to fear from the narrower scope of political jurisdictions?

CAUGHT IN AN INTERNATIONAL TRILEMMA

A familiar result of open-economy macroeconomics is that countries cannot simultaneously maintain independent monetary policies, fixed exchange rates, and an open capital account. This result is fondly known to the cognoscenti as the "impossible trinity," or in Obstfeld and Taylor's (1998) terms, as the "open-economy trilemma." The trilemma is represented schematically in the top panel of figure 7.1. If a government chooses fixed exchange rates and capital mobility, it has to give up monetary autonomy. If it wants monetary autonomy and capital mobility, it has to go with floating exchange rates. If it wants to combine fixed exchange rates with monetary autonomy (at least in the short run), it better restrict capital mobility.

The bottom panel of figure 7.1 suggests, by analogy, a different kind of trilemma, one that we might call the *political* trilemma of the world economy. The three nodes of the extended trilemma are international economic integration, the nation-state, and mass politics. I use the term

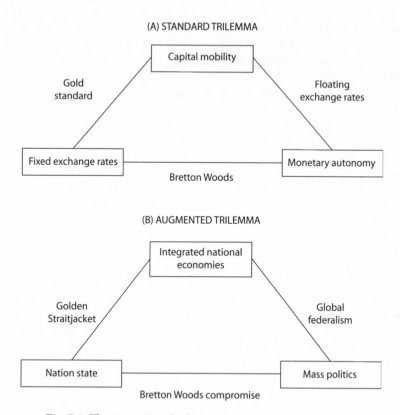

Fig. 7.1. The international trilemma

nation-state to refer to territorial-jurisdictional entities with independent powers of making and administering the law. I use the term *mass politics* to refer to political systems where (*a*) the franchise is unrestricted; (*b*) there is a high degree of political mobilization; and (*c*) political institutions are responsive to mobilized groups.

The implied claim, as in the standard trilemma, is that we can have at most two of these three things. If we want true international economic integration, we have to go either with the nation-state, in which case the domain of national politics will have to be significantly restricted, or else with mass politics, in which case we will have to give up the nation-state in favor of global federalism. If we want highly participatory political regimes, we have to choose between the nation-state and international economic integration. If we want to keep the nation-state, we have to choose between mass politics and international economic integration.

None of this is immediately obvious. But to see that there may be some logic in it, consider our hypothetical perfectly integrated world economy. This would be a world economy in which national jurisdictions do not interfere with arbitrage in markets for goods, services or capital. Transaction costs and tax differentials would be minor; product and regulatory standards would be harmonized; there would be a common monetary system; and convergence in commodity prices and factor returns would be almost complete.

The most obvious way we can attain such a world is by instituting federalism on a global scale. Global federalism would align jurisdictions with the market, and remove the "border" effects. In the United States, for example, despite the continuing existence of differences in regulatory and taxation practices among states, the presence of a national constitution, national government, a nationwide Federal Reserve System, and a federal judiciary ensures that markets are truly national.[7] The European Union, while very far from a federal system at present, seems to be headed in the same direction. Under a model of global federalism, the entire world—or at least the parts that matter economically—would be organized along the lines of the U.S. system. National governments would not necessarily disappear, but their powers would be severely circumscribed by supranational legislative, executive, and judicial authorities. A world government would take care of a world market.

But global federalism is not the only way to achieve complete international economic integration. An alternative is to maintain the nation-state system largely as is, but to ensure that national jurisdictions—and the differences among them—do not get in the way of economic transactions. The overarching goal of nation-states in this world would be to appear attractive to international markets. National jurisdictions, far from acting as an obstacle, would be geared toward facilitating international commerce and capital mobility. Domestic regulations and tax policies would be either harmonized according to international standards, or structured such that they posed the least hindrance to international economic integration. The only local public goods provided would be those that are compatible with integrated markets.

It is possible to envisage a world of this sort; in fact, many commentators seem to believe we are already there. Governments today actively compete with each other by pursuing policies that they believe will earn them market confidence and attract trade and capital inflows: tight money, small government, low taxes, flexible labor legislation, deregulation, privatization, and openness all around. These are the policies that comprise what Thomas Friedman (1999) has aptly termed the Golden Straitjacket.

---

[7] However, Wolf (1997) finds that state borders within the United States still have some deterrent effects on trade.

The price of maintaining national jurisdictional sovereignty while markets become international is that politics have to be exercised over a much narrower domain. "As your country puts on the Golden Straitjacket," Friedman notes (1999, 87),

> two things tend to happen: your economy grows and your politics shrinks. ... [The] Golden Straitjacket narrows the political and economic policy choices of those in power to relatively tight parameters. That is why it is increasingly difficult these days to find any real differences between ruling and opposition parties in those countries that have put on the Golden Straitjacket. Once your country puts on the Golden Straitjacket, its political choices get reduced to Pepsi or Coke—to slight nuances of tastes, slight nuances of policy, slight alterations in design to account for local traditions, some loosening here or there, but never any major deviation from the core golden rules.

Whether this description accurately characterizes our present world is debatable. But Friedman is on to something. His argument carries considerable force in a world where national markets are fully integrated yet politics remains organized nationally. In such a world, the shrinkage of politics would be reflected in the insulation of economic policymaking bodies (central banks, fiscal authorities, and so on) from political participation and debate, the disappearance (or privatization) of social insurance, and the replacement of developmental goals with the need to maintain market confidence. The essential point is this: once the rules of the game are set by the requirements of the global economy, the ability of mobilized popular groups to access and influence national economic policymaking has to be restricted.

The experience with the classical gold standard, and its eventual demise, provides an apt illustration of the incompatibility. At the height of the gold standard, the limited domain of national politics (and its elite-based nature) ensured that domestic monetary policy could be entirely subjugated to the needs of maintaining the gold parities. By the interwar period, as the franchise was fully extended and labor became organized, national governments found that they could no longer pursue gold standard economic orthodoxy. When the needs of full employment clashed with those of the gold standard, the latter gave way.

The same is true of the Argentinian experience of the 1990s, which was a conscious attempt to emulate the Golden Straitjacket. By linking the value of the peso one-for-one to the U.S. dollar in 1991, and putting monetary policy on automatic pilot, the Argentine government sought to remove the "sovereign risk" associated with investing in Argentina and integrate itself fully with international capital markets. For a while, it looked as though the strategy might work. In the first half of the 1990s, capital inflows did increase substantially and the economy expanded at unprecedented rates. But then Argentina was hit with a series of external shocks—the Mexican peso crisis of 1995, the Asian crisis in 1997–98, and most damagingly, the Brazilian devaluation of January 1999. The last left Argentina's economy looking hopelessly uncompetitive relative to its regional rival. Economic growth turned negative in 1999, and foreign investors began to worry about the repayment of the huge liabilities incurred during the course of the decade.

By the end of the summer of 2001, markets were demanding a huge interest premium for fear that Argentina might default on its debt. And, of course, with interest rates so high, default was virtually assured. The Argentina leaders were willing to abrogate their contracts with virtually all domestic constituencies—public employees, pensioners, provincial governments, bank depositors—so as to not skip a cent of their obligations to foreign creditors and to undertake increasingly restrictive economic policies. Yet in the end, investors still wound up thinking that Argentina was a worse credit risk than Nigeria. The reason is that markets became increasingly skeptical that the Argentine congress, provinces, and common people would tolerate such policies for long. And the markets were right. After a couple of days of mass protests and riots just before Christmas, the economy minister Cavallo and President de la Rúa had to resign and the currency board system collapsed.

Having donned the Golden Straitjacket so enthusiastically, the Argentina of the 1990s looked like the perfect illustration of Friedman's point about the shrinkage of political space. But Argentina's real lesson proved to be a different one: democratic politics casts a long shadow on international capital flows, even when political leaders are oblivious to it.

Note the contrast with global federalism. Under global federalism, politics need not, and would not, shrink: it would relocate to the global level. The United States provides a useful way of thinking about this: the most contentious political battles in the United States are fought not at the state level, but at the federal level.

Figure 7.1 shows a third option, which becomes available if we sacrifice the objective of complete international economic integration. I have termed this the Bretton Woods compromise. The essence of the Bretton Woods–GATT regime was that countries were free to dance to their own tune as long as they removed a number of border restrictions on trade and generally did not discriminate among their trade partners.[8] In the area of international finance, countries were allowed (indeed encouraged) to maintain restrictions on capital flows. In the area of trade, the rules frowned

---

[8] Ruggie (1994) has written insightfully on this, describing the system that emerged as "embedded liberalism."

upon quantitative restrictions but not import tariffs. Even though an impressive amount of trade liberalization was undertaken during successive rounds of GATT negotiations, there were also gaping exceptions. Agriculture and textiles were effectively left out of the negotiations. Various clauses in the GATT (on antidumping and safeguards, in particular) permitted countries to erect trade barriers when their industries came under severe competition from imports. Developing country trade policies were effectively left outside the scope of international discipline.[9]

Until roughly the 1980s, these loose rules left enough space for countries to follow their own, possibly divergent paths of development. Hence, western Europe chose to integrate within itself and to erect an extensive system of social insurance. Japan caught up with the developed economies using its own distinctive brand of capitalism, combining a dynamic export machine with large doses of inefficiency in services and agriculture. China grew by leaps and bounds once it recognized the importance of private initiative, even though it flouted every other rule in the guidebook. Much of the rest of East Asia generated an economic miracle relying on industrial policies that have since been banned by the World Trade Organization. Scores of countries in Latin America, the Middle East, and Africa generated unprecedented economic growth rates until the late 1970s under import-substitution policies that insulated their economies from the world economy.

The Bretton Woods compromise was largely abandoned in the 1980s, for several reasons. Improvements in communication and transportation technologies undermined the old regime by making globalization easier. International trade agreements began to reach behind national borders; for example, policies on antitrust or health and safety, which had previously been left to domestic politics, now became issues in international trade discussions. Finally, there was a shift in attitudes in favor of openness, as many developing nations came to believe that they would be better served by a policy of openness. The upshot is that we are left somewhere in between the three nodes of the augmented trilemma of figure 7.1. Which one shall we eventually give up?

In what follows I suggest two different paths, one appropriate for the short to medium term, and the other for the long term. The first path consists of re-creating the Bretton Woods compromise: under this scenario, we would accept the continued centrality of the nation-state, and therefore combine international rules and standards with built-in opt-out schemes. The rationale of such a system, and what it may look like, is laid

---

[9] Lawrence (1996) has termed the model of integration followed under the Bretton Woods-GATT system as "shallow integration," to distinguish it from the "deep integration" that requires behind-the-border harmonization of regulatory policies.

out in the following section. The long-term path is one of global federalism: since this scenario obviously lies far in the future, it allows our imagination to run freely.

GENERALIZED OPT-OUT SCHEMES IN THE SHORT RUN

As long as the nation-state remains the decisive actor, any stable regime of international economic governance has to be incentive-compatible with respect to national preferences. Since national policymakers always have the option of going it alone, the regime must contain incentives for them not to do so. Therefore, the challenge of international economic governance is twofold. On the one hand, we must have a set of rules that encourages greater convergence of policies and standards on a *voluntary* basis. This helps narrow the effect of jurisdictional differences and thereby encourages greater economic integration. At the same time, sufficient flexibility needs to be built into the rules that govern international economic relations to allow selective disengagement from multilateral disciplines. This flexibility is needed to leave room for divergence in national norms and preferences and for dealing with uncertainty and changing circumstances.

Consider as an example the Agreement on Safeguards in the World Trade Organization. This agreement allows a member state to impose temporary trade restrictions following an increase in imports, but under a very stringent set of conditions. My argument is essentially that there is a generic case for such "escape-clause" action, and that it should be allowed under a much broader range of circumstances and in areas going beyond trade. As I will show below, building opt-outs into the rules generally does better than the alternatives, which are either not to have rules or to have rules that are frequently flouted.

The Analytics of Temporary Opt-Outs

When will governments give up some of their sovereignty and choose to empower intergovernmental organizations? There is a simple answer in game-theoretic terms: when the long-run benefits of "cooperation" outweigh the short-run benefits of "defection" (i.e., unilateral action).[10]

More concretely, consider cooperation between two countries in the context of a repeated game, where the one-shot Nash equilibrium is all-around defection. Let tariffs be the policy action in question (bearing in mind that the logic applies to any aspect of international economic policy).

[10] This discussion draws on Rodrik 1998b.

Both countries would prefer to be in the low-tariff equilibrium, but the one-shot Nash equilibrium entails high tariffs in both countries. (This is the case of a prisoner's dilemma applied to trade policy.) We know that cooperation can be sustained in an infinitely repeated setting under certain conditions. In particular, cooperation will be the equilibrium strategy for any player at time t if at that time

> short-term benefits of defection
> < (discount term) × (future net benefits of cooperation).

Hence, for cooperation to be sustainable, the short-term benefits of defection must be small, the discount rate low, and the future benefits from cooperation high. One form of such cooperation is the case in which each player employs a trigger-strategy of the form, "Start by cooperating, cooperate if the other side cooperated last period, defect for k periods otherwise." In a static environment, that is the end of the story. Either the underlying parameters produce cooperation, or they do not.

But consider what happens when conditions change. Think of the tariff game analyzed by Bagwell and Staiger (1990), where there are exogenous (i.i.d., identically and independently distributed) shocks to the volume of trade. When the trade volume is (unexpectedly) high, the benefits to short-term opportunism (imposing a tariff for terms-of-trade reasons) are also high. The left-hand side of the above expression increases, while the right-hand side remains unchanged. At that point, cooperation may no longer be an equilibrium strategy, even if it had been one previously. We will therefore get defection by both parties (a trade war) for at least k periods.

It would have been far better to allow for this possibility by altering the strategies to read, "Start by cooperating, cooperate if other side cooperated last period *or if the other side defected when the trade volume exceeded a certain threshold*, and defect for k periods otherwise." The outcome with these strategies is that long periods of trade wars are avoided. The game now explicitly allows for an "escape clause." A government is not penalized for withdrawing from the rules when there is insufficient incentive for it to have played by the rules. The outcome is better for all parties because unnecessary trade conflicts do not take place.

The point of this example generalizes beyond surges in trade volumes and the use of tariffs for terms-of-trade reasons. Whenever conditions change and free trade becomes incompatible with domestic social or political objectives, the system is better off allowing "defections" than treating the "defections" as instances of rule-breaking. This point has been made also by Milner and Rosendorff (1998), in a setting where uncertainty originates from domestic political pressures (rather than demand conditions abroad, as in Bagwell and Staiger 1990). Thinking in these terms makes it clear that escape clauses ("safeguards," "opt-outs," etc.) are an integral part of sustainable international agreements. I will return to these issues in the next chapter in the context of development-friendly trade policies.

The Analytics of Permanent Opt-Outs

The opt-outs in the discussion above were temporary. There is also a strong case for *permanent* opt-outs when national preferences differ. For example, there is no reason why all countries should have identical environmental standards, labor rules, product-safety standards, or tax regulations. In cases such as these, giving national authorities some latitude makes a lot of sense. However, a free-for-all is unlikely to be optimal, since there will be spillovers across countries. By establishing less stringent labor standards or lower taxes on capital, some countries can divert trade and capital flows in their direction. In general, whenever there are externalities involved in setting standards (whether of the standard or network kind), we know that decentralized behavior will result in suboptimal outcomes.

An important paper by Piketty (1996) develops a useful guiding principle for such situations. Piketty proves that a two-stage procedure of the following kind always improves on decentralized behavior among nation-states.

1. In stage 1, countries collectively vote on a common standard.
2. In stage 2, each country that wishes to depart from the common stadard can do so by paying a cost.

This scheme Pareto-dominates the Nash equilibrium in which each nation behaves independently.

A simple model helps illustrate how this works. Denote by t_i a policy that is under the control of national authorities. (This could be a labor standard, a tax on capital, or financial regulation.) We express the welfare function for country i as follows:

$$W_i = -\frac{1}{2}(a_i - t_i)^2 + b(\bar{t} - a_i)^{1/2}$$

with $b > 0$. This formulation captures two ideas: first, each country has a distinct ideal standard, here denoted by a_i; and second, each country's welfare is also affected by the "average" standard maintained in the other countries (denoted by $\bar{t}$). In particular, the second term has the interpretation that country i suffers a utility loss whenever other countries maintain (on average) a lower standard than country i's most preferred level. (Think again of capital taxation or banking standards for concreteness.) I assume that there is a continuum of countries, indexed by their ideal policies, and that a_i is distributed uniformly in the interval $[0, 1]$.[11] In the decentralized, noncooperative equilibrium, each country would select its ideal policy without regard to the externality imposed on the others. This yields the noncooperative (*nc*) solutions $t_k = a_k$ for all k, and $\bar{t}^{nc} = \frac{1}{2}$.

In principle, the first-best outcome can be achieved by implementing a Pigovian tax/subsidy scheme to counter the externality in the choice of t. But this would require knowledge of the entire distribution of national preferences, as well as an international tax authority. I will show that an alternative modeled after Piketty's suggestion is guaranteed to be Pareto-superior to the noncooperative, Nash equilibrium, with minimal informational requirements.

The alternative scheme consists of the following rule. In stage 1, countries select a common t^c by simple majority vote (with c denoting the common standard under cooperation). In stage 2, countries are required to set their $t_i \geq t^c$ or else pay a cost $k \geq 0$. This cost k is selected subject to the participation constraint that no country is left worse off than under the noncooperative equilibrium.

To show that there is always a t^c and k under which every country does at least as well, we proceed in two steps. First, we derive the cutoff level of a, denoted a_s, below which all countries will choose to pay k and depart from the standard t^c. This cutoff value of a_s is a function of t^c and k, and is defined implicitly by the equation

$$-\frac{1}{2}(a_s - t_s)^2 + b(\bar{t}^c - a_s)^{1/2} - k = -\frac{1}{2}(a_s - t^c)^2 + b(\bar{t}^c - a_s)^{1/2}.$$

The left-hand side of the equality is the utility level when the country indexed by s selects its own most-preferred t, t_s, and pays the cost k. The right-hand side is the utility level when this country sticks with the common standard t^c. By assumption, country s is indifferent between the two options. Solving this equation (and noting $t_s = a_s$), we get $a_s = t^c - \sqrt{2k}$. Note that countries with $a_k > t^c$ are not constrained by the rules, so they simply pick their most preferred standards, $t_k = a_k$.

Given a certain t^c and k, the outcome is as depicted in figure 7.2. The thick line shows choices of t as a function of a. Countries with a's in the range $[0, a_s]$ pay the cost k and select their most preferred t's. Countries in the range $(a_s, t^c]$ select t^c. And countries in the range $(t^c, 1]$ select their most preferred t's. The effect of the scheme is to lift the standards adopted

---

[11] The assumption of uniform distribution is for convenience only. Other distributional assumptions yield qualitatively similar results, although closed-form solutions are more difficult to derive.

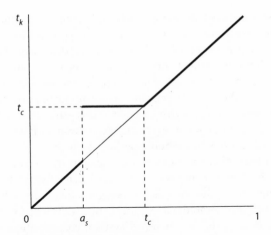

Fig. 7.2. Equilibrium of the model

in the second (middle) of these ranges. It can be shown that the average standard is thereby raised to $\bar{t}^c = \frac{1}{2} + k$, which is at least as large as $\bar{t}^{nc} = \frac{1}{2}$.

In step 2, we derive the equilibrium levels of t^c and k. Since t^c is selected by majority voting among countries and k by the constraint that no country is left worse off, the solutions are easy. Note first that the worst-off country under the scheme is the one with lowest a, that is, $a_k = 0$. For this country to be as well off under the scheme as under the noncooperative outcome, the following criterion has to be satisfied: $k \leq b^2$. Maximizing the median country's welfare subject to that constraint in turn yields the results $k = b^2$ and $t^c = \frac{1}{2}$. (The latter follows from the fact that the median equals the average, given the uniform distribution of a's.)

In fact, any k in the interval $(0, b^2]$ is a Pareto improvement compared to the noncooperative equilibrium. So for a small enough k this scheme will always work, without requiring any knowledge of b. Harmonization coupled with an opt-out clause (the latter exercised at a cost) is a flexible way of combining standardization with diversity.

Discussion

The analytical frameworks described above provide a useful way to think about the governance of economic globalization. The opt-out principle is in fact already in use in the WTO, albeit in a limited way. As mentioned before, the GATT and the WTO contain explicit safeguard schemes that allow countries to impose temporary tariffs in response to import surges. These safeguard measures have not been used much, because taking advantage of antidumping (AD) procedures is considerably easier. In practice, AD duties have served as the safeguard mechanism of choice. The GATT also allows permanent escapes under specific conditions for non-trade and foreign policy reasons. More to the point, the GATT has recognized the need in the past for relaxing or not imposing disciplines in the areas of agriculture, textiles (Multi-Fiber Arrangement) and in selected industrial products (VERs, voluntary export restraints). Rather than viewing these as "derogations," one should perhaps view them as part and parcel of the broader logic of achieving international cooperation.

As the disciplines of the international trade and financial regimes expand into new areas, the analysis here suggests that there will be a parallel need to build reinvigorated opt-out mechanisms. As long as nation-states remain at the core of the international system, considerations of sustainability and diversity require that the rules allow selective disengagement from multilateral disciplines.

In the area of trade, one could imagine expanding the scope of the current Agreement on Safeguards to a broader range of circumstances, such as those arising from concern over labor standards, the environment, or human rights. The purpose of such an expanded escape clause mechanism would be to allow countries, under well-specified contingencies and subject to multilaterally approved procedures, greater breathing room to fulfill domestic requirements that conflict with trade. To prevent abuse, the mechanism would have to ensure that domestic proceedings would be transparent, democratic, and open to all interests (including those that benefit from trade), and that the results would be subject to periodic reviews. (These procedural requirements can be interpreted as corresponding to the k in the model discussed previously.) If this could be achieved *in exchange* for a tightening of rules on antidumping action, which have a highly corrosive effect on the world trading system, the benefits could be substantial. I will discuss such an expanded escape-clause mechanism in the next chapter.

In the area of international finance, we need to think of similar mechanisms. In the wake of recent financial crises, international institutions have developed a formidable list of codes and standards to which countries are expected to adhere. These cover fiscal transparency, monetary and financial policy, banking supervision, data dissemination, corporate governance and structure, and accounting standards. These codes may often be inappropriate to the needs of developing countries. They rule out development banking and many industrial policies of the type discussed in chapter 4. They typically require a large investment in resources and administrative capability. In practice, the real question is this: will opt-outs be allowed on an informal, ad hoc manner, or will they be built into the rules explicitly? The discussion here suggests that the latter strategy is far preferable.

GLOBAL FEDERALISM IN THE LONG RUN?

Over the long run, can we envisage a world in which the reach of markets, jurisdictions, and politics is truly and commensurately global—a world of global federalism?

Perhaps we could, based on the following reasoning. First, continuing technological progress will both foster international economic integration and remove some of the traditional obstacles (such as distance) to global government. Second, short of global wars or natural disasters of major proportions, it is hard to envisage that a substantial part of the world's population will want to give up the goodies that an increasingly integrated (hence efficient) world market can deliver. Third, hard-won citizenship rights (of representation and self-government) are also unlikely to be given up easily, keeping pressure on politicians to remain accountable to the wishes of their electorate.

Further, we can perhaps project an alliance of convenience in favor of global governance between those who perceive themselves to be the "losers" from economic integration, like labor groups and environmentalists, and those who perceive themselves as the "winners," like exporters, multinational enterprises, and financial interests. The alliance would be underpinned by the mutual realization that both sets of interests are best served by the supranational promulgation of rules, regulations, and standards. Labor advocates and environmentalists would get a shot at international labor and environmental rules. Multinational enterprises would be able to operate under global accounting standards. Investors would benefit from common disclosure, bankruptcy, and financial regulations. A global fiscal authority would provide public goods, and a global lender-of-last-resort would stabilize the financial system. Part of the bargain would be to make international policymakers accountable through democratic elections, with due regard to the preeminence of the economically more powerful countries. National bureaucrats and politicians, the only remaining beneficiaries of the nation-state, would either refashion themselves as global officials or they would be shouldered aside.

Global federalism would not mean that the United Nations turns itself into a world government. What we would be likely to get is a combination of traditional forms of governance (an elected global legislative body) with regulatory institutions spanning multiple jurisdictions and accountable to perhaps multiple types of representative bodies. In an age of rapid technological change, the form of governance itself can be expected to be subject to considerable innovation.[12]

Many things can go wrong with this scenario. One alternative possibility is that an ongoing series of financial crises will leave national electorates sufficiently shell-shocked that they willingly, if unhappily, don the Golden Straitjacket for the long run. Another possibility is that governments will resort to protectionism to deal with the distributive and governance difficulties posed by economic integration. For the near term, either one of these scenarios should be regarded as more likely than global federalism. But a longer time horizon leaves room for greater optimism.

CONCLUDING REMARKS

This chapter provides a framework for thinking about the governance of economic globalization. I have argued that we are presently nowhere near complete international economic integration, and that traveling the remaining distance will require either an expansion of our jurisdictions or a shrinking of our politics. We can envisage a long run in which politics and jurisdictions expand to match the scope of a truly integrated global economy. This is my scenario of global federalism. Reaping the efficiency benefits of complete international economic integration requires the further empowering of multilateral institutions and greater reliance on international standards. But in the short run, more realistic solutions are needed and we need to scale down our ambitions. As long as nation-states predominate, neither is likely to be sustainable unless escape-clause or opt-out mechanisms are explicitly built into international economic rules. In a famous passage from *The Economic Consequences of the Peace*, Keynes (1920) drew a vivid picture of an integrated world economy at the pinnacle of the gold standard. While sipping his morning tea in bed, Keynes reminisced nostalgically, the Englishmen of his time could order by telephone various commodities of the world, invest in far-off places, purchase unlimited amounts of foreign currency or precious metals, and arrange for international travel without even requiring a passport. Keynes, who was writing in the aftermath of a devastating world war and was anticipating a period of economic turbulence and protectionism—correctly, as it turned out—considered this a lost era of great magnificence.

Will we experience a similar rebound from globalization in the first decades of the twenty-first century? The answer depends on our ability to devise domestic and international institutions that render economic globalism compatible with the principles of the mixed economy.

[12] See Frey 1996 on some intriguing ideas for the design of federal political systems.

8

The Global Governance of Trade As If Development Really Mattered

WHAT objectives does (or should) the World Trade Organization serve? The first substantive paragraph of the agreement establishing the WTO lists the following aspirations:

> raising standards of living, ensuring full employment and a large and steadily growing volume of real income and effective demand, and expanding the production of and trade in goods and services, while allowing for the optimal use of the world's resources in accordance with the objective of sustainable development, seeking both to protect and preserve the environment and to enhance the means for doing so in a manner consistent with their respective needs and concerns at different levels of economic development.

A subsequent paragraph cites "mutually advantageous arrangements directed to the substantial reduction of tariffs and other barriers to trade and to the elimination of discriminatory treatment in international trade relations" as a means of "contributing to these objectives."[1] It is clear from this preamble that the WTO's framers placed priority on raising standards of living and on sustainable development. Expanding trade was viewed as a means toward that end, rather than an end in itself. Promoting economic development has acquired an even higher standing in the official rhetoric of the WTO recently, partly in response to its critics.

That the purpose of the world trade regime is to raise living standards all around the world—rather than to maximize trade per se—has never been controversial. In practice, however, these two goals—promoting development and maximizing trade—have come to be viewed as synonymous by the WTO and multilateral lending agencies, such that the latter

---

[1] Agreement Establishing the World Trade Organization, available on the WTO web site at http://www.wto.org/english/docs_e/legal_e/final_e.htm.

substitutes for the former.[2] As the WTO's former director general, Mike Moore (2000) put it, "The surest way to do more to help the poor is to continue to open markets." This view has the apparent merit that it is backed by a voluminous empirical literature that claims to identify trade as a key determinant of economic growth. It also fits nicely with the traditional modus operandi of the WTO, which is to focus predominantly on reciprocal market access (instead of development-friendly trade rules). However, the net result is a confounding of ends and means. Trade becomes the lens through which development is perceived, rather than the other way around.

Imagine a trading regime that is true to the preamble of the WTO. This would be a regime in which trade rules are determined so as to maximize development potential, particularly of the poorest nations in the world. Instead of asking, "How do we maximize trade and market access?" negotiators would ask, "How do we enable countries to grow out of poverty?" Would such a regime look different from the one that exists currently?

The answer depends critically on how one interprets recent economic history and the role that trade openness plays in the course of economic development. The prevailing view in G7 capitals and multilateral lending agencies is that integration into the global economy is an essential determinant of economic growth. Successful integration in turn requires both enhanced market access in the advanced industrial countries and a range of institutional reforms at home (ranging from legal and administrative reform to safety nets) to render economic openness viable and growth promoting. I shall call this the "enlightened standard view"—enlightened because of its recognition that there is more to integration than simply lowering tariff and nontariff barriers to trade, and standard because it represents the prevailing conventional wisdom. In this conception, today's WTO represents what the doctor ordered: the WTO's focus on expanding market access and deepening integration through the harmonization of a wide range of "trade-related" practices is precisely what development requires.

There is an alternative account of economic development—one that I have presented earlier (see especially Chapter 1). This is an account that questions the centrality of trade and trade policy and emphasizes instead the critical role of domestic institutional innovations that often depart from prevailing orthodoxy. In this view, transitions to high economic growth are rarely sparked by blueprints imported from abroad. Opening up the economy is hardly ever a key factor at the outset. The initiating reforms

---

[2] The slippage is evident in the WTO's own promotional material. According to the WTO's web site, the organization's "main function is to ensure that trade flows as smoothly, predictably and freely as possible." See http://www.wto.org/english/thewto_e/ whatis_e/inbrief_e/ inbr00_e.htm.

instead tend to be a combination of unconventional institutional innovations with some of the elements drawn from the orthodox recipe. These combinations tend to be country-specific, requiring local knowledge and experimentation for successful implementation. They are targeted at domestic investors and tailored to domestic institutional realities.

In this alternative view, a development-friendly international trading regime is one not purely focused on enhancing poor countries' access to markets in the advanced industrial countries. It is one that enables poor countries to experiment with institutional arrangements and leaves room for them to devise their own, possibly divergent solutions to the developmental bottlenecks that they face. It is one that evaluates the demands of institutional reform not from the perspective of integration ("What do countries need to do to integrate?") but from the perspective of development ("What do countries need to do to achieve broad-based, equitable economic growth?"). In this vision, the WTO would serve no longer as an instrument for the harmonization of economic policies and practices across countries, but as an organization that manages the interface between different national practices and institutions.

Therefore, a reinvigorated focus on development and poverty alleviation, along with a nuanced, empirically based understanding of the development process, would have far-reaching implications for the manner in which the international trading regime and the WTO function. This chapter is devoted to making the case for such a reorientation. My focus will be on the broad principles, rather than specific recommendations, because it is only through a change in the overall mind-set of trade negotiations that significant change can be accomplished.

One of the key arguments of the chapter is that developing countries shortchange themselves when they focus their complaints on specific asymmetries in market access (tariff peaks against developing country exports, industrial country protection in agriculture and textiles, and so on). This way of posing their grievances reflects acceptance of a market-access mind-set that does developing countries limited good. They would be far better served by pressing for changes that enshrine development at the top of the WTO's agenda, and correspondingly provide them with a better mix of enhanced market access and maneuvering room to pursue appropriate development strategies.

I begin in the next section by discussing the evidence on the links between trade policy and economic performance. The voluminous literature in this area, which forms the basis for the extravagant statements on the benefits of trade openness one often hears, has to be approached with extreme care. A close look at this literature, and the evidence underlying the conclusions drawn, suggests that the issues are hardly clear-cut. Essentially, there is no convincing evidence that trade liberalization is predictably associated with subsequent economic growth. In the third section, I argue that this raises serious questions about the priority that the integrationist policy agenda typically receives in orthodox reform programs. The problem is not trade liberalization per se, but the diversion of financial resources and political capital from more urgent and deserving developmental priorities. I illustrate some of these trade-offs in the fourth section.

The fifth section develops some general principles for a world trade regime that puts development first. I emphasize that the trade regime has to accept institutional diversity, rather than seek to eliminate it, and that correspondingly it must accept the right of countries to "protect" their institutional arrangements. However, the right to protect one's own social arrangements is distinct from, and does not extend to, the right to impose it on others. Once these simple principles are accepted and internalized in trade rules, developmental priorities of poor nations and the needs of the industrial countries can be rendered compatible and mutually supportive. This section discusses an opt-out mechanism to operationalize these ideas. The final section offers concluding remarks.

Trade Liberalization, Growth, and Poverty
Alleviation: What Do the Facts Really Show?

Consider two countries that I shall call A and B. Country A engages in state trading, maintains import monopolies, retains quantitative restrictions and high tariffs (in the range of 30–50 percent) on imports of agricultural and industrial products, and is not a member of the WTO. Country B, a WTO member, has slashed import tariffs to a maximum of 15 percent and removed all quantitative restrictions, earning a rare commendation from the U.S. State Department, "There are few significant barriers to U.S. exports."[3] One of the two economies has experienced GDP growth rates in excess of 8 percent per annum, has sharply reduced poverty, has expanded trade at double-digit rates, and has attracted large amounts of foreign investment. The other economy has stagnated, suffered deteriorating social indicators, and made little progress in integrating with the world economy, as judged by trade and foreign investment flows.

Country A is Vietnam, which since the mid-1980s has followed Chinese-style gradualism and a two-track reform program. Vietnam has been phenomenally successful, achieving not only high growth and poverty alleviation, but also a rapid pace of integration into the world economy

[3] See "1999 Country Report on Economic Policy and Trade Practices: Haiti," http://www.state.gov/www/issues/economic/trade_reports/1999/haiti.pdf.

despite high barriers to trade. County B is Haiti. Haiti has gone nowhere even though the country undertook a comprehensive trade liberalization in 1994–95.

The contrasting experiences of these two countries highlight two important points. First, a leadership committed to development and standing behind a coherent growth strategy counts for a lot more than trade liberalization, even when the strategy departs sharply from the enlightened standard view on reform. Second, integration with the world economy is an outcome, and not a prerequisite, of a successful growth strategy. Protected Vietnam is integrating with the world economy significantly more rapidly than open Haiti, because Vietnam is growing and Haiti is not.

I have started with this example because it illustrates a common misdiagnosis. A typical exercise at the World Bank consists of classifying developing countries into "globalizers" and "nonglobalizers" based on their rates of growth of trade volumes. Next, the analyst asks whether globalizers (i.e., those with the highest rates of trade growth) have experienced faster income growth, greater poverty reduction, and worsened income distribution.[4] The answers tends to be yes, yes, and no. As the Vietnam and Haiti examples show, however, this is a highly misleading exercise. Trade volumes are the outcome of many different things, including, most importantly, an economy's overall performance. They are not something that governments control directly. What governments control are trade *policies*: the level of tariff and nontariff barriers, membership in the WTO, compliance with its agreements, and so on. The relevant question is this: do open trade *policies* reliably produce higher economic growth and greater poverty reduction?

The cross-national evidence on this issue is easily summarized. The available studies reveal no systematic relationship between a country's average level of tariff and nontariff restrictions and its subsequent economic growth rate. If anything, the evidence for the 1990s indicates a *positive* (but statistically insignificant) relationship between tariffs and economic growth (see figure 8.1). The only systematic relationship is that countries dismantle trade restrictions as they get richer. That accounts for the fact that today's rich countries, with few exceptions, embarked on modern economic growth behind protective barriers, but now have low trade barriers.

The absence of a robust positive relationship between open trade policies and economic growth may come as a surprise in view of the ubiquitous claim that trade liberalization promotes higher growth. Indeed, the literature is replete with cross-national studies concluding that growth and

---

[4] See, for example, Dollar and Kraay 2000. A critique of this paper can be found at http://ksghome.harvard.edu/~.drodrik.academic.ksg/Rodrik%20on%20Dollar-Kraay.PDF.

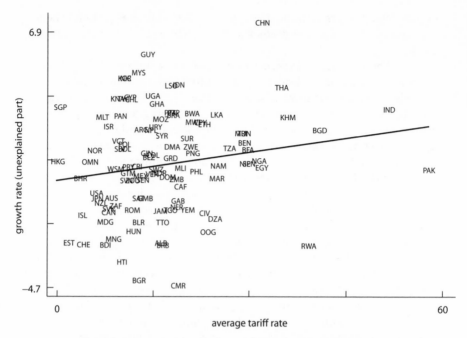

Fig. 8.1. Low import tariffs are good for growth? Think again

Note: All data are averages for the 1990s and come from the Dollar and Kraay 2000 data set. I base my specification on Dollar and Kraay 2000, replacing trade/GDP with tariff levels. As in Dollar and Kraay 2000, initial income, government consumption/GDP, and inflation rate are separately controlled for.

economic dynamism are strongly linked to more liberal trade policies. For example, a particularly influential study by Sachs and Warner (1995) finds that economies that are open, by the study's own definition, grew 2.4 percentage points faster annually than closed ones—an enormous difference. Without such studies, organizations such as the World Bank, IMF, and WTO could not have been as vociferous in their promotion of trade-centric development strategies.

Upon closer look, however, these studies turn out to be flawed. The classification of countries as "open" or "closed" in the Sachs-Warner (1995) study, for example, is not based on actual trade policies but largely on indicators related to exchange rate policy and location in sub-Saharan Africa. The Sachs-Warner classification of countries in effect conflates macroeconomics, geography, and institutions with trade policy. It is so correlated with plausible groupings of alternative explanatory variables— macroeconomic instability, poor institutions, location in Africa—that one cannot draw from the subsequent empirical analysis any strong inferences about the effects of openness on growth (see Rodríguez and Rodrik 2001).

The problem is a general one. In a detailed review of the empirical literature, Francisco Rodríguez and I have found that there is a major gap between the policy conclusions that are typically drawn and what the research has actually shown.[5] A common problem in this line of research has been the misattribution of either macroeconomic phenomena (overvalued currencies or macroeconomic instability) or geographic determinants (e.g., location in the tropical zone) to trade policies proper. Once these problems are corrected, any meaningful relationship across countries between the level of trade barriers and economic growth evaporates.[6]

There are in fact reasons to be skeptical about the existence of a general, unambiguous relationship between trade openness and growth. The relationship is likely to be a contingent on a host of country and external characteristics. The fact that practically all of today's advanced countries embarked on their growth behind tariff barriers, and reduced protection only subsequently, surely offers a clue of sorts. Moreover, the modern theory of endogenous growth yields an ambiguous answer to the question of whether trade liberalization promotes growth. The answer varies depending on whether the forces of comparative advantage push the economy's resources in the direction of activities that generate long-run growth (via externalities in research and development, expanding product variety, upgrading product quality, and so on) or divert them from such activities.

No country has developed successfully by turning its back on international trade and long-term capital flows. Very few countries have grown over long periods of time without experiencing an increase in the share of foreign trade in their national product. In practice, the most compelling mechanism that links trade with growth in developing countries is that imported capital goods are likely to be significantly cheaper than those manufactured at home. Policies that restrict imports of capital equipment, raise the price of capital goods at home, and thereby reduce real investment levels have to be viewed as undesirable prima facie.[7] Exports, in turn, are important since they allow purchases of imported capital equipment.

But it is equally true that no country has developed simply by opening itself up to foreign trade and investment. The trick in the successful cases has been to combine the opportunities offered by world markets with a domestic investment and institution-building strategy to stimulate the animal spirits of domestic entrepreneurs. Almost all of the outstanding

---

[5] Besides Sachs and Warner 1995, our detailed analysis covers four other papers that together constitute the best-known in the field: Dollar 1992; Ben-David 1993; Edwards 1998; and Frankel and Romer 1999.

[6] This is also the conclusion of the careful country studies collected in Helleiner 1994.

[7] This does not rule out the possibility of selective infant industry policies in certain segments of capital-goods industries.

cases—East Asia, China, India since the early 1980s—involve partial and gradual opening up to imports and foreign investment.

The experiences of China and India are particularly noteworthy, as these are two huge countries that have done extremely well recently, and are often pointed to as examples of what openness can achieve.[8] The reality, once again, is more complicated. In both China and India, the main trade reforms took place about a decade *after* the onset of higher growth. Moreover, these countries' trade restrictions remained (as late as the mid-1990s) among the highest in the world. As I discussed in earlier chapters, the increase in China's growth started in the late 1970s with the introduction of the household responsibility system in agriculture and of two-tier pricing. Trade liberalization did not start in earnest until much later, during the second half of the 1980s and especially during the 1990s, once the trend growth rate had already increased substantially.

As figure 8.2 makes clear, India's trend growth rate increased substantially in the early 1980s (a fact that stands out clearly when one benchmarks India's growth against other developing countries, as is done in the figure). Meanwhile, serious trade reform did not start until 1991–93. The tariff averages displayed in the figure show that tariffs were actually higher in the rising growth period of the 1980s than in the low-growth 1970s. Of course, tariffs hardly constitute the most serious trade restrictions in India, but they nonetheless display the trends in Indian trade policy.

Of course, both India and China did "participate in international trade," and by that measure they are both globalizers. But the relevant question for policymakers is not whether trade per se is good or bad—countries that do well also increase their trade/GDP ratios as a by-product—but what the correct sequencing of policies is and how much priority deep trade liberalization should receive early on in the reform process. With regard to the latter questions, the experiences of India and China suggest the benefits of a gradual, sequenced approach.

An important reason for delaying significant import liberalization until after economic dynamism has set roots is that doing so shelters employment in the transition. In rapidly liberalizing economies (such as those in Latin America and eastern Europe), the labor released by previously protected sectors has ended up not in tradable activities with higher productivity but in informal activities with even lower productivity (or in unemployment). This explains why economy-wide productivity has suffered in these countries (even as labor productivity in the shrinking modern sector has increased). Countries (such as those in Asia) that have promoted

---

[8] Here is a typical statement: "Growth rates for these recent globalizers have generally accelerated as they have become more open. This trend is clearest for China and India" (Stern 2000, 3).

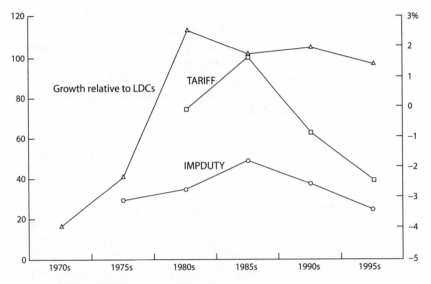

Fig. 8.2. Tariffs and growth in India
Source: Author's calculations from data in Dollar and Kraay 2000 (tariff) and World Bank, World Development Indicators 2000 CD-ROM.

export orientation through promotion of new activities and export incentives at the margin (rather than import liberalization across the board) have avoided this fate.[9]

To repeat, the appropriate conclusion is not that trade protection is inherently preferable to trade liberalization; certainly, there is scant evidence from the last 50 years that inward-looking economies experience systematically faster economic growth than open ones. The relevant point is that the benefits of trade openness are now greatly oversold. Deep trade liberalization cannot be relied on to deliver high rates of economic growth and therefore does not deserve the high priority it typically receives in the development strategies pushed by leading multilateral organizations.[10]

[9] The model I have in mind is one where there are three types of tradable goods: import-competing activities, traditional exportables, and nontraditional exportables. The Latin American model is premised on the idea that removing protection from the first category of goods will spur enough new production of both types of the other two goods. But when the supply elasticity of traditional exports is limited (and their labor intensity low) and new exports do not arise automatically (for reasons discussed in chapter 4), this expectation may not be realized. The Asian model, by contrast, is based on direct support for nontraditional exports.

[10] Much the same can be said about the promotion and subsidization of inward flows of direct foreign investment. See Hanson 2001 for a good overview of the evidence and the policy issues.

As Helleiner (2000, 3) puts it, there are "few reputable developing country analysts or governments who question the positive potential roles of international trade or capital inflow in economic growth and overall development. How *could* they question the inevitable need for participation in, indeed a considerable degree of integration with, the global economy?" The real debate is not over whether integration is good or bad, but over matters of policy and priorities.

THE LIMITED BENEFITS FROM (FURTHER) MARKET ACCESS IN DEVELOPED COUNTRY MARKETS

But what about access to markets in rich countries? Wouldn't developing countries be far worse off if they were unable to export goods to industrial country markets? Surely yes. A world with high import barriers in rich countries would be one that is far less hospitable to developing countries than the one that we live in currently. What is not clear is that developing countries stand to gain much from *further* liberalization in advanced county markets. The world economy is more open today than it has ever been, and will remain so even if the Doha talks can never be resuscitated. Barriers to trade on manufactured goods and in many services are at a historic low in rich countries. (The most significant exception relates to labor services, a topic I will pick up in chapter 9.) It would be hard to identify any poor country whose development prospects are seriously blocked by restrictions on market access abroad. Any country with a sensible development strategy has the opportunity to grow its economy, with assistance from trade.

The Doha Round has made much of global liberalization in agriculture. One often hears the claim that farm supports in the United States and European Union undercut the livelihood of millions of poor farmers, and that their phasing out would make a significant dent in world poverty. The reality is that the global impact of agricultural liberalization in the rich countries would be relatively small and highly uneven. These policies may hurt agricultural producers elsewhere, but they also benefit poor urban consumers. The balance depends on the poverty profile of individual countries and on whether they are food exporters or importers. Most sensible estimates suggest that complete trade liberalization (including in manufactures and by developing nations themselves) would produce a net gain to the developing world of one percentage point of their income or less—a meager impact that the World Bank and the WTO do their best to hide behind more impressive-sounding claims.

To be sure, there are some big gainers from agricultural reform, but these are chiefly consumers and taxpayers in the rich countries themselves. Some large middle-income food exporters (such as Brazil and Argentina) will also reap gains. Such outcomes are not unimportant, but they represent a far cry from the picture painted by trade fundamentalists.

THE INTEGRATIONIST AGENDA AND THE CROWDING OUT OF DEVELOPMENT PRIORITIES

Priorities are important because in the enlightened standard view integration with the world economy is no longer a matter simply of removing trade and investment barriers. Countries have to satisfy a long list of institutional requirements, so that they can, as the cliché goes, maximize the gains and minimize the risks of participation in the world economy. Global integration remains the key prerequisite for economic development, but there is now a lot more to it than just throwing the borders open. Reaping the gains from openness requires a full complement of institutional reforms.

So trade liberalization entails not only the lowering of tariff and nontariff barriers, but compliance with WTO requirements on subsidies, intellectual property, customs procedures, sanitary standards, and policies vis-à-vis foreign investors. Moreover, these legal requirements have to be complemented with additional reforms to ensure favorable economic outcomes: tax reform to make up for lost tariff revenues; social safety nets to compensate displaced workers; credibility enhancing institutional innovations to quell doubts about the permanence of the reforms; labor market reform to enhance labor mobility across industries; technological assistance to upgrade firms adversely affected by import competition; training programs to ensure that export-oriented firms and investors have access to skilled workers; and so on. Reading World Bank reports on trade policy, one can be excused for thinking that the list of complementary reforms is virtually endless.

Many of the institutional reforms on the integrationist agenda are perfectly sensible ones,[11] and in a world without financial, administrative, or political constraints, there would be little argument about the need to adopt them. But in the real world, fiscal resources, administrative capabilities, and political capital are all scarce, and choices need to be made about how to deploy them. In such a world, viewing institutional priorities from the vantage point of insertion in the global economy has real opportunity costs (Rodrik 2001b).

---

[11] Many, but not all. As argued earlier, the Washington agenda for integrationist reform is influenced too heavily by an Anglo-American conception of institutional possibilities.

Here are some illustrative trade-offs. It has been estimated that it costs a typical developing country $150 million to implement requirements under just three of the WTO agreements (those on customs valuation, sanitary and phytosanitary measures (SPS), and intellectual property rights (TRIPS). As the World Bank's Michael Finger points out, this is a sum equal to a year's development budget for many of the least-developed countries (Finger and Schuler 1999).

In the area of legal reform, should the government focus its energies on "importing" legal codes and standards, or on improving existing domestic legal institutions? In Turkey, a weak coalition government spent several months in the 1990s gathering political support for a bill that would provide foreign investors the protection of international arbitration. Wouldn't it have been a better strategy for the long run to reform the existing legal regime for the benefit of foreign *and* domestic investors alike?

In public health, should the government pursue tough policies on compulsory licensing and parallel importation of basic medicines, even if that means running afoul of existing WTO rules? The United States has charged in the past that Brazil's highly successful anti-AIDS program violates WTO rules because it allows the government to seek compulsory licensing when a foreign patent holder does not "work" the patent locally.[12]

In industrial strategy, should the government simply open up and let the chips drop wherever they might, or should it emulate East Asian experience of industrial policies through export subsidies, directed credit, and selective protection?

How should the government focus its anticorruption strategy? Should it target the "grand" corruption that foreign investors complain about, or the petty corruption that affects the poor? Perhaps, as the proponents of permanent normal trade relations (PNTR) with China used to argue in U.S. debates, a government that is forced to protect the rights of foreign investors becomes more inclined to protect the human rights of its own citizens too. But isn't this, at best, a trickle-down strategy of institutional reform? Shouldn't institutional reform be targeted on the desired ends directly—whether those ends are the rule of law, improved observance of human rights, or reduced corruption for all?

The rules for admission into the world economy not only reflect little awareness of development priorities, they are often completely unrelated to sensible economic principles. WTO rules on antidumping, subsidies and countervailing measures, agriculture, textiles, TRIMs (Trade Related Investment Measures), and TRIPS are utterly devoid of economic rationale beyond the mercantilist interests of a narrow set of powerful

---

[12] Since the adoption of the Doha Declaration on the TRIPS Agreement and Public Health in 2001, these have become less serious problems.

groups in the advanced industrial countries. The developmental payoff of most of these requirements is hard to see.

As I discussed in chapter 4, bilateral and regional trade agreements are often far worse, as they impose even tighter prerequisites on developing countries in return for crumbs of enhanced "market access" in the larger partners. The Africa Growth and Opportunity Act signed by President Clinton in May 2000 contains a long list of eligibility criteria, including the specific requirement that African governments minimize interference in the economy. It provides free market access into the United States only under strict rules of origin, thereby ensuring that few economic linkages are generated in the African countries themselves. The United States–Jordan Free Trade Agreement imposes more restrictive intellectual property rules on Jordan than exist under the WTO. In its free-trade agreement with Chile, the United States successfully obtained severe restrictions on Chile's ability to employ capital controls.

In each of these areas, a strategy focused on integration crowds out alternatives that may be more development-friendly. Many of the institutional reforms needed for insertion in the world economy can be independently desirable, or produce broader spillovers. But these priorities do not necessarily coincide with the priorities of an agenda that is more fully developmental. A strategy that focuses on getting the state out of the way of the market overlooks the important functions that the state needs to play during the process of economic transformation. What belongs on the agenda of institutional reform is building up state capacity—not diminishing it (Evans 2000).

World markets are a source of technology and capital; it would be silly for the developing world not to exploit these opportunities. But, as I have argued throughout this book, successful development strategies have always required a judicious blend of imported practices with domestic institutional innovations. Policymakers need to forge a *domestic* growth strategy, relying on domestic investors and domestic institutions. The most costly downside of the integrationist agenda is that it is crowding out serious thinking and efforts along such lines.

An International Trade Regime That Puts Development First: General Principles and Illustrations

Access to the markets of the industrial countries matters for development. But so does the autonomy to experiment with institutional innovations that diverge from orthodoxy. Given the level of openness of the world economy, the exchange of reduced policy autonomy in the South for even better market access in the North is a bad bargain so far as development is concerned.

Consider the old GATT system. Under the GATT, the international trade regime did not reach much beyond tariff and nontariff barriers to trade. The developing countries were effectively exempt from prevailing disciplines. The MFN (most-favored nation) principle ensured that they benefited from the tariff cuts negotiated among the industrial countries, while they themselves "gave up" little in return. The resulting pattern of liberalization may have been asymmetric (with many products of interest to developing countries either excluded or receiving less beneficial treatment), but the net effect for the developing world was highly salutary.

It is in such an external environment that the most successful "globalizers" of an earlier era—the East Asian tigers—managed to prosper. South Korea, Taiwan, and the other East Asian countries had the freedom to do their own thing, and they used it abundantly. As I discussed previously, they combined their reliance on trade with unorthodox policies—export subsidies, domestic-content requirements, import-export linkages, patent and copyright infringements, restrictions on capital flows (including direct foreign investment), directed credit, and so on—that are either precluded by today's rules or highly frowned upon.[13] In fact, such policies were part of the arsenal of today's advanced industrial countries until quite recently.[14] The environment for today's globalizers is quite different and significantly more restrictive.

For the world's poorest economies (the so-called least-developed countries), something along the old GATT lines is still achievable, and would constitute a more development-friendly regime than the one that exists currently. These are economies that are individually and collectively small enough that "adjustment" issues in the advanced countries are not a serious obstacle to the provision of one-sided free market access in the North to the vast majority of products of interest to them. Instead of encumbering these countries with all kinds of institutional requirements that come attached to a "single undertaking," it would be far better to leave them the room to follow their own institutional priorities, while providing

---

[13] See Amsden 2000 for a more optimistic reading of WTO rules. Amsden argues that WTO rules remain permissive insofar as industrial policies are concerned, and that what developing countries lack is a "vision" for transforming their economies. While I agree with her on the issue of vision, I also think that current WTO regulations do preclude many of the strategies that were usefully employed by the East Asian countries. A recent illustration is the dispute between Brazil and Canada over Brazil's subsidization of its aircraft manufacturer, Embraer. Brazil lost this case in the WTO, and will either remove the subsidies or have to put up with retaliation from Canada. Successful performers such as South Korea, Taiwan, and Mauritius subsidized their export industries for years without incurring similar sanctions.

[14] On patents and compulsory licensing, for example, see Scherer and Watal 2001.

them with duty- and quota-free access in Northern markets. In practice, this can be done either by extending existing "phase-in" periods until certain income thresholds are reached, or by incorporating a general least-developed-country exception.

In the case of middle-income and other developing nations, it is unrealistic to expect that advanced industrial countries would be willing to accept a similar arrangement. The amount of political opposition that imports from developing countries generate in the advanced industrial countries is already disproportionate to the volume of trade in question. Some of these objections have a legitimate core, and it is important that developing nations understand and accept this.[15] Under a sensible set of global trade rules, industrialized countries would have as much right to "protect" their own social arrangements—in areas such as labor and environmental standards, welfare-state arrangements, rural communities, or industrial organization—as developing nations have to adopt divergent institutional practices. Countries such as India, Brazil, or China, whose exports can have a sizable impact on, say, labor-market institutions and employment relations within the advanced countries, cannot ask importing countries to overlook these effects while demanding at the same time that the constraints on their own developmental agenda be lifted. Middle-income developing countries have to accept a more balanced set of rights and obligations.

Is it possible to preserve developing countries' autonomy while also respecting the legitimate objectives of advanced industrial countries to maintain high labor, social, and environmental standards at home? Would such a regime of world trade avoid collapsing into protectionism, bilateralism, or regional trade blocs? Would it be development-friendly after all? The answer to all these questions is yes, provided we accept five simple principles.

1. *Trade is a means to an end, not an end in itself.* Step number 1 is to move away from attaching normative significance to trade itself. The scope of market access generated by the international trade regime and the volume of trade thereby stimulated are poor measures of how well the system functions. As I have argued throughout, and as the WTO's own preamble emphasizes, trade is useful only insofar as it serves broader developmental and social goals. Developing countries should not be obsessed with market access abroad, at the cost of overlooking more fundamental developmental challenges at home. Industrial countries should balance the

---

[15] See Mayda and Rodrik 2005 for an empirical analysis of the determinants of individuals' attitudes toward trade in the rich countries. We show in this paper that these attitudes are shaped by values having to do with communitiarian and patriotic feelings as well as narrow material self-interest.

interests of their exporters and multinational companies with those of their workers and consumers.

Advocates of globalization lecture the rest of the world incessantly about the adjustments countries have to undertake in their policies and institutions in order to expand their international trade and become more attractive to foreign investors. This is another instance of confusing means for ends. Trade serves at best as an instrument for achieving the goals that societies seek: prosperity, stability, freedom, and quality of life. Nothing enrages WTO bashers more than the suspicion that, when push comes to shove, the WTO allows trade to trump the environment or human rights. And developing countries are right to resist a system that evaluates their needs from the perspective of expanding world trade instead of alleviating poverty.

Reversing our priorities would have a simple but powerful implication. Instead of asking what kind of multilateral trading system maximizes foreign trade and investment opportunities, we would ask what kind of multilateral system best enables nations around the world to pursue their own values and developmental objectives.

2. *Trade rules have to allow for diversity in national institutions and standards.* As I have repeatedly emphasized, there is no single recipe for economic advancement. This does not mean that anything and everything works: market-based incentives, effective property rights, competition, macroeconomic stability are key everywhere. More broadly, political freedom, civil liberties, and human rights are universal principles. But even these universal requirements and principles can, and have been, embodied in diverse institutional forms. Investment strategies, needed to jump-start economies, can also take different forms. Moreover, citizens of different countries have varying preferences over the regulations that should govern new technologies (such as genetically modified organisms), restrictiveness of environmental regulations, intrusiveness of government policies, extensiveness of social safety nets, or the relationship between efficiency and equity more broadly.[16] Rich and poor nations have very different needs in the areas of labor standards or patent protection. Poor countries need the space to follow developmental policies that richer countries no longer require.

When countries use the trade system to impose their institutional preferences on others, the result is erosion of the system's legitimacy and efficacy. Trade rules should seek peaceful coexistence among national practices, not harmonization.

---

[16] This is not to deny that in practice these preferences are aggregated through social choice mechanisms that can be highly imperfect, sometimes reflecting the excessive power of organized lobbies. But the appropriate response to these shortcomings is to enhance the working of representative and participatory democracy, not to undercut it.

3. *Nondemocratic countries cannot count on the same trade privileges as democratic ones.* National standards that deviate from those in trade partners and provide "trade advantages" are legitimate only to the extent that they are grounded in free choices made by citizens. Think of labor and environmental standards, for example. Poor countries argue that they cannot afford to have the same stringent standards in these areas as the advanced countries. Indeed, tough emission standards or regulations against the use of child labor can easily backfire if they lead to fewer jobs and greater poverty. Democratic countries such as India and Brazil can legitimately argue that their practices are consistent with the wishes of their own citizens, and that therefore it is inappropriate for labor groups or NGOs *in advanced countries* to tell them what standard they should have. Democratic governments are presumptively accountable to *their own* NGOs and electorates, which is as it should be. Of course democracy never works perfectly (even in the advanced countries), and one would not want to make the stronger argument that there are no human rights abuses in the countries just mentioned. The point is simply that the presence of civil liberties and political freedoms provides a presumptive cover against the charge that labor, environmental, and other standards in the developing nations are inappropriately low.

But nondemocratic countries, such as China, do not pass the same prima facie test. The assertion that labor rights and the environment are trampled for the benefit of commercial advantage cannot be as easily dismissed in those countries. Consequently, exports of nondemocratic countries deserve greater scrutiny when they entail costly dislocations or adverse distributional consequences in importing countries. In the absence of the presumptive cover provided by democratic rights, such countries need to make a "developmental" case for policies that generate adjustment difficulties in the importing countries. For example, minimum wages that are significantly lower than in rich countries or health and other benefits that are less generous can easily be justified by pointing to lower labor productivity and living standards in poor nations. Lax child labor regulations can often be justified by the argument that under conditions of widespread poverty it is not feasible or desirable to withdraw young workers from the labor force. In other cases, the "affordability" argument carries less weight: nondiscrimination, freedom of association, collective bargaining, prohibition of forced labor do not "cost" anything; compliance with these "core labor rights" does not harm, and indeed possibly benefits, economic development. The latter are examples that do not pass the "development test."

4. *Countries have the right to protect their own institutions and development priorities.* Opponents of today's trade regime argue that trade sets off a "race to the bottom," with nations converging toward the lowest levels of environmental, labor, and consumer protections. Advocates

counter that there is little evidence trade leads to the erosion of national standards. Developing nations complain that current trade laws are too intrusive, and leave little room for development-friendly policies. Advocates of the WTO reply that these rules provide useful discipline to rein in harmful policies that would otherwise end up wasting resources and hampering development.

One way to cut through this morass is to accept that countries can uphold national standards and policies in these areas, by withholding market access or suspending WTO obligations if necessary, when trade demonstrably undermines domestic practices enjoying broad popular support. For example, poor nations might be allowed to subsidize industrial activities (and indirectly their exports) when this is part of a broadly supported development strategy aimed at stimulating technological capabilities. This approach would render the international trade system more compatible with the goal of local ownership of development programs. Advanced countries might seek temporary protection against imports originating from countries with weak enforcement of labor rights when such imports worsen working conditions at home. The WTO already has a "safeguard" system in place to protect firms from import surges. An extension of this principle to protect developmental priorities or environmental, labor, and consumer-safety standards at home—with appropriate procedural restraints against abuse—might make the world trading system more development-friendly, more resilient, and more resistant to ad hoc protectionism.

Currently the Agreement on Safeguards allows (temporary) increase in trade restrictions under a very narrow set of conditions.[17] It requires determination that *increased* imports "cause or threaten to cause serious injury to the domestic industry," that causality be firmly established, and that injury be not attributed to imports if there are multiple causes for it. Safeguards cannot be applied to developing-country exporters unless their share of imports of the product concerned is above a threshold. A country applying safeguard measures has to compensate the affected exporters by providing "equivalent concessions," lacking which the exporter is free to retaliate.

A broader interpretation of safeguards would acknowledge that countries may legitimately wish to restrict trade or suspend existing WTO obligations—exercise what I will call "opt-outs"—for reasons going beyond competitive threats to their industries. As I have discussed, developmental priorities are among such reasons, as are distributional concerns or conflicts with domestic norms or social arrangements in the industrial countries. We could imagine recasting the current agreement into an Agreement on *Developmental and Social Safeguards*, which would permit the

---

[17] This discussion draws on Rodrik 1997b.

application of opt-outs under a broader range of circumstances. This would require recasting the "serious injury" test. I would replace the injury criterion with another hurdle: the need to demonstrate broad domestic support, *among all concerned parties*, for the proposed measure.

To see how that might work in practice, consider what the current agreement says:

> A Member may apply a safeguard measure only following an investigation by the competent authorities of that Member pursuant to procedures previously established and made public in consonance with Article X of the GATT 1994. This investigation shall include reasonable public notice to all interested parties and public hearings or other appropriate means in which *importers, exporters and other interested parties could present evidence and their views*, including the opportunity to respond to the presentations of other parties and to submit their views, inter alia, as to *whether or not the application of a safeguard measure would be in the public interest*. The competent authorities shall publish a report setting forth their findings and reasoned conclusions reached on all pertinent issues of fact and law. (Emphasis added)

The main shortcoming of this clause is that while it allows all relevant groups, exporters and importers in particular, to make their views known, it does not actually compel them to do so. Consequently, it results in a strong bias in the domestic investigative process toward the interests of import-competing groups, who are the petitioners for import relief and its obvious beneficiaries. Indeed, this is a key problem with hearings in antidumping proceedings, where testimony from other groups besides the import-competing industry is typically not allowed.

The most significant and reliable guarantee against the abuse of opt-outs is informed deliberation at the national level. A key reform, then, would be to require the investigative process in each country to (*a*) gather testimony and views from *all* relevant parties, including consumer and public-interest groups, importers and exporters, civil society organizations, and (*b*) determine whether there exists *broad enough support* among these groups for the exercise of the opt-out or safeguard in question. The requirements that groups whose incomes might be adversely affected by the opt-out—importers and exporters—be compelled to testify, and that the investigative body balance the competing interests in a transparent manner would help ensure that protectionist measures that benefit a small segment of industry at large cost to society would not have much chance of success. When the opt-out in question is part of a broader development strategy that has already been adopted after broad debate and participation, an additional investigative process need not be launched. This last point deserves special emphasis in view of the emphasis placed on "local ownership" and "participatory mechanisms" in strategies of poverty reduction and growth promoted by the international financial institutions.

The main advantage of the proposed procedure is that it would force a public debate on the legitimacy of trade rules and when they may appropriately be suspended. It ensures that all sides would be heard. This is something that rarely happens even in the industrial countries, let alone the developing nations. This procedure could also be complemented with a strengthened monitoring and surveillance role for the WTO, to ensure that domestic opt-out procedures comply with the expanded safeguard clause. An automatic sunset clause could ensure that trade restrictions and opt-outs do not become entrenched long after their perceived need has disappeared.

Allowing opt-outs in this manner would not be without its risks. The possibility that the new procedures would be abused for protectionist ends and open the door to unilateral action on a broad front, despite the high threshold envisaged here, has to be taken into account. But as I have already argued, the current arrangements are not riskless. The "more of the same" approach that is embodied in current practice is unlikely to produce many benefits for developing nations. Absent creative thinking and novel institutional designs, the narrowing of the room for institutional divergence will continue to harm development prospects. It may also lead to the emergence of a new set of "gray area" measures entirely outside multilateral discipline. These consequences are worse than the expanded safeguard regime I have just described.

5. *But countries do not have the right to impose their institutional preferences on others.* The exercise of opt-outs to uphold a country's own priorities has to be sharply distinguished from using them to impose these priorities on other countries. Trade rules should not force Americans to consume shrimp that are caught in ways that most Americans find unacceptable; but neither should they allow the United States to use trade sanctions to alter the way that foreign nations go about their fishing business. Citizens of rich countries who are genuinely concerned about the state of the environment or of workers in the developing world can be more effective through channels other than trade—via diplomacy or foreign aid, for example. Trade sanctions to promote a country's own preferences are rarely effective, and have no moral legitimacy (except for when they are used against repressive political regimes).

This and the previous principle help us draw a useful distinction between two styles of "unilateralism"—one that is aimed at protecting differences, and another aimed at reducing them. When the European Union drags its feet on agricultural trade liberalization, it is out of a desire to "protect" a set of domestic social arrangements that Europeans, through their democratic procedures, have decided are worth maintaining. When, on the other hand, the United States threatens trade sanctions against Japan because its retailing practices are perceived to harm American exporters or against South Africa because its patent laws are perceived as too lax, it does so out of a desire to bring these countries' practices into line with its own. A well-designed world trade regime would leave room for the former, but prohibit the latter.

6. *Other development-friendly measures.* In addition to providing unrestricted access to least developed countries' exports and enabling developing countries greater autonomy in the use of subsidies, "trade-related" investment measures, patent regulations, and other measures, a development-friendly trade regime would have the following features:[18]

- It would greatly restrict the use of antidumping (AD) measures in advanced industrial countries when exports originate from developing countries. A small, but important step would be to require that the relevant investigating bodies take fully into account the consumer costs of AD action.
- It would allow greater mobility of workers across international boundaries, by liberalizing, for example, the movement of natural persons connected to trade in labor-intensive services (such as construction), as discussed in the next chapter.
- It would require that all existing and future WTO agreements be fully costed out (in terms of implementation and other costs). It would condition the phasing in of these agreements in the developing countries on the provision of commensurate financial assistance.
- When a dispute settlement panel rules in favor of a developing country complainant, it would require additional compensation or (when compensation is not forthcoming) that other countries join in the retaliation.
- It would provide expanded legal and fact-finding assistance to developing country members of the WTO in prospective dispute settlement cases.

CONCLUSIONS: FROM A MARKET-EXCHANGE MIND-SET TO A DEVELOPMENT MIND-SET

Economists think of the WTO as an institution designed to expand free trade and thereby enhance consumer welfare, in the South no less than the North. In reality it is an institution enabling countries to bargain about market access. "Free trade" is *not* the typical outcome of this process; nor is consumer welfare (much less development) what the negotiators have chiefly in mind. Traditionally, the agenda of multilateral trade negotiations

---

[18] For a comprehensive compendium of proposals from the perspective of developing countries, see UNCTAD 2000. Raghavan (1996) presents developing countries' perspective on the so-called new issues.

has been shaped in response to a tug-of-war between exporters and multinational corporations in the advanced industrial countries (which have had the upper hand), on one side, and import-competing interests (typically, but not solely, labor) on the other. The chief beneficiaries of free trade mentioned in textbooks—consumers—sit nowhere at the table. The features of the WTO can best be understood in this context, as the product of intense lobbying by specific exporter groups in the United States or Europe or of specific compromises between such groups and other domestic groups. The differential treatment of manufactures and agriculture, or of clothing and other goods within manufacturing, the antidumping regime, and the IPR (intellectual property rights) regime, just to pick some of the key anomalies, are all the results of this *political* process. Understanding this is essential since it underscores the important point that there is very little in the structure of multilateral trade negotiations to ensure that their outcomes are consistent with developmental goals, let alone that they are designed to further development.

Hence, there are at least three sources of slippage between what development requires and what the WTO does. First, even if free trade were optimal for development in its broad sense, the WTO does not fundamentally pursue free trade. Second, even if free trade were what the WTO was about, there is no guarantee that free trade is the best trade policy for countries at low levels of development. Third, compliance with WTO rules, even when they are not harmful in themselves, crowds outs a more fully developmental agenda—both at the international and national level. I have developed the second and third of these arguments more fully in the main body of this chapter.

My key argument has been that the world trading regime has to shift from a "market access" mind-set to a "development" mind-set. Essentially, the shift means that we stop evaluating the trade regime from the perspective of whether it maximizes the flow of trade in goods and services, and ask instead, "Do the trading arrangements—current and proposed—maximize the possibilities of development at the national level?" I have discussed why these two perspectives are *not* the same, even though they sometimes overlap, and have outlined some of the operational implications of such a shift. One key implication is that developing nations have to articulate their needs not in terms of market access, but in terms of the policy autonomy that will allow them to exercise institutional innovations that depart from prevailing orthodoxies. A second implication is that the WTO should be conceived of not as an institution devoted to harmonization and the reduction of national institutional differences, but as an institution that manages the interface between different national systems.

The Doha "development round" falls far short of this goal, as it focuses on agricultural reform and is based largely on a market-access

mind-set. Indeed, one of the mysteries of the current round of trade negotiations is that developing nations have let themselves be bamboozled into
accepting an agenda centered on agricultural liberalization as a "development round." In fact, the developing countries' interest in agricultural liberalization has always been ambiguous. Aside from a few middle-income
members of the Cairns group, such as Argentina, Brazil, Chile and Thailand,
which are important agricultural exporters, few developing countries have
traditionally looked at this area as a major source of gain. Research done at
the World Bank during the Uruguay Round highlighted the possibility that
most sub-Saharan African nations could actually end up *worse off* as a result
of the rise in world food prices produced by the reduction in European
export subsidies. More recently, a range of careful, microeconomic studies
have shown that the poverty impact of increases in relative agricultural
prices tends to be heterogeneous and uncertain, even for the producers
themselves.

Moreover, most global trade models predict very modest increases
in agricultural prices—increases that are likely to be swamped by the sheer
volatility in commodity prices. Consider cotton for example. The *largest*
estimate of the price impact of the eventual and complete removal of U.S.
cotton subsidies is around 15 percent. Compare this to the impact of the
devaluation of the CFA franc in 1994 by 50 percent, which in principle
should have raised agricultural incomes in countries such as Burkina Faso
and Benin by a full 50 percent. There is little evidence that such a boost in
incomes actually took place, however, since the most direct beneficiaries of
increases in border prices tend to be traders and intermediaries, rather
than farmers. In all likelihood, poor farmers will reap very few of the gains
generated by agricultural liberalization in the North. The real (economic)
winners will be taxpayers and consumers in the North and traders and
intermediaries in the South.

A shift to a real developmental mind-set in trade negotiations
would have several important advantages. The first, and the most obvious
one, is that this would provide for a more development-friendly international economic environment. Countries would be able to use trade as a
means for development, rather than being forced to view trade as an end in
itself (and being forced to sacrifice developmental goals in the bargain). It
would save developing countries precious political capital by obviating the
need to bargain for "special and differential treatment"—a principle that in
any case is more form than substance at this point.

Second, viewing the WTO as an institution that manages institutional diversity (rather than imposing uniformity) gets the developing
countries out of a conundrum inherent in their current negotiating stance.
The conundrum arises from the inconsistency between their demands for
maneuvering space to implement their development policies, on the one

hand, and their complaints about Northern protectionism in agriculture, textiles, and labor and environmental standards, on the other. As long as the issues are viewed in market-access terms, developing countries will remain unable to make a sound and principled defense of their legitimate need for space. And the only way they can gain enhanced market access is by restricting their own policy autonomy in exchange. Once one views the objective of the trading regime differently—to let different national economic systems prosper side by side—the debate can become a more fruitful one about each nation's institutional priorities and how they may be rendered compatible in a development-friendly way.

The third advantage is that this shift in perspective provides a way out of the impasse in which the trading system finds itself. At present, two groups feel excluded from the decision-making machinery of the global trade regime: developing country governments and Northern NGOs. The former complain about the asymmetry in trade rules, while the latter charge that the system pays inadequate attention to fundamental values such as transparency, accountability, human rights, and environmental sustainability. The demands of these two disenfranchised groups are often perceived to be conflicting—over questions such as labor and environmental standards or the transparency of the dispute settlement procedures—allowing the advanced industrial countries and the leadership of the WTO to seize the "middle" ground. It is the demands of these two groups, and the apparent tension between them, that has paralyzed the process of multi lateral trade negotiations.

But once one views the trade regime—and the governance challenges it poses—from a developmental perspective, it becomes clear that the developing country governments and many of the Northern NGOs share the same goals: policy autonomy to pursue one's own values and priorities, poverty alleviation, and human development in an environmentally sustainable manner. The tensions over issues such as labor standards become manageable if the debate is couched in terms of developmental processes—broadly defined—instead of the requirements of market access. On all counts, then, the shift in perspective provides a better foundation for the multilateral trading regime.

9

Globalization for Whom?

GLOBALIZATION has brought little but good news to those with the products, skills, and resources to market worldwide. But does it also work for the world's poor?

That is the central question around which the debate over globalization revolves. Antiglobalization protesters may have had only limited success in blocking world trade negotiations or disrupting the meetings of the International Monetary Fund (IMF), but they have irrevocably altered the terms of the debate. Poverty is now *the* defining issue for both sides. The captains of the world economy have conceded that progress in international trade and finance has to be measured against the yardsticks of poverty alleviation and sustainable development.

For most of the world's developing countries, the 1990s were a decade of frustration and disappointment. The economies of sub-Saharan Africa, with few exceptions, stubbornly refused to respond to the medicine meted out by the World Bank and the IMF. Latin American countries were buffeted by a never-ending series of boom-and-bust cycles in capital markets and experienced growth rates significantly below their historical averages. Most of the former socialist economies ended the decade at *lower* levels of per capita income than they started it—and even in the rare successes, such as Poland, poverty rates remained higher than under Communism. East Asian economies such as South Korea, Thailand, and Malaysia, which had been hailed previously as "miracles," were dealt a humiliating blow in the financial crisis of 1997. That this was also the decade in which globalization came into full swing is more than a minor inconvenience for its advocates. If globalization is such a boon for poor countries, why so many setbacks?

THE ARGUMENTS

Globalizers deploy two counterarguments against such complaints. One is that global poverty has actually decreased. The reason is simple: while *most* countries have seen lower income growth, the world's two largest countries, China and India, have had the opposite experience. As an empirical matter, economic growth tends to be correlated with poverty reduction. China's growth since the late 1970s—averaging almost 8 percent per annum per capita—has been nothing short of spectacular. India's performance has not been as extraordinary, but the country's growth rate has more than doubled since the early 1980s—from 1.5 percent per capita to 3.7 percent. These two countries house more than half of the world's poor, and their experience is perhaps enough to dispel the collective doom elsewhere.

The second counterargument is that it is precisely those countries that have experienced the greatest integration with the world economy that have managed to grow fastest and reduce poverty the most. A typical exercise in this vein consists of dividing developing countries into two groups on the basis of the increase in their trade—"globalizers" versus "nonglobalizers"—and to show that the first group did much better than the second. Here too, China, India, and a few other high performers like Vietnam and Uganda are the key exhibits for the proglobalization argument. The intended message from such studies is that countries that have the best shot at lifting themselves out of poverty are those that open themselves up to the world economy.

How we read globalization's record in alleviating poverty hinges critically, therefore, on what we make of the experience of a small number of countries that have done well in the last decade or two—China in particular. In 1960, the average Chinese expected to live only 36 years. By 1999, life expectancy had risen to 70 years, not far below the level of the United States. Literacy has risen from less than 50 percent to more than 80 percent. Even though economic development has been uneven, with the coastal regions doing much better than the interior, there has been a striking reduction in poverty rates almost everywhere.

What does this impressive experience tell us about what globalization can do for poor countries? There is little doubt that exports and foreign investment have played an important role in China's development. By selling its products on world markets, China has been able to purchase the capital equipment and inputs needed for its modernization. And the surge in foreign investment has brought much-needed managerial and technical expertise. The regions of China that have grown fastest are those that took the greatest advantage of foreign trade and investment.

INCONVENIENT FACTS

But look closer at the Chinese experience, and you discover that it is hardly a poster child for globalization. China's economic policies have violated virtually every rule by which the proselytizers of globalization would like the game to be played. China did *not* liberalize its trade regime to any significant extent, and it joined the World Trade Organization (WTO) only in 2001. Chinese currency markets were *not* unified until 1994. China resolutely refused to open its financial markets to foreigners, again until very recently. Most striking of all, China achieved its transformation without adopting private-property rights, let alone privatizing its state enterprises. China's policymakers were practical enough to understand the role that private incentives and markets could play in producing results. But they were also smart enough to realize that the solution to their problems lay in institutional innovations suited to the local conditions—the household responsibility system, township and village enterprises, special economic zones, partial liberalization in agriculture and industry—rather than in off-the-shelf blueprints and Western rules of good behavior.

The remarkable thing about China is that it has achieved integration with the world economy *despite* having ignored these rules—and indeed because it did so. If China were a basket case today, rather than the stunning success that it is, officials of the WTO and the World Bank would have fewer difficulties fitting it within their worldview than they do now.

China's experience may represent an extreme case, but it is by no means an exception. Earlier successes such as South Korea and Taiwan tell a similar story. Economic development often requires unconventional strategies that fit awkwardly with the ideology of free trade and free capital flows. South Korea and Taiwan made extensive use of import quotas, local-content requirements, patent infringements, and export subsidies—all of which are currently prohibited by the WTO. Both countries heavily regulated capital flows well into the 1990s. India managed to increase its growth rate through the adoption of more probusiness policies, despite having one of the world's most protectionist trade regimes. Its comparatively mild import liberalization in the 1990s came a decade *after* the onset of higher growth in the early 1980s. And India has *yet* to open itself up to world financial markets—which is why it emerged unscathed from the Asian financial crisis of 1997.

By contrast, many of the countries that have opened themselves up to trade and capital flows with abandon have been rewarded with financial crises and disappointing performance. Latin America, the region that adopted the globalization agenda with the greatest enthusiasm in the 1990s, has suffered rising inequality, enormous volatility, and economic growth rates significantly below those of the post-World War II decades. Argentina represents a particularly tragic case. It tried harder in the 1990s than virtually any country to endear itself to international capital markets, only to be the victim of an abrupt reversal in "market sentiment" by the end of the decade. The Argentine strategy may have had elements of a gamble, but it was solidly grounded in the theories expounded by U.S.-based economists and multilateral agencies such as the World Bank and the IMF. When Argentina's economy took off in the early 1990s after decades of stagnation, the reaction from these quarters was not puzzlement—it was that reform pays off.

What these countries' experience tells us, therefore, is that while global markets are good for poor countries, the rules according to which they are being asked to play the game are often not. Caught between WTO agreements, World Bank strictures, IMF conditions, and the need to maintain the confidence of financial markets, developing countries are increasingly deprived of the room they need to devise their own paths out of poverty. They are being asked to implement an agenda of institutional reform that took today's advanced countries generations to accomplish. The United States, to take a particularly telling example, was hardly a paragon of free-trade virtue while catching up with and surpassing Britain. In fact, U.S. import tariffs during the latter half of the nineteenth century were higher than in all but a few developing countries today. Today's rules are not only impractical, they divert attention and resources from more urgent developmental priorities. Turning away from world markets is surely not a good way to alleviate domestic poverty—but countries that have scored the most impressive gains are those that have developed their *own* version of the rulebook while taking advantage of world markets. The regulations that developing nations confront in those markets are highly asymmetric. Import barriers tend to be highest for manufactured products of greatest interest to poor countries, such as garments. The global intellectual-property-rights regime tends to raise prices of essential medicines in poor countries.

GOING FOR THE REAL GAINS

But the disconnect between trade rules and development needs is nowhere greater than in the area of international labor mobility. Thanks to the efforts of the United States and other rich countries, barriers to trade in goods, financial services, and investment flows have now been brought down to historic lows. But the one market where poor nations have something in abundance to sell—the market for labor services—has remained untouched by this liberalizing trend. Rules on cross-border labor flows are determined almost always unilaterally (rather than multilaterally as in other areas of economic exchange) and remain highly restrictive. Even a small relaxation of these rules would produce huge gains for the world economy, and for poor nations in particular.

Consider, for example, instituting a system that would allot temporary work permits to skilled and unskilled workers from poorer nations, amounting to, say, 3 percent of the rich countries' labor force. Under the scheme, these workers would be allowed to obtain employment in the rich countries for a period of three to five years, after which they would be expected to return to their home countries and be replaced by new workers. (While many workers, no doubt, will want to remain in the host countries permanently, it would be possible to achieve acceptable rates of return by building specific incentives into the scheme. For example, a portion of workers' earnings could be withheld until repatriation takes place. Or there could be penalties for home governments whose nationals failed to comply with return requirements: sending countries' quotas could be reduced in proportion to the numbers who fail to return.) A back-of-the-envelope calculation indicates that such a system would easily yield $200 billion of income annually for the citizens of developing nations—vastly more than the existing WTO trade agenda is expected to produce. The positive spillovers that the returnees would generate for their home countries—the experience, entrepreneurship, investment, and work ethic they would bring back with them—would add considerably to these gains. What is equally important, the economic benefits would accrue directly to workers from developing nations. There would be no need for "trickle down."

If the political leaders of the advanced countries have chosen to champion trade liberalization but not international labor mobility, the reason is not that the former is popular with voters at home while the latter is not. They are *both* unpopular. When asked their views on trade policy, fewer than one in five Americans rejects import restrictions. In most advanced countries, including the United States, the proportion of respondents who want to expand imports tends to be about the same or lower than the proportion who believe immigration is good for the economy. The main difference seems to be that the beneficiaries of trade and investment liberalization have managed to become politically effective. Multinational firms and financial enterprises have been successful in setting the agenda of multilateral trade negotiations because they have been quick to see the link between enhanced market access abroad and increased profits at home. Cross-border labor flows, by contrast, usually have not had a well-defined constituency in the advanced countries. Rules on foreign workers have been relaxed only in those rare instances where there has been intense lobbying from special interests. When Silicon Valley firms became concerned about labor costs, for example, they pushed Congress hard to be allowed to import software engineers from India and other developing nations.

CONCLUDING REMARKS

It will take a lot of work to make globalization's rules friendlier to poor nations. Leaders of the advanced countries will have to stop dressing up policies championed by special interests at home as responses to the needs of the poor in the developing world. Remembering their own history, they will have to provide room for poor nations to develop their own strategies of institution-building and economic catch-up. For their part, developing nations will have to stop looking to financial markets and multilateral agencies for the recipes of economic growth. Perhaps most difficult of all, economists will have to learn to be more humble!

References

Acemoglu, Daron, Philippe Aghion, and Fabrizio Zilibotti. 2002. "Distance to Frontier, Selection, and Economic Growth." NBER Working Paper no. 9066. National Bureau of Economic Research, July.

Acemoglu, Daron, Simon Johnson, and James A. Robinson. 2001. "The Colonial Origins of Comparative Development: An Empirical Investigation." *American Economic Review* 91.5: 1369–1401.

———. 2003. "Botswana: An African Success Story." In *In Search of Prosperity: Analytic Narratives on Economic Growth*. Ed. Dani Rodrik. Princeton, NJ: Princeton University Press.

Aghion, Philippe, Robin Burgess, Stephen Redding, and Fabrizio Zilibotti. 2003. "The Unequal Effects of Liberalization: Theory and Evidence from India." Department of Economics, London School of Economics, March.

Agosin, Manuel. 1999. "Trade and Growth in Chile: Past Performance and Future Prospects." Department of Economics, University of Chile, June.

Alesina, Alberto, and Allan Drazen. 1991. "Why Are Stabilizations Delayed?" *American Economic Review* 81.5: 1170–88.

Amsden, Alice H. 1989. *Asia's Next Giant: South Korea and Late Industrialization.* New York: Oxford University Press.

———. 2000. "Industrialization under New WTO Law." Paper prepared for the High-Level Round Table on Trade and Development, UNCTAD X, Bangkok, February 12.

Anderson, James E., and Douglas Marcouiller. 2002. "Insecurity and the Pattern of Trade: An Empirical Investigation." *Review of Economics and Statistics* 84.2: 342–52.

Anderson, James E., and J. Peter Neary. 1992. "Trade Reform with Quotas, Partial Rent Retention, and Tariffs." *Econometrica* 60: 57–76.

Anderson, James E., and Eric van Wincoop. 2004. "Trade Costs." *Journal of Economic Literature* 42.3: 691–751.

Aoki, Masahiko. 1997. "Unintended Fit: Organizational Evolution and Government Design of Institutions in Japan." In *The Role of Government in East Asian Economic Development: Comparative Institutional Analysis.* Ed. M. Aoki et al. Oxford: Clarendon Press.

Aslund, Anders, Peter Boone, and Simon Johnson. 1996. "How to Stabilize: Lessons from Post-Communist Countries." *Brookings Papers on Economic Activity* 1: 217–313.

Aslund, Anders, and Simon Johnson. 2003. "Small Enterprises and Economic Policy." Working paper, Sloan School, MIT.

Azariadis C., and A. Drazen. 1990. "Threshold Externalities in Economic Development." *Quarterly Journal of Economics* 105.2: 501–26.

Bagwell, Kyle, and Robert Staiger. 1990. "A Theory of Managed Trade." *American Economic Review* 80.4: 779–95.

Barro, Robert. 1996. "Determinants of Economic Growth: A Cross-Country Empirical Study." NBER Working Paper no. 5698. National Bureau of Economic Research, August.

Barth, G. Caprio, and S. Levine. 2001. "The Regulation and Supervision of Banks Around the World: A New Database." World Bank Working Paper Series no. 2588.

Ben-David, Dan. 1993. "Equalizing Exchange: Trade Liberalization and Income Convergence." *Quarterly Journal of Economics* 108.3: 653–79.

Berkowitz, Daniel, Katharina Pistor, and Jean-Francois Richard. 2003. "Economic Development, Legality, and the Transplant Effect." *European Economic Review* 47.1: 165–95.

Besley, Timothy, and Robin Burgess. 2002. "Halving Global Poverty." Department of Economics, London School of Economics, August.

Birdsall, Nancy, and Augusto de la Torre. 2001. *Washington Contentious: Economic Policies for Social Equity in Latin America*. Washington, DC: Carnegie Endowment for International Peace.

Bordo, Michael D., Claudia Goldin, and Eugene N. White, eds. 1998. *The Defining Moment: The Great Depression and the American Economy in the Twentieth Century*. Chicago: University of Chicago Press.

Bosworth, Barry, and Susan M. Collins. 2003. "The Empirics of Growth: An Update." Brookings Institution, March 7.

Brock, William A., and Steven N. Durlauf. 2001. "Growth Empirics and Reality." *World Bank Economic Review* 15.2: 229–72.

Caballero, Ricardo J., and Arvind Krishnamurthy. 2003. "Excessive Dollar Debt: Financial Development and Underinsurance." *Journal of Finance* 58.2: 867–94.

Calvo, Guillermo. 1989. "Incredible Reforms." In *Debt, Stabilization and Development*. Ed. Calvo et al. New York: Basil Blackwell.

Casella, Alessandra, and James Rauch. 2002. "Anonymous Market and Group Ties in International Trade." *Journal of International Economics* 58: 19–47.

Chandra, Siddharth. 1998. "On Pillars of Democracy and Economic Growth." Graduate School of Public and International Affairs, University of Pittsburgh, February.

Chen, Shaohua, and Martin Ravallion. 2004. "How Have the World's Poor Fared since the Early 1980s." Policy Research Working Paper no. WPS 3341, World Bank, July.

Chowdhurie-Aziz, Monali. 1997. "Political Openness and Economic Performance." University of Minnesota, January.

Clapp, Roger Alex. 1995. "Creating Comparative Advantage: Forest Policy as Industrial Policy in Chile." *Economic Geography* 71.3: 273–96.

Collins, Susan, and Barry Bosworth. 1996. "Economic Growth in East Asia: Accumulation versus Assimilation." *Brookings Papers on Economic Activity* 2: 135–91.

de Ferranti, David, Guillermo E. Perry, Daniel Lederman, and William F. Maloney. 2002. *From Natural Resources to the Knowledge Economy*. Washington, DC: World Bank.

de Menil, Georges. 2003. "History, Policy, and Performance in Two Transition Economies: Poland and Romania." In *In Search of Prosperity: Analytic Narratives of Economic Growth*. Ed. Dani Rodrik. Princeton, NJ: Princeton University Press.

DeLong, Brad. 2003. "India since Independence: An Analytic Growth Narrative." In *In Search of Prosperity: Analytic Narratives of Economic Growth*. Ed. Dani Rodrik. Princeton, NJ: Princeton University Press.

Dewatripont, Mathias, and Gerard Roland. 1995. "The Design of Reform Packages Under Uncertainty." *American Economic Review* 85.5: 1207–23.

Diamond, J. 1997. *Guns, Germs, and Steel*. New York: W. W. Norton.

Dixit, Avinash. 2004. *Lawlessness and Economics: Alternative Modes of Economic Governance*. Princeton, NJ: Princeton University Press.

Djankov, Simeon, Edward Glaeser, Rafael LaPorta, Florencio Lopez-de-Silanes, and Andrei Shleifer. 2003. "The New Comparative Economics." *Journal of Comparative Economics* 31.4: 595–619.

Dollar, David, and Aart Kraay. 2004. "Trade, Growth, and Poverty." *Economic Journal* 114: F22–F49.

———. 2000. Dataset for *Trade, Growth, and Poverty*. Washington, DC: World Bank.

Easterly, William. 2001. *The Elusive Quest for Growth*. Cambridge: MIT Press.

———. 2005. "National Policies and Economic Growth: A Reappraisal." In *Handbook of Economic Growth*. Ed. Philippe Aghion and Steven Durlauf. Vol. 1. Amsterdam: Elsevier.

Easterly, William, Michael Kremer, Lant Pritchett, and Lawrence H. Summers. 1993. "Good Policy or Good Luck? Country Growth Performance and Temporary Shocks." *Journal of Monetary Economics* 32.3: 459–83.

Easterly, William, and R. Levine. 2003. "Tropics, Germs, and Crops: How Endowments Influence Economic Development." *Journal of Monetary Economics* 50.1: 3–39.

Eaton, Jonathan, and Mark Gersovitz. 1981. "Debt with Potential Repudiation: Theoretical and Empirical Analysis." *Review of Economic Studies* 48.2: 289–309.

———. 1998. "Openness, Productivity and Growth: What Do We Really Know?" *Economic Journal* 108: 383–98.

Engerman, Stanley, and Kenneth L. Sokoloff. 1994. "Factor Endowments, Institutions, and Differential Paths of Growth Among New World Economies: A View from Economic Historians of the United States." NBER Working Paper no. H0066. National Bureau of Economic Research, December.

Evans, Peter. 1995. *Embedded Autonomy: States and Industrial Transformation.* Princeton, NJ: Princeton University Press.

———. 2000. "Economic Governance Institutions in a Global Political Economy: Implications for Developing Countries." Paper prepared for the High-Level Round Table on Trade and Development, UNCTAD X, Bangkok, February 12.

Feldstein, Martin S., and Charles Horioka. 1980. "Domestic Saving and International Capital Flows." *Economic Journal* 90: 314–29.

Feynman, Richard P. 1985. *Surely You're Joking Mr. Feynman! (Adventures of a Curious Character).* New York: W. W. Norton.

Finger, Michael J., and Philip Schuler. 1999. "Implementation of Uruguay Round Commitments: the Development Challenge." World Bank Policy Research Working Paper no. 2215. September.

Frankel, Jeffrey. 2000a. "The Asian Model, the Miracle, the Crisis, and the Fund." In *Currency Crises.* Ed. Paul Krugman. Chicago: University of Chicago Press.

———. 2000b. "Globalization of the Economy." In *Governance in a Globalizing World.* Ed. Joseph S. Nye and John D. Donahue. Washington, DC: Brookings Institution Press.

Frankel, Jeffrey, and David Romer. 1999. "Does Trade Cause Growth?" *American Economic Review* 89.3: 379–99.

Freeman, Richard B. 2000. "Single Peaked vs. Diversified Capitalism: The Relation Between Economic Institutions and Outcomes." NBER Working Paper No. W7556. National Bureau of Economic Research, February.

Frey, Bruno. 1996. "FOCJ: Competitive Governments for Europe." *International Review of Law and Economics* 16.3: 315–27.

Friedman, Eric, Simon Johnson, Daniel Kaufmann, and Pablo Zoido-Lobaton. 2000. "Dodging the Grabbing Hand: The Determinants of Unofficial Activity in 69 Countries." *Journal of Public Economics* 76.3: 459–93.

Friedman, Thomas L. 1999. *The Lexus and the Olive Tree: Understanding Globalization.* New York: Farrar, Straus and Giroux.

Gallup J. L., J. D. Sachs, and A. D. Mellinger. 1998. "Geography and Economic Development." NBER Working Paper no. W6849. National Bureau of Economic Research, December.

Gerschenkron, Alexander. 1962. *Economic Backwardness in Historical Perspective: A Book of Essays.* Cambridge: Harvard University Press.

Gilbert, Christopher L., and Panos Varangis. 2003. "Globalization and International Commodity Trade with Specific Reference to the West African Cocoa Producers." NBER Working Paper no. W9668. National Bureau of Economic Research, May.

Glaeser, Edward L., Rafael La Porta, Florencio Lopez-de-Silanes, and Andrei Shleifer. 2004. "Do Institutions Cause Growth?" *Journal of Economic Growth* 9.3: 271–303.

Goldstone, Jack A. Forthcoming. *The Happy Chance: The Rise of the West in Global Context, 1500–1850.* Cambridge: Harvard University Press.

Greider, William. 1997. *One World Ready or Not: The Manic Logic of Global Capitalism.* New York, Simon and Schuster.

Gulhati, Ravi. 1990. *The Making of Economic Policy in Africa.* Washington, DC: Economic Development Institute, World Bank.

Haggard, Stephan. 2004. "Institutions and Growth in East Asia." *Studies in Comparative International Development* 38.4: 53–81.

Haggard, Stephan, and Robert Kaufman, eds. 1983. *The Politics of Economic Adjustment.* Princeton, NJ: Princeton University Press.

Hall, Robert E., and Charles I. Jones. 1999. "Why Do Some Countries Produce So Much More Output per Worker than Others?" *Quarterly Journal of Economics* 114.1: 83–116.

Hanson, Gordon H. 2001. "Should Countries Promote Foreign Direct Investment?" G-24 Discussion Paper No. 9, United Nations, Geneva, February.

———. 2003. "Interview with Arnold Harberger: Sound Policies Can Free Up Natural Forces of Growth." *IMF Survey* 32.19: 213–16.

Harrison, Glenn W., Thomas F. Rutherford, and David G . Tarr. 1993. "Trade Reform in the Partially Liberalized Economy of Turkey." *World Bank Economic Review* 7.2: 191–218.

Hatta, Tatsuo. 1977a. "A Recommendation for a Better Tariff Structure." *Econometrica* 45: 1859–69.

———. 1977b. "A Theory of Piecemeal Policy Recommendations." *Review of Economic Studies* 44: 1–21.

Hausmann, Ricardo, and Michael Gavin. 1996. "Securing Stability and Growth in a Shock Prone Region: The Policy Challenge for Latin America." Inter-American Development Bank, Washington, DC.

Hausmann, Ricardo, Lant Pritchett, and Dani Rodrik. 2004. "Growth Accelerations." Harvard University, May.

———. 2005. "Growth Accelerations." *Journal of Economic Growth* 10: 303–29.

Hausmann, Ricardo, and Dani Rodrik. 2003. "Economic Development as Self-Discovery." *Journal of Development Economics* 72: 603–33.

———. 2005. "Self-Discovery in a Development Strategy for El Salvador." *Economia* 6.1: 43–102.

Hausmann, Ricardo, Andres Velasco, and Dani Rodrik. 2005. "Growth Diagnostics." In *The Washington Consensus Reconsidered: Towards a New Global Governance.* Ed. J. Stiglitz and N. Serra. Oxford University Press, forthcoming

Heckman, James J., and Carmen Pages. 2000. "The Cost of Job Security Regulation: Evidence from Latin American Labor Markets." NBER Working Paper no. 7773. National Bureau of Economic Research, June.

Helleiner, Gerald K. 2000. "Markets, Politics, and the Global Economy: Can the Global Economy Be Civilized?" Prebisch Lecture, UNCTAD, December.

Helleiner, Gerald K. ed. 1994. *Trade Policy and Industrialization in Turbulent Times.* London: Routledge.

Helliwell, John F. 1994. "Empirical Linkages Between Democracy and Economic Growth." *British Journal of Political Science* 24: 225–48.

———. 1998. *How Much Do National Borders Matter?* Washington, DC: Brookings Institution.

Hellmann, Thomas, Kevin Murdock, and Joseph Stiglitz. 1997. "Financial Restraint: Toward a New Paradigm." In *The Role of Government in East Asian Economic Development: Comparative Institutional Analysis.* Eds. M. Aoki et al. Oxford: Clarendon Press.

Hibbs, Douglas A., Jr., and Ola Olsson. 2004. "Geography, Biogeography, and Why Some Countries Are Rich and Others Are Poor." *Proceedings of the National Academy of Sciences* 101.10: 3715–20.

Hirschman, Albert O. 1958. *The Strategy of Economic Development.* New Haven: Yale University Press.

Hoekman, Bernard. 2005. "Operationalizing the Concept of Policy Space in the WTO: Beyond Special and Differential Treatment." *Journal of International Economic Law* 8.2: 405–24.

Hoff, Karla, and Joseph Stiglitz. 2001. "Modern Economic Theory and Development." In *Frontiers of Development Economics.* Ed. G. M. Meier and J. E. Stiglitz. New York: Oxford University Press.

Imbs, Jean, and Romain Wacziarg. 2003. "Stages of Diversification." *American Economic Review* 93.1: 63–86.

Isham, Jonathan, Daniel Kaufmann, and Lant Pritchett. 1997. "Civil Liberties, Democracy, and the Performance of Government Projects." *World Bank Economic Review* 11.2: 219–42.

Jacoby, Sanford M. 1998. "Risk and the Labor Market: Societal Past as Economic Prologue." Institute of Industrial Relations, UCLA.

Jaggers K., and T. R. Gurr. 1995. "Tracking Democracy's Third Wave with Polity III Data." *Journal of Peace Research* 32.4: 469–82.

Jarvis, Lovell S. 1994. "Changing Private and Public Roles in Technological Development: Lessons from the Chilean Fruit Sector." In *Agricultural Technology: Policy Issues for the International Community.* Ed. J. R. Anderson. Wallingford, England: CAB International.

Johnson, Simon, John McMillan, and Chris Woodruff. 2000. "Entrepreneurs and the Ordering of Institutional Reform: Poland, Slovakia, Romania, Russia, and Ukraine Compared." *Economics of Transition* 8.1: 1–36.

Johnson, Simon, and Andrei Shleifer. 1999. "Coase v. the Coasians: The Regulation and Development of Securities Markets in Poland and the Czech Republic." MIT and Harvard University, September.

Kapur, Devesh, and John McHale. 2005. *Give Us Your Best and Brightest: The Global Hunt for Talent and Its Impact on the Developing World.* Washington, DC: Center for Global Development.

Kaufmann, Daniel. 2002. "Rethinking Governance." World Bank Institute, World Bank, Washington, DC, December.

Kaufmann, Daniel, Aart Kraay, and Pablo Zoido-Lobatón. 1999. "Governance Matters." World Bank Policy Research Department Paper no. 2196. May.

———. 2002. "Governance Matters II—Updated Indicators for 2000/01." World Bank Policy Research Department Working Paper no. 2772.

Keohane, Robert O., and Joseph S. Nye. 1999. "Power, Interdependence, and Globalism." Unpublished paper, November 16.

Keynes, John Maynard. 1920. *The Economic Consequences of the Peace.* New York: Harcourt, Brace, and Howe.

Klinger, Bailey, and Daniel Lederman. 2006. "Diversification, Innovation, and Imitation inside the Global Technological Frontier." World Bank Policy Research Department Working Paper no. 3872. April.

Knack, Stephen, and Philip Keefer. 1995. "Institutions and Economic Performance: Cross-Country Tests Using Alternative Institutional Measures." *Economics and Politics* 7: 207–28.

———. 1997. "Does Social Capital Have an Economic Payoff? A Cross-Country Investigation." *Quarterly Journal of Economics* 112.4: 1251–88.

Krueger, Anne O. 1997. "Trade Policy and Development: How We Learn" *American Economic Review* 87.1: 1–22.

Krugman, Paul. 1995. "Dutch Tulips and Emerging Markets." *Foreign Affairs* 74.4: 36–37.

Kuczynski, Pedro-Pablo, and John Williamson, eds. 2003. *After the Washington Consensus: Restarting Growth and Reform in Latin America.* Washington, DC: Institute for International Economics.

Lall, Sanjaya. 2004. "Reinventing Industrial Strategy: The Role of Government Policy in Building Industrial Competitiveness." G-24 Discussion Paper no. 28, United Nations, Geneva, April.

Lau, Lawrence, J., Yingyi Qian, and Gerard Roland. 2000. "Reform Without Losers: An Interpretation of China's Dual-Track Approach to Transition." *Journal of Political Economy* 108.1: 120–43.

Lawrence, Robert Z. 1996. *Regionalism, Multilateralism, and Deeper Integration.* Washington, DC: Brookings Institution.

Li, Shuhe. 1999. "The Benefits and Costs of Relation-Based Governance: An Explanation of the East Asian Miracle and Crisis." City University of Hong Kong, October.

Lin, Justin Yifu, Fang Cai, and Zhou Li. 1996. *The China Miracle: Development Strategy and Economic Reform,* Shatin, NT, Hong Kong: Chinese University Press.

Lin, Justin Yifu, and Jeffrey B. Nugent. 1995. "Institutions and Economic Development." *Handbook of Economic Development.* Ed. J. Behrman and T. N. Srinivasan. Vol. 3A. Amsterdam: North-Holland.

Lindauer, David L., and Lant Pritchett. 2002. "What's the Big Idea? The Third Generation of Policies for Economic Growth." *Economia* 3.1: 1–40.

Lipton, David, and Jeffrey Sachs. 1990. "Creating a Market Economy in Eastern Europe: The Case of Poland." *Brookings Papers on Economic Activity* 1: 75–133.

Loayza, Norman, Pablo Fajnzylber, and Cesar Calderón. 2002. "Economic Growth in Latin America and the Caribbean: Stylized Facts, Explanations, and Forecasts." World Bank, Washington, DC, June.

López E. 2003. "El Salvador: Growing in the Millennium." World Bank, May 21.

Lopez, Ramon. 1997. "Environmental Externalities in Traditional Agriculture and the Impact of Trade Liberalization: The Case of Ghana." *Journal of Development Economics* 53.1: 17–39.

Lopez, Ramon, and Arvind Panagariya. 1992. "On the Theory of Piecemeal Tariff Reform: The Case of Pure Imported Intermediate Inputs." *American Economic Review* 82.3: 615–25.

Lora, Eduardo. 2001a. "Structural Reforms in Latin America: What Has Been Reformed and How to Measure It." Inter-American Development Bank, Washington, DC, December.

———. 2001b. "El crecimiento económico en América Latina después de una década de reformas estructurales." Research Department, Inter-American Development Bank, Washington, DC.

MacLean, Brian K. 1999. "The Rise and Fall of the 'Crony Capitalism' Hypothesis: Causes and Consequences." Department of Economics, Laurentian University, Ontario, March.

Madani, Dorsati. 1998. "A Review of the Role and Impact of Export Processing Zones." World Bank.

Maddison, Angus. 2001. *The World Economy: A Millennial Perspective.* Paris: OECD.

Matsuyama, Kiminori. 1992. "Agricultural Productivity, Comparative Advantage, and Economic Growth." *Journal of Economic Theory.* 58.2: 317–34.

Mayda, Anna Maria, and Dani Rodrik. 2005. "Why Are Some Individuals (and Countries) More Protectionist than Others?" *European Economic Review* 49:1393–1430.

Meade J. E., et al. 1961. *The Economics and Social Structure of Mauritius—Report to the Government of Mauritius.* London: Methuen.

Melo, Alberto. 2001. "Industrial Policy in Latin America at the Turn of the Century." Research Department Working Paper no. 459. Inter-American Development Bank.

Milanovic, Branko. 2003. "The Two Faces of Globalization: Against Globalization as We Know It." *World Development* 31.4: 667–83.

Miles, William F. S. 1999. "The Mauritius Enigma." *Journal of Democracy* 10.2: 91–104.

Milner, Helen V., and B. Peter Rosendorff. 1998. "The Optimal Design of International Trade Institutions: Uncertainty and Escape." Department of Political Science, Columbia University, August.

Mishkin, Frederick S. 2006. *The Next Great Globalization: How Disadvantaged Nations Can Harness Their Financial Systems to Get Rich.* Princeton, NJ: Princeton University Press.

Moore, Mike. 2000. "The WTO Is a Friend of the Poor." *Financial Times,* June 19.

Mukand, Sharun, and Dani Rodrik. 2005. "In Search of the Holy Grail: Policy Convergence, Experimentation, and Economic Performance." *American Economic Review* 95.1: 374–83.

Murphy, Kevin M., Andrei Shleifer, and Robert W. Vishny. 1989. "Industrialization and the Big Push." *Journal of Political Economy* 97.5: 1003–26.

———. 1992. "The Transition to a Market Economy: Pitfalls of Partial Reform." *Quarterly Journal of Economics* 107.3: 889–906.

Naim, Moises. 1999. "Fads and Fashion in Economic Reforms: Washington Consensus or Washington Confusion?" Paper prepared for the IMF Conference on Second Generation Reforms, Washington, DC, October.

Nelson, Richard R. 2004. "The Changing Institutional Requirements for Technological and Economic Catch Up." Columbia University, June.

North, Douglass C. 1990. *Institutions, Institutional Change and Economic Performance.* New York: Cambridge University Press.

———. 1994. "Economic Performance Through Time." *American Economic Review* 84.3: 359–68.

North, Douglass C., and R. Thomas. 1973. *The Rise of the Western World: A New Economic History.* Cambridge: Cambridge University Press.

North, Douglass C., and Barry Weingast. 1989. "Constitutions and Commitment: The Evolution of Institutions Governing Public Choice in Seventeenth Century England." *Journal of Economic History* 49.4: 803–32.

Obstfeld, Maurice, and Alan Taylor. 1998. "The Great Depression as a Watershed: International Capital Mobility over the Long Run." In *The Defining Moment: The Great Depression and the American Economy in the Twentieth Century.* Ed. Michael D. Bordo, Claudia D. Goldin, and Eugene N. White. Chicago: University of Chicago Press.

Ocampo, José Antonio. 2002. "Rethinking the Development Agenda." United Nations Economic Commission for Latin America and the Caribbean (ECLAC), Santiago, Chile.

———. 2003. "Structural Dynamics and Economic Growth in Developing Countries." United Nations Economic Commission for Latin America and the Caribbean (ECLAC), Santiago, Chile.

Persson, Torsten, and Guido Tabellini. 2006. "Democracy and Development: The Devil in the Details." *American Economic Review Papers and Proceedings* 96.2: 319–24.

Piketty, Thomas. 1996. "A Federal Voting Mechanism to Solve the Fiscal-Externality Problem." *European Economic Review* 40.1: 3–18.

Pistor, Katharina. 2002. "The Standardization of Law and its Effect on Developing Economies." *American Journal of Comparative Law* 50: 101–34.

Polterovich, Victor, and Vladimir Popov. 2002. "Accumulation of Foreign Exchange Reserves and Long Term Growth." New Economic School, Moscow.

Pritchett, Lant. 1997. "Economic Growth: Hills, Plains, Mountains, Plateaus and Cliffs." World Bank, October.

———. 2004. "Does Learning to Add Up Add Up? The Returns to Schooling in Aggregate Data." Kennedy School of Government, Harvard University.

Qian, Yingyi. 2003. "How Reform Worked in China." In *In Search of Prosperity: Analytic Narratives of Economic Growth.* Ed. Dani Rodrik. Princeton, NJ: Princeton University Press.

Qian, Yingyi, Gerard Roland, and Chenggang Xu. 1999. "Coordinating Changes in M-Form and U-Form Organizations." Paper prepared for the Nobel Symposium, August.

Quinn, Dennis P., and John T. Woolley. 1998. "Democracy and National Economic Performance: The Search for Stability." School of Business, Georgetown University, June.

Raghavan, Chakravarthi. 1996. "The New Issues and Developing Countries." In *TWN Trade & Development Series.* No. 4. Penang, Malaysia: Third World Network.

Rodríguez, Francisco. 2005. "Cleaning up the Kitchen Sink: On the Consequences of the Linearity Assumption for Cross-Country Growth Empirics." Department of Economics, Wesleyan University, September.

Rodríguez, Francisco, and Dani Rodrik. 2001. "Trade Policy and Economic Growth: A Skeptic's Guide to the Cross-National Evidence." In *NBER Macroeconomics Annual 2000.* Ed. Ben Bernanke and Kenneth S. Rogoff. Cambridge: MIT Press.

Rodríguez-Clare, Andrés. 1996. "The Division of Labor and Economic Development." *Journal of Development Economics* 49.1: 3–32.

———. 2004. "Clusters and Comparative Advantage: Implications for Industrial Policy." Inter-American Development Bank, June.

Rodrik, Dani. 1991. "Policy Uncertainty and Private Investment in Developing Countries." *Journal of Development Economics* 36: 229–42.

———. 1995a. "Getting Interventions Right: How South Korea and Taiwan Grew Rich." *Economic Policy* 20: 55–107.

———. 1995b. "Taking Trade Policy Seriously: Export Subsidization as a Case Study in Policy Effectiveness." In *New Directions in Trade Theory.* Ed. A. Deardorff, J. Levinson, and R. Stern. Ann Arbor: University of Michigan Press.

———. 1996a. "Understanding Economic Policy Reform." *Journal of Economic Literature* 34.1: 9–41.

———. 1996b. "Coordination Failures and Government Policy: A Model with Applications to East Asia and Eastern Europe." *Journal of International Economics* 40.1–2: 1–22.

———. 1997a. "Democracy and Economic Performance." Unpublished paper, December.

———. 1997b. *Has Globalization Gone Too Far?* Washington, DC: Institute for International Economics.

Rodrik, Dani. 1998a. "Why Do More Open Economies Have Bigger Governments?" *Journal of Political Economy* 106.5: 997–1032.

———. 1998b. "The Debate over Globalization: How to Move Forward by Looking Backward." In *Launching New Global Trade Talks: An Action Agenda.* Special

Report no. 12. Ed. Jeffrey J. Schott. Washington, DC: Institute for International Economics.

———. 1999a. *The New Global Economy and Developing Countries: Making Openness Work*. Washington, DC: Overseas Development Council.

———. 1999b. "Where Did All the Growth Go? External Shocks, Social Conflict, and Growth Collapses." *Journal of Economic Growth* 4.4: 385–412.

———. 1999c. "Democracies Pay Higher Wages." *Quarterly Journal of Economics* 114.3: 707–38.

———. 2001a. "Why Is There So Much Economic Insecurity in Latin America?" *CEPAL Review* 73: 7–30.

———. 2001b. "Trading in Illusions." *Foreign Policy* 123: 55–62.

Rodrik, Dani, and Arvind Subramanian. 2005. "From Hindu Growth to Productivity Surge: The Mystery of the Indian Growth Transition." *IMF Staff Papers* 52.2.

Rodrik, Dani, Arvind Subramanian, and Francesco Trebbi. 2004. "Institutions Rule: The Primacy of Institutions over Geography and Integration in Economic Development." *Journal of Economic Growth* 9.2: 131–65.

Rose, Andrew K. 1999. "One Money, One Market: Estimating the Effect of Common Currencies on Trade." NBER Working Paper no. 7432. National Bureau of Economic Research, December.

Rosenstein-Rodan, Paul. 1943. "Problems of Industrialization of Eastern and Southeastern Europe." *Economic Journal* 53: 202–11.

Rostow, Walt W. 1965. *The Stages of Economic Growth: A Non-Communist Manifesto*. Cambridge: Cambridge University Press.

Ruggie, John G. 1994. "Trade, Protectionism and the Future of Welfare Capitalism." *Journal of International Affairs* 48.1: 1–11.

Sabel, Charles F. 2004a. "Beyond Principal-Agent Governance: Experimentalist Organizations, Learning and Accountability." In *Democratie voorbij de Staat*. Ed. Ewald Engelen and Monika Sie Dhian Ho. Amsterdam: Amsterdam University Press.

———. 2004b. "Theory of a Real-Time Revolution." Columbia University, July 2003.

Sabel, Charles F., and Sanjay Reddy. N.d. "Learning to Learn: Undoing the Gordian Knot of Development Today." Columbia University.

Sachs, Jeffrey. 2003. "Institutions Don't Rule: Direct Effects of Geography on Per Capita Income." NBER Working Paper no. 9490. National Bureau of Economic Research, February.

Sachs, Jeffrey, and Andrew Warner. 1995. "Economic Reform and the Process of Global Integration." *Brookings Papers on Economic Activity* 1: 1–118.

Sachs, Jeffrey, and Wing Whye Woo. 2000. "Understanding China's Economic Performance." *Journal of Policy Reform* 4.1: 1–50.

Sah, Raaj K. 1991. "Fallibility in Human Organizations and Political Systems." *Journal of Economic Perspectives* 5.2: 67–88.

Sala-i-Martin X., and A. Subramanian. 2003. "Addressing the Natural Resource Curse: An Illustration from Nigeria." NBER Working Paper no. 9804. National Bureau of Economic Research, June.

Saxenian, AnnaLee. 2002. *The New Argonauts: How Entrepreneurs are Linking Technology Markets in a Global Economy*. Cambridge: Harvard University Press.

Scherer, F. M., and Jayashree Watal. 2001. "Post-TRIPS Options for Access to Patented Medicines in Developing Countries." John F. Kennedy School of Government, Harvard University, January.

Shleifer, Andrei, and Robert W. Vishny. 1998. *The Grabbing Hand: Government Pathologies and Their Cures*. Cambridge: Harvard University Press.

Soon, Cho. 1994. *The Dynamics of Korean Development*. Washington, DC: Institute for International Economics.

Stern, Nicholas. 2000. "Globalization and Poverty." Address, Institute of Economic and Social Research, Faculty of Economics, University of Indonesia, December 15.

———. 2001. "A Strategy for Development." Keynote Address. Annual Bank Conference on Development Economics, World Bank, Washington, DC, May.

Stiglitz, Joseph E. 1998. "More Instruments and Broader Goals Moving toward the Post-Washington Consensus." United Nations University/WIDER, Helsinki.

Subramanian, Arvind, and Devesh Roy. 2003. "Who Can Explain the Mauritian Miracle? Meade, Romer, Sachs, or Rodrik?" *In Search of Prosperity: Analytic Narratives of Economic Growth*. Ed. Dani Rodrik. Princeton, NJ: Princeton University Press.

Summers, Lawrence H. 2003. Godkin Lectures. John F. Kennedy School of Government, Harvard University, April.

Tavares, Jose, and Romain Wacziarg. 2001. "How Democracy Affects Growth." *European Economic Review* 45.8: 1341–78.

Temple, Jonathan. 1999. "The New Growth Evidence." *Journal of Economic Literature* 37.1: 112–56.

———. 2003. "Growing into Trouble: Indonesia After 1966." In *In Search of Prosperity: Analytic Narratives of Economic Growth*. Ed. Dani Rodrik. Princeton, NJ: Princeton University Press.

Temple, Jonathan, and Paul Johnson. 1998. "Social Capability and Economic Growth." *Quarterly Journal of Economics* 113.3: 965–90.

Tirole, Jean. 1989. *The Theory of Industrial Organization*. Cambridge: MIT Press.

Tornell, Aaron, and Philip R. Lane. 1999. "The Voracity Effect." *American Economic Review* 89.1: 22–46.

Trindade, Vitor. 2005. "The Big Push, Industrialization, and International Trade: The Role of Exports." *Journal of Development Economics* 78.1: 22–48.

Tybout, James R. 2000. "Manufacturing Firms in Developing Countries: How Well Do They Do, and Why?" *Journal of Economic Literature* 38.1: 11–44.

UNCTAD. 2000. *Positive Agenda and Future Trade Negotiations*. Geneva: UNCTAD.

Unger, Roberto Mangabeira. 1998. *Democracy Realized: The Progressive Alternative*. London: Verso.

Vamvakidis, Athanasios. 2002. "How Robust is the Growth-Openness Connection? Historical Evidence." *Journal of Economic Growth* 7.1: 57–80.

Van Arkadie, Brian, and Raymond Mallon. 2003. *Vietnam: A Transition Tiger?* Canberra: Asia Pacific Press.

Wade, Robert. 1990. *Governing the Market.* Princeton, NJ: Princeton University Press.

Wei, Shang-Jin. 1997. "Gradualism versus Big Bang: Speed and Sustainability of Reforms." *Canadian Journal of Economics* 30.4B: 1234–47.

Wellisz, Stanislaw, and Philippe Lam Shin Saw. 1993. "Mauritius." In *The Political Economy of Poverty, Equity, and Growth: Five Open Economies.* Ed. Ronald Findlay and Stanislaw Wellisz. New York: Oxford University Press.

Williamson, John. 1990. "What Washington Means by Policy Reform." In *Latin American Adjustment: How Much Has Happened?* Ed. J. Williamson. Washington, DC: Institute for International Economics.

———, ed. 1994. *The Political Economy of Policy Reform.* Washington, DC: Institute for International Economics.

Williamson, John, and Roberto Zagha. 2002. "From Slow Growth to Slow Reform." Institute for International Economics, Washington, DC, July.

Wolf, Holger C. 1997. "Patterns of Intra- and Inter-State Trade." NBER Working Paper no. W5939. National Bureuau of Economic Research, February.

World Bank. 1993. *The East Asian Miracle: Economic Growth and Public Policies.* New York: Oxford University Press.

———. 1998. "Beyond the Washington Consensus: Institutions Matter." World Bank, Washington, DC.

———. 2002. *Development, Trade and WTO: A Handbook.* Ed. Bernard Hoekman, Aaditya Mattoo, and Philip English. Washington, DC: World Bank

Yanikkaya, Halit. 2003. "Trade Openness and Economic Growth: A Cross-Country Empirical Investigation." *Journal of Development Economics* 72.1: 57–89.

Young, Alwyn. 1992. "A Tale of Two Cities: Factor Accumulation and Technical Change in Hong Kong and Singapore." In *NBER Macroeconomics Annual.* Cambridge: MIT Press.

———. 2000. "The Razor's Edge: Distortions and Incremental Reform in the People's Republic of China." NBER Working Paper no. 7828. National Bureau of Economic Research, August.

Index